THE GOOD NEWS OF SAINT PAUL
FOR TODAY

To Martin and Mary,

RICHARD PARSONS

The Good News of Saint Paul for Today

With good wishes,

Richard

16 Nov. 2009.

ST PAULS

Nihil Obstat:
Fr Anton Cowan

Imprimatur:
Rt Revd Alan Hopes, v.g.
Auxiliary Bishop in Westminster

The Nihil Obstat and Imprimatur are a declaration that a book or pamphlet is considered to be free from doctrinal or moral error. It is not implied that those who have granted the Nihil Obstat and Imprimatur agree with the contents, opinions or statements expressed.

ST PAULS Publishing
187 Battersea Bridge Road, London SW11 3AS, UK
www.stpaulspublishing.com

Copyright © ST PAULS 2009

ISBN 978-0-85439-755-6

A catalogue record is available for this book from the British Library.

Set by Tukan DTP, Stubbington, Fareham, UK
Printed and bound in Great Britain by Athenaeum Press Ltd, Gateshead, Tyne & Wear, UK

ST PAULS is an activity of the priests and brothers of the Society of St Paul who proclaim the Gospel through the media of social communication.

CONTENTS

All proceeds due to me from the sale of this book will be donated to The Sick and Retired Priests' Fund of the Archdiocese of Westminster.

Richard Parsons
Parish Administrator of St Theresa of the Child Jesus, Headstone Lane, Hatch End, Archdiocese of Westminster. Advisor to the Institute for Work-Based Learning, Middlesex University.

FOREWORD

The Holy Father, Pope Benedict XVI, proclaimed 28 June 2008 – 29 June 2009 a Jubilee year to celebrate the 2000th anniversary of the birth of the apostle Paul. The Holy Father expressed the hope that this Pauline year would be enriched by 'special publications on the Pauline texts... to make ever more widely known the immense wealth of the teaching they contain, a true patrimony of humanity redeemed by Christ.' Fr Richard Parsons' thoughtful study of the theology of St Paul, as expressed in the canonical Pauline corpus of letters, provides a publication of considerable value in response to the call of his Holiness.

I wholeheartedly welcome this astute and judicious study of the Pauline epistles, which offers a range of insights that can benefit the diverse membership that comprise the body of Christ (1 Cor 12): students of Pauline literature and theology can attune their ears and eyes to the careful study of the flow of Paul's arguments; parish Bible-study groups can use their lips to discuss the contemporary relevance of the pastoral theology of the apostle; lay faithful can use their feet to 'walk' in the way of the Lord, guided by a clearer appreciation of the apostle's ethical principles.

Fr Richard deserves our grateful thanks. This scholarly work will, I hope, be of great benefit to all its readers.

+ Cormac Murphy-O'Connor

Cardinal Cormac Murphy-O'Connor
Archbishop of Westminster
The Immaculate Conception of the Blessed Virgin Mary, 2008

Pope Benedict's declaration of 2009-2010 as a Year for Priests can be seen as a natural progression from the Year of St Paul. When we priests consider our ministry – its foundation, role and purpose – we should return to the basis of the apostolic ministry which St Paul proclaims. Fundamentally, he identifies his ministry, and ours, with Christ's life, death and resurrection. In this regard I commend Fr Richard Parsons' book as one way of entering St Paul's teaching on the apostolic ministry and the entire mystery of our salvation.

Archbishop Vincent Nichols, Archbishop of Westminster
Assumption of the Blessed Virgin Mary, 2009

ABBREVIATIONS

BIBLICAL COMMENTARIES

NJBC   *The New Jerome Biblical Commentary*, eds. R.E Brown,
J.A. Fitzmyer, R.E. Murphy, 1989, London, Chapman.

OBC   *The Oxford Bible Commentary*, eds. J. Barton and
J. Muddiman, 2001, Oxford, Oxford University Press.

BOOKS OF INTRODUCTION

CNT   A. E. Harvey, *A Companion to the New Testament*,
Second edition, 2004, Cambridge, Cambridge
University Press.

INT   Raymond E. Brown, *An Introduction to the New
Testament*, 1997, New York, Doubleday.

ARTICLES

CCStP   *The Cambridge Companion to St Paul*, ed. James D.G.
Dunn, 2003, Cambridge, Cambridge University Press.

DBI   *A Dictionary of Biblical Interpretation*, eds. R.J. Coggins
and J.L. Houlden, 1990, reissue 2003, London, SCM
Press.

DPL   *Dictionary of Paul and his Letters*, eds. G.F. Hawthorne,
R.P. Martin and D.G. Reid, 1993, Leicester, InterVarsity
Press.

FNTS   *The Face of New Testament Studies: A Survey of Recent
Research*, eds. Scot McKnight and Grant R. Osborne,
2004, Michigan, Grand Rapids, Baker Academic.

FOR ARCHAEOLOGICAL SITES

BSGT   Glyde E. Fant and Mitchell G. Reddish, *A Guide to
Biblical Sites in Greece and Turkey*, 2003, Oxford,
Oxford University Press.

PREFACE

My serious critical research of the historical, theological and literary issues relating to the study of St Paul began in 1963. In this context I should like to express my thanks to the teachers at my school (George Abbot School, Guildford) in particular Mr John Rogers; at my university (Kings College, London) in particular Christopher Evans, Morna Hooker, Colin Hickling, Anthony Harvey and Graham Stanton and at Leuven where I studied from 1998-2000, in particular Adelbert Denaux.

Since 1970 I have shared my insights into Pauline literature and thought with numerous groups: sixth formers, college students, many of whom were destined for the ordained ministry, doctoral students, church groups, together with inter-faith seminars and those who are studying Paul from the context of classical Roman history. From this continuing dialogue I have learnt an enormous amount in relation to knowledge, perception and application. Much of this book has been informed by the principles of 'work-based' learning. In this context I am most grateful to my colleagues involved in the Institute for Work-Based Learning at Middlesex University, in particular to: Profs. Ken Goulding, Margaret House, Derek Portwood, Jonathan Garnett and his staff for all the valuable insights which I have received from them in connection with the communication and application of Paul in the work-based learning environment: school, college, university and church. Coupled with the notion of the learning environment is the nature of the professionalism of those who work and operate in that environment. Reflection upon Paul's ministry therefore is vital in our consideration of the teaching and clerical professions and their contemporary roles in terms of mission and education.

For my present context my deep gratitude goes to Cardinal Cormac Murphy O'Connor, for not merely agreeing to write the foreword but also for all his pastoral support and interest, and to Archbishop Vincent Nichols for agreeing to include his own reflections on this publication in connection with *The Year for Priests*. My thanks go also to other Westminster Diocesan clergy, among them Bishop Alan Hopes, Mgr Seamus O'Boyle, Mgr Mark O'Toole, Mgr Martin Hayes, Fr Anton Cowan and Dr Michael Cullinan for their help and encouragement. Some of my ideas on Paul have been used in connection with the work done within the Westminster Diocesan Agency for Evangelisation. It has been a joy to share perceptions with such creative minds as those possessed by Dr Michael O'Boy and Dr Mark Nash. I am also most grateful to Dr Martin Kitchen for sharing his considerable knowledge and understanding with me. Particular thanks go to Dr Sean Ryan who has provided much material from contemporary scholarship, read much of the work but, above all, offers true support and friendship. Sean is one of a number of younger scholars who have so much to contribute to biblical research and who are a constant source of refreshment and encouragement to us, more ageing, brethren. As she has done many times before Brenda Maxwell has typed, corrected and e-mailed some of this text. I am very grateful to her. My greatest thanks go to my wife, Elaine who reads all my material with a critical awareness in relation to the issues raised, provides many of the references to Classical Studies and, more importantly as always, has given to me her love.

Richard Parsons, 8 December 2008 & 28 June 2009
In honour of St Paul, St Peter and the Blessed Virgin Mary
(Gal 4:4; Acts 1:14)

INTRODUCTION

The overall aim of this book is to encourage as many people as possible, either individually or in a group setting, or both, to engage in the study of St Paul's life and writings. Accordingly, this work is written to aid the study of the Pauline writings by a diverse readership, reflecting on these letters in a variety of contexts:

- Lay faithful (individuals and groups)– encouraged by Pope Benedict XVI's declaration of a year of St Paul (June 2008-2009) to encourage Christians, especially Roman Catholic Christians, to study and reflect on the writings of St Paul, either through individual study or in parish study-groups.

- Seminarians – concerned to study the theological, pastoral and ethical insights of St Paul as reflected in his situational letters to various early Christian communities in the first century AD.

- Clergy – interested in renewing their acquaintance with the content and context of the Pauline epistles to inform their preaching on St Paul.

- Students of theology/history/classics – striving to engage more closely with the individual texts of the Pauline corpus as part of a programme of theological or historical study.

This publication functions as a bridge between the diverse range of introductory studies to the life and letters of St Paul (e.g. James D.G. Dunn (Ed.) *The Cambridge Companion to St Paul*, (Cambridge, CUP, 2003)) and more detailed commentaries focusing on a single Pauline epistle (e.g. *Black's New Testament Commentaries* series). This work provides an overview of the breadth of Pauline literature in a single volume, introducing the interested reader to the social and historical context of each letter, the flow of Paul's argument as it weaves through the text, and concluding with a more focussed reflection on central theological and ethical issues that arise in each epistle.

Accordingly, this work has been carefully structured to tailor to the variety of different needs and uses that such a diverse readership may have in approaching the life and letters of St Paul. Each of the major chapters on individual letters, or letter collections, in the Pauline corpus (Chapters one to six) follows an identical tripartite structure:

Section One – Structure. In which the reader is invited to become familiar with the general outline of the letter and to follow the Lines of Argument that develop (and recur) as the letter progresses. Central words and concepts will be highlighted (in transliterated Greek) to aid the reader's grasp of items of recurring interest and concern.

Section Two – Environment. In which the reader is invited to consider the context in which Paul is operating and where a particular event may be placed within the chronology of his missionary material.

Section Three – Theological, Pastoral and Hermeneutical Issues. In which the reader is invited to consider the theological and pastoral issues that Paul engaged with in the first century AD, and to reflect on how such issues may inform contemporary ethical and pastoral concerns.

Each reader will approach the Pauline epistles with his/her own interests and concerns, and may tailor the use of this book accordingly to best serve such needs.

- *Lay faithful (groups)* – parish groups may wish to focus on a single letter (or group of letters) as part of a series of Bible study sessions. Such readers may wish to concentrate exclusively on a single chapter (e.g. The Corinthian correspondence, ch 3) within this book, which functions as a 'stand-alone' section, providing an introduction to the context, argument and theological issues that arise from these particular epistles. Such readers may find that Section Three, Theological and Pastoral Issues offer a useful starting-point for reflection on contemporary ethical issues.

- *Lay faithful (individuals)* – individual readers may be concerned to consider changes and developments within the Pauline corpus and prefer to work through the chapters more systematically as a companion to private study of the Pauline corpus as a whole.

- *Seminarians* – seminary students may find that the detailed outline of the 'lines of argument' of the individual letters are a helpful guide to an engagement with the flow of Paul's theological reflections, and provide a helpful supplement to critical commentaries focussed more closely on individual passages within the text.

- *Clergy* – may find that Section Three (Theological and Pastoral Issues) inform and enliven their own reflection on the Pauline epistles in sermons and private reflection

- *Students* – undergraduate students (of theology and history) may wish to reflect on Section Two (Environment) as a window into the first century AD Graeco-Roman context of the Pauline epistles.

Such suggestions are illustrative, rather than prescriptive, and are intended merely to highlight the many and various ways in which this study may be used by a wide readership.

Chapter 7 of this study offers an alternative perspective on the interpretation of the Pauline epistles, considering the diversity of approaches to this emerging corpus of letters in the second and third centuries AD. The purpose of this chapter is to enable the reader to perceive the continuing discussion of Paul's writings within the framework of Early Christianity as an alternative, yet related, lens to contemporary discussions on the interpretation of the Pauline corpus.

In whatever ways an individual reader may choose to engage with this study, the overarching aim is to provide an informative and helpful guide to the context, content and relevance of the Pauline corpus in both its original and contemporary setting so that these letters may continue to afford 'Good News' of St Paul for today.

CHAPTER 1

TO THE THESSALONIANS

St Paul's First Letter to the Thessalonians is generally believed to be 'the oldest preserved Christian writing' (Brown, *INT*, 456). Therefore, it should be the starting point for our study and although a debatable issue, to be followed by a discussion of 2 Thessalonians.

SECTION 1 – STRUCTURE

A. OUTLINE – 1 THESSALONIANS

1:1	Opening greeting.
1:2-10	Thanksgiving to God for the Thessalonian Church.
2:1-16	The ministry in Thessalonica.
2:17-20	Paul's concern for their welfare.
3:1-13	Timothy's mission and Paul's prayer.
4:1-12	Exhortation on chastity (4:1-8) and charity (4:9-12).
4:13-5:11	Discussion of eschatology in relation to the *parousia* (4:13-18) and living in the eschatological age (5:1-11).
5:12-22	Discussion of Church life in relation to ministerial order (5:12-13) and ethical living (5:14-22).
5:23-28	Concluding blessing and greeting.

B. LINES OF ARGUMENT

Opening greeting, 1:1

As was the custom with the Graeco-Roman letters of the period both the senders and the recipients to whom greetings are offered are indicated. In 1 Thessalonians the names of three senders are given: Paul, Silvanus and Timothy, although their ecclesial status (cf. 1 Cor 1:1) is not mentioned. The first person plural is generally used throughout the letter with the exception of 2:18; 3:5 and 5:27. An oscillation occurs, therefore, between the corporate voice of the three missionaries and Paul's personal aspirations (3:18) although it is to be assumed that all three adhere to the contents of the letter. Rather than portraying Paul as a lone figure it is clear that the view of the ministry presented is collegiate (1:1). The Thessalonian believers are described corporately as church (*ekklesia*, 1:2). This term would have been used in connection with the civic assembly but for the believers it would indicate the Semitic usage of being 'called out' by God into fellowship with him through Jesus Christ. The greeting of grace (*charis*) and peace (*eirene*) originate from God and Jesus and may have developed into Christian liturgical vocabulary from the Aaronic blessing recorded in Numbers 6:22-25. The greeting also enshrines matters of theological and Christological importance. God is described as Father while Jesus is attributed with Messianic status and Lordship with the Father (1:3).

Thanksgiving to God for the Thessalonian Church, 1:2-10

The thanksgiving for the community is enshrined within prayers to God, to whom any advancement in evangelisation is attributed (1:2). The divine origin of the Gospel is affirmed, as is the powerfully positive relationship between the missionaries and the believers. These believers are named as brethren (1:4) and, as result, find themselves in a new relationship with God, their evangelising missionaries (1:6) and with the other believers in the region (1:7, see map 3). Despite the joy which belief in Christ brings, afflication accompanies it. This is a feature of the final age and linked to Christ's death and resurrection. The section concludes with a summary of the preaching offered to a largely Gentile audience. Turning to the one God from idols was typical of Jewish preaching to non-Jews to which the Christian proclamation of Jesus' resurrection and subsequent return as judge (1:9-10) have been added.

The ministry in Thessalonica, 2:1-16

Chapter two begins with an autobiographical statement. The language of 2:1 extends that of 1:5. The fruitfulness of the missionaries' evangelising ministry is emphasised and placed within the wider context of the Macedonian ministry (for example at Philippi, Acts 16:19-40; Phil 1:30). The sincerity of their proclamation (2:4) is explained as is their concept of their Thessalonican ministry in terms of the metaphor of a mother caring for her children (2:7b). The parental metaphor is extended to include fatherhood – both the apostles' care for the community and the over-arching theological perception of the fatherhood of God (2:11; 1:1). The Thessalonians are praised for imitating the original Judaean churches which places the community in an organic relationship with the origin of Christianity in Jerusalem (2:14). The enmity which the new Messianic community have generated and the persecution which they have received from within Judaism is explained in terms of the Jewish leadership who were instrumental, not only in the crucifixion of Jesus, but whose forefathers were responsible also for the persecution of the prophets (2:14; Mt 23:30). These different levels of persecution in the apostolic age represent the attempt to hinder the totality of Christian evangelisation (2:16) and, as a result, mean that some Jews will incur the divine wrath (2:16; 1:10).

Paul's concern for their welfare, 2:17-20

Within the context of the apostolic ministry Paul expresses his personal anxiety for being unable to visit the Thessalonian community. This prevention is attributed, somewhat enigmatically, to 'Satan' (2:18), a personified description for evil in Jewish theology. A rhetorical question follows which introduces the concept of 'presence' (*parousia*, 2:19) in terms of the biblical language of hope and joy and of the athletic metaphor of victory (see 1 Cor 9:25) and which in turn leads to the declaration that the Thessalonian community is the glory and joy of the apostolic mission (2:20).

Timothy's mission and Paul's prayer, 3:1-13

In chapter three the idealism of 2:20 is confronted by the realism of the operation of the tempter (3:5, cf. 2:18). Timothy, as co-worker (3:2), is sent to encourage the community. His report is generally positive and thanksgiving to God results (3:9) but a further visit is desired in order to rectify any shortcomings in the Thessalonians' faith (3:10). A prayer of intercession follows whose petitions include the increase of love (3:12) and holiness (3:13). The purpose of this intercession is in order that the Thessalonian Christians might be prepared theologically and ethically to receive the 'presence' (*parousia*, 3:13, see 2:19) of the exalted Lord Jesus (see 1:1). As a result the saints (3:13) are placed in the closest possible relationship with Jesus.

Exhortation on chastity and charity, 4:1-12

The 'finally, therefore' ensures that the ethical exhortations in chapter 4 are linked intrinsically to the earlier theological and pastoral sections. Three points emerge: first, that ethical injunctions and the apostolic teaching relating to them are based on the ministry and authority of 'the Lord Jesus' (4:1-2). Thus ethical teaching is related directly to that of Jesus. Secondly, this teaching is conceived within a Jewish framework, the way the believers should walk (a Hebraic concept describing ethical behaviour) and please God. Thirdly, this teaching includes an underlying injunction to preserve the sanctity of marriage (see later, 1 Cor 7:14) with its overt reference to avoid sexual immorality (4:3), the sin of lust (4:5) and the necessity of regarding the body as the place where the Holy Spirit dwells (see later, 1 Cor 6:18-20). This teaching is therefore a Christianised form of the Jewish injunctions (note the biblical allusions in this section: 4:5 to Psalm 79:6 and 4:8 to Ezek 37:14) addressed both to Jews living within a Graeco-Roman environment and to Gentiles who wished to understand the theology and ethics of Judaism.

4:9-12 place these sexual ethical injunctions within a wider framework. The theme of 'brotherly love' recounts the concept as expressed already in 1:4-8 while the reference to the necessity of hard work and of not causing offence within the wider social community is linked to the injunction to demonstrate respect (note the 'walk' concept in 4:12 used earlier in 4:1) to outsiders. While it is both theologically and socially clear as to those who can be considered as belonging within the Christian community, nevertheless this belonging involves a recognition of the role that Christians ought to play, and to be perceived to be playing, in relation to the civic community (Esler, *OBC*, 1208-9).

Discussion of Eschatology, 4:13–5:11

The consideration of the theological and pastoral problems relating to the ultimate issues concerning the deaths of the believers before the Lord's coming (*parousia*, 4:15: also 3:13 and 2:19) and the proper attitude of believers awaiting this coming are discussed in two sections: 4:13-18 and 5:1-11. In order to understand the first problem the hearers are told to return to the basic facts of the Christian Gospel: Jesus' death and resurrection (4:14). It is belief in Jesus' resurrection which will ensure that believers, both living and departed, will share in the Lord's eternal presence (4:17) as a result of their own resurrection. The explanation of this theology is couched in the language of Jewish apocalyptic imagery (4:16-17) and with a sense of ordered progression: first the dead then the living. This exposition should be a cause for encouragement (4:18) rather than of grieving (4:13). The second section relates to attitudes and behaviour in the light of the imminence of the Lord's coming. This coming is again described in terms of the language of Jewish apocalyptic and the variety of well known metaphors which that language contains: 'the Day of the Lord' (Amos 5:18; Joel 2:1; Zeph 1:7); 'the thief in the night' and the labour pains of pregnancy before childbirth (5:1-2). The purpose of this imagery is to demonstrate both the suddenness of the coming and the need for believers to live and behave as if they exist in the light rather than the darkness (5:4-5). This dualism (note this familiar theme within the Dead Sea scrolls) has both an actual and metaphoric character: to avoid drunkenness (5:7), to keep working (4:11) but also to be armed with the equipment of a soldier (5:8) in order that the battle for the faith may be won. The purpose of this endurance is to be prepared to receive God's salvation (5:8 and 9) rather than his wrath (1:10), salvation which has been achieved as

23

a result of the mission of 'our Lord Jesus' (5:9; 5:10 returns to the theme of 4:13-14). The section concludes with the encouragement theme which concluded the first of these sections at 4:18.

Discussion of Church life, 5:12-22

This final exhortation (5:12-22) provides a summary of some of the issues raised already in the letter. First, esteem for ministerial leaders is demanded (5:12-13). This injunction is to be seen in the context of all that has been said earlier in the letter about the apostolic ministry to the Thessalonians (e.g. 2:7-12). Secondly, there follows a number of short ethical injunctions relating to such topics as peaceful living (5:14), supporting the weak (5:14), continual rejoicing (5:16) and discerning the activity of the prophetic Spirit (5:19-21a). The purpose of these injunctions is to summarise what has been written in chapter 4 (5:22), to place them within the context of the shortly expected *parousia* (5:13) and to leave open the possibility of the discussion of further topics such as that relating to the Spirit (5:19, later 1 Cor 12:10). Their objective is to provide ethical and social norms by which the Christian community can be defined and recognised.

Concluding blessing and greeting, 5:23-28

As with the opening greetings, the conclusions of the Pauline literature, although based on contemporary models from the Graeco-Roman world, both vary from letter to letter, and have been Christianised. The prayer for God's peace recalls the opening of the letter (1:1) and thus has the effect of taking its contents and arguments full circle. The circle, however, has been considerably enlarged. Through hearing, studying and living the contents of the letter it is envisaged that the Thessalonian Christians will be completely sanctified (5:23) in all aspects of their being (5:23). This process will be based on the action of God (5:24). The *parousia* language relating to the Lord Jesus Christ is also recalled, accompanied by the prayer that the Thessalonians will be blameness (5:23) when the *parousia* arrives. The unity of the church with the apostolic mission is to be strengthened by prayer (5:25; 1:2; 3:11-13; also Rom 15:30-32; Philem 22) and by the public reading of the letter (5:27; Col 4:16). In this latter regard the first person is utilised by Paul (see also 2:18; 3:5) to reinforce the sense of personal apostolic authority and command. Brotherly concord (1:5b) is to be symbolised by the liturgical act of the 'holy kiss' (5:26; 1 Cor 16:20; 2 Cor 13:12 and later, Justin 1 Apol. 65:2). Again, by the use of the word grace, 1:1 is recalled in 5:28, not, however, as a human greeting, but in the form of a blessing from our Lord Jesus Christ, thus giving the letter its Christological climax.

C. THE QUESTION OF 2 THESSALONIANS

There is no uniform agreement as to the dating of 2 Thessalonians. On one hand there are similarities between 1 and 2 Thessalonians in structure and contents while there are differences in both tone and theology in particular relating to Christology and eschatology. Several theses are possible: (i) 2 Thessalonians may have been written before 1 Thessalonians (the view of T.W. Manson); (ii) 2 Thessalonians was composed some months after 1 Thessalonians in order to give the eschatological teaching contained in that letter further clarification (see the comments of Kreitzer, *DBI*, 696 and those of Harvey, *CNT,* 655) and (iii) that 2 Thessalonians was not written by Paul and his companions as stated in 1:1 but by a later disciple who modelled his general letter concerning eschatology on 1 Thessalonians (Mitchell, *CCStP*, 59). As a result the dating of 2 Thessalonians can be placed between AD 50 and 80 which, in turn, raises considerable difficulty as to where the letter should be placed within the development of Paul's thought. Although it is doubtful as to whether the issue of authorship and dating will be resolved it is, however, necessary to analyse the structure of 2 Thessalonians and to review the eschatological teaching which it contains both in relationship to 1 Thessalonians and to early Christianity in general.

STRUCTURE

A. OUTLINE – 2 THESSALONIANS

1:1-2	Opening greeting.
1:3-4	Thanksgiving.
1:5-12	Persecution of the faithful, vengeance upon unbelievers, prayer for the community.
2:1-12	How the *parousia* should be understood.
2:13-17	Declaration of thanksgiving, the need for endurance.
3:1-5	Request for prayer and exhortation.
3:6-16	Ethical injunctions and blessing.
3:17-18	Paul's concluding blessing.

B. LINES OF ARGUMENT

Opening greeting, thanksgiving and persecution of the faithful, 1:1-12

A similar pattern is found here to that used in 1 Thessalonians: greeting (1:1-2); thanksgiving for the church (1:3) and praise for their endurance (1:4) under persecution. Differences from 1 Thessalonians begin to emerge from 1:6 onwards. First, using contemporary Jewish apocalyptic imagery, the heavenly revelation of 'the Lord Jesus' is to be accompanied by powerful angels (1:7) and secondly there is a series of statements emphasising the dualism between the believers and the unbelievers: the believers will be glorified (1:10) while the unbelievers will be destroyed and excluded from the presence (lit. the face) of the Lord (1:9).

The section concludes with a prayer that the community may be worthy and filled with God's power through the exhibition of their goodness and faith (1:11-12).

How the *parousia* should be understood, 2:1-12

The authors are concerned that the community is not shaken through its discussion of the *parousia* of 'our Lord Jesus Christ' (2:1) or by any misinformation that the Day of the Lord has arrived already (2:2). Compared with 1 Thessalonians 4:13-

5:11 further details are added which give the apocalyptic picture more precision. Similar to Jewish apocalyptic literature allusions are made to biblical passages for confirmation of the symbols offered and the teaching given. In 2 Thessalonians reference is made in particular to the Isaianic material (2:8 uses Isaiah 66:15, God coming as fire; 2:9 uses Isaiah 2:10-17; 49:3; 66:5) and to Jeremiah (2:8 uses Jer 10:25 against those who refuse to accept the message). The *parousia* is to be preceded by apostasy (2:3) and by the presence of the figure of the man of lawlessness, the son of perdition (2:3) who will both place himself in God's Temple and proclaim himself as God (2:4). I shall discuss the purpose of introducing this figure in a later section and the possible historical and theological background utilised; for the time being it should be noted that the 'Lord Jesus' will slay this lawless one (2:8) and that the dualism between the righteous followers of Jesus and the unrighteous adherents of the lawless one has been intensified (2:9-12).

Declaration of thanksgiving, the need for endurance, 2:13-17

The authors now turn to the theme of thanksgiving which is offered to God for the sanctification and salvation of the community (2:13; cf. 1 Thess 2:13). The brothers (2:15) are exhorted to hold firm to the traditions (2:15; 3:6; Gal 1:14; 1 Cor 11:2; Col 2:8) which they have been taught. The section ends with the prayer that 'our Lord Jesus' and 'God our Father' who loved and gave comfort, hope and grace to every believer (us, 2:16) may comfort and strengthen the community particularly (you, 2:17).

Prayer and ethical injunctions, 3:1-16

As with 1 Thessalonians 4:1 this section begins with 'finally' (3:1). Prayer for the apostolic missionaries is requested (3:1), in particular that they may be preserved from evil men (3:2). The 'work-ethic' of 1 Thessalonians 4:11b and 5:14 is extended in 3:6-12 together with the injunction to adhere to apostolic authority (cf. 1 Thess 5:12). The section concludes with the benediction for peace (1 Thess 1:1; 2 Thess 1:2) thus moving the letter full circle (3:16).

Paul's concluding blessing, 3:17-18

Compared with 1 Thessalonians 5:25-28, in 2 Thessalonians Paul's hand in writing the concluding greeting of the letter (as opposed to a secretary) is emphasised here as a sign of the authenticity of all Paul's letters. As with 1 Thessalonians 5:28 the blessing of grace from 'our Lord Jesus Christ' forms the Christological climax.

SECTION 2 – CONTEXT

A. THE ENVIRONMENT

The city of Thessalonica was situated on a prime location on the Via Egnatia, an important highway which connected the Balkans to Asia Minor. The city served as a port at the head of the Thermaic gulf of the Aegean Sea and, as a result of its geographical location, was a centre of trade and commerce. The city was also of historical importance. It was founded in 316 BC by Cassander, a general in Alexander the Great's army. Cassander was the son-in-law of Philip II of Macedonia having married his daughter, Thessalonikeia, after whom he named the city. When the Romans annexed the province of Macedonia in 146 BC Thessalonica became its capital and the major city of northern Greece. Cicero was exiled here in 58-57 BC and in 49 BC it became Pompey's military headquarters in his attempt to escape Julius Caesar. Like some other Graeco-Roman cities there was a Jewish minority here who congregated around the local synagogue (Acts 17:1). This congregation considered itself part of the Diaspora, communities of Jews who lived away from Jerusalem (see Map 1). Generally Jewish relationships with the local population were ambivalent. While considered strange for not sharing in the political and social life of the city, nevertheless the Jews were generally respected. There was a fascination about their religious beliefs and practices and it was thought that Jewish expertise in education and trade might be utilised for the common good. When Paul and his companions arrived in Thessalonica in c. AD 49-50 he entered into a vibrant environment proud of its historical antecedents and of its contemporary prosperity.

Within the Roman Empire Thessalonica was considered a free city. Although a Roman procurator was based here the city's government was under the control of local officials. Considering the archaeological evidence of ancient Thessalonica provides a picture of the political, social and religious environment of one of the Graeco-Roman cities in which Paul first preached the Christian Gospel (Cf. *BSGT,* 132-140). As will be seen, each of the centres of Paul's missionary activity, for example Philippi, Athens, Corinth and Ephesus, had different historical foundations and also variable social and economic structures. We shall consider how Paul conceptualised the Gospel in each particular environment.

B. THESSALONICA WITHIN PAUL'S MISSIONARY ACTIVITY

The context for the apostolic mission to Thessalonica is placed by Luke within Paul's second missionary journey (see Map 3). This journey begins after the Council of Jerusalem (Acts 15:36) with Paul and Silas progressing through Galatia, Timothy joining them at Lystra (Acts 16:3), before moving onto Troas (ancient Troy) in Asia Minor. Responding to the divine call to evangelise in Macedonia (Acts 16:9-10) they journeyed to Philippi (Acts 16:12) and thence to Thessalonica (Acts 17:1). After the disturbance in Thessalonica, Paul, Silas and Timothy went to Beroea (Acts 17:10) and then Paul journeyed to Athens where, for a while, he lived alone (Acts 17:15). From Athens, Paul journeyed to Corinth (Acts 18:1) where he was joined by Aquila and Priscilla who, like all Jews, were recently exiled from Italy on the order of the Emperor Claudius (Acts 18:2, see also Suetonius, *Life of Claudius,* 25:4). Latterly Paul was joined by Silas and Timothy (Acts 18:5). After Paul's stay in Corinth, and accompanied by Aquila and Priscilla, they journeyed to Syria via Ephesus (Acts 18:18-21).

This second journey concludes at Antioch (Acts 18:22) from where the first missionary journey began (Acts 13:2-3).

1 Thessalonians has provided some of these details: first, that the apostolic missionaries were treated shamefully at Philippi (1 Thess 2:2; Acts 16:37, where the point about Roman citizenship is included), secondly that Paul was alone in Athens (1 Thess 3:1; Acts 17:15) and thirdly that the main reason why the Thessalonian ministry proved difficult was due to the hostility of the Jewish population (1 Thess 2:2; 2:16; Acts 17:5). Luke adds information about Jason who had offered the missionaries hospitality. It is possible that Jason was a wealthy Jew (bearing the name of a Jewish high priest, 2 Macc. 4:7, also Rom 16:21). He was dragged before the city authorities (Acts 17:6 and 8; also inscription on Vartar Gate, *BSGT,* 135) on a political charge relating to Jesus' kingship in relation to that of Caesar and forced to offer financial security apparently in lieu of future good conduct. These difficulties did not apparently hinder the growth of the Church or the support for the Pauline mission (Phil 4:16; 2 Tim 4:10). It is likely therefore that 1 Thessalonians was written by Paul from Corinth. The purpose of the letter is clear: to discuss the issue of the Lord's *parousia*; to elaborate the apostolic belief about church and ministry and their inter-relationship and to probe the nature of Christian preaching and its implications for Gentiles believers, in particular as they attempt to fulfil their civic duties within Thessalonian society. The setting of 2 Thessalonians remains uncertain (Brown, *INT,* 592-596 is particularly helpful in this regard). What can be said however is that the Thessalonian correspondence offers important insights into Pauline thought and its development, especially in relation to eschatology, ethics and ministry.

SECTION 3 – THEOLOGICAL, PASTORAL AND HERMENEUTICAL ISSUES

A. ESCHATOLOGY

Why should Paul's advice to the Thessalonian Christians relating to eschatology be good news for us? To attempt to answer this question we need to define eschatology as used in early Christian writings and then to analyse the different philosophical contemporary world-views which our research into the concept generates.

Eschatology means a study of the last things (*eschatos, logos*), that is issues relating to the end of the world, whether political or cosmic in scope, and the end of the individual, death (and afterlife). The fundamental background for reflection on these issues in Christian circles is the death and resurrection of Jesus (1 Thess 4:14) and the implications of these events for theology and salvation. Paul's own reflections draw on his Jewish heritage, most notably a view that God would transform the world politically and ecologically, to free his people from the present (Roman imperial) system, and inaugurate a new age (which some Jews believed would be arriving imminently).

A dominant twenty-first-century Western world view, however, relates to progress, from childhood to adulthood during which time we hope to grow in both wealth and prosperity and in intellectual understanding. Yet there exists another perception, that of cyclical advance. Both in employment and in spiritual matters, for example, we are doing many of the same things through life but in the doing of them we are able to progress spiritually thus advancing in Christian understanding.

For the Thessalonian Christians their philosophical world view was interventionist. They were waiting for the imminent coming of Jesus which aroused in them issues about the dead and the manner and time scale for Jesus' arrival. In order to explain these issues Paul uses the concept of *parousia* (1 Thess 2:19; 3:13; 4:15; 5:23; 2 Thess 2:1; 2:8; note also 1 Cor 1:8; 15:23; Mt 24:27; 2 Pet 3:12). This non-Septuagintal word was used in Graeco-Roman culture as the official term for the visitation of a high ranking official, a king or emperor, to a province, thus providing a mixture of meanings: arrival, coming and presence. As a result, both for the Thessalonians and for ourselves, the concept of eschatology contains within it a series of tensions; first, between the expected coming of Jesus and his presence within the Christian community (note here Matthew's Emmanuel theology, Mt 1:23; 18:20; 28:20) and secondly between the present and the future. We experience salvation in the present (1 Thess 5:9) but its totality will be revealed and experienced later. As we shall see this balance between a present fragmentary experience and the totality of future glory which is to be awaited is fundamental to Paul's thought (see, for example, 1 Cor 15:22; 2 Cor 1:22; Rom 6:5). Furthermore it is a concept which can be grasped within our twenty-first-century world view: progress but ever expectant of God's revelation of Jesus, the Christ whether in this world or the next.

The problem with this tension humanly is one of time; when will Jesus' *parousia* arrive? Paul's answer is that we must rely only upon God's time (1 Thess 5:1). Christians must be prepared for its suddenness (1 Thess 3:10), live ethically, work hard as normal (1 Thess 5:12-22; 2 Thess 3:6-13, created from the norms of Jewish ethics) and be continually serving the community. To describe this situation a series of metaphors is utilised: burglary, women waiting to give birth, darkness and light and being asleep and being awake (1 Thess 5:2-7). These metaphors, which provide the symbolic images for expectation, come from the language of Jewish apocalyptic (*apokalypsis*, revelation or in its verb form, *apokalupto*, to uncover, note the use of the term in 2 Thess 2:3; 2:6; 2:8). Apocalyptic is both a concept and a form of literature. The concept concerns the revealing of the mysterious plan of God, while apocalyptic literature in its various forms, through its numerous symbolic images, provides the literary form for the concept. Paul has interpreted both concept and literature to demonstrate that God's supreme plan for the world and its purification has been revealed totally in Jesus, but because Christians are awaiting the finality of this revelation for themselves apocalyptic language provides a useful way of highlighting the eschatological tension. Thus within contemporary ideas about progress and cyclical renewal the expectation about Jesus' *parousia* ought to be maintained.

The problem in 2 Thessalonians is that some teachers (attempting to imitate Paul) desired to remove the eschatological tension of present and future by maintaining that 'the day of the Lord had come already' (2 Thess 2:1). This day, however, will be first preceded by rebellion, apostasy (2 Thess 2:3) and the arrival of 'the man of lawlessness' (2 Thess 2:3). Numerous attempts have been made to identify historically this figure (details, Brown, *INT*, 597). It could be, however, that he represents a generalised personification of evil based either on the Prince of Tyre as represented by Ezekiel 28 or on Antiochus IV Epiphanes who persecuted the Jewish people of Jerusalem between 167 and 164 BC and who is represented within the apocalyptic sections of the book of Daniel (e.g. Dan 7:19-27; 11:29-45). The language relating this ruler's god-like pretensions and violation of true worship (2 Thess 2:4) could be used both of certain Roman Emperors in Paul's time and of modern rulers in our own. In either case 'the man of lawlessness' is the antithesis of the image of the Davidic king portrayed in the 'Royal Psalms' (e.g. Ps 72:1-4; 12-14) of whom Jesus is the ultimate fulfilment. Thus a clear contrast exists between the 'secular', evil, tyrannical ruler and the Lordship of Christ.

It is sometimes suggested that 2 Thessalonians 'corrects' the *parousia* theology of 1 Thessalonians. Perhaps rather 2 Thessalonians complements 1 Thessalonians, given that we are dealing with the mysterious action of God. Why this variety of approaches to the *parousia* of the Lord is important as good news for today is that it provides a wider vision of the earth/ heaven relationship in Christian thought and allows a further tension in eschatology understanding, this time between the imminent and the long-term dimension, to remain. The Thessalonian correspondence challenges us to live with these eschatological tensions and, as a result, to be ever watchful for the presence of Christ in all its aspects.

B. CHURCH AND APOSTOLIC MINISTRY

The Thessalonian correspondence challenges the contemporary Church to re-examine the nature of itself in terms of Church with regard to its self-perception, its relationship to the apostolic ministry and the models of ethical conduct demanded from its members. This re-examination demands the acknowledgment of the series of interlocking relationships involved in the Church's ministry and mission. In the Thessalonian correspondence there is first the relationship between the apostolic missionaries themselves: Paul, Silvanus and Timothy (1 Thess 1:1). This relationship concerned the recognition of the operation of a common brotherhood and servant-hood in the service of Gospel.

These categories are reflective of the ministry of Jesus (e.g. Mt 23:8; Mk 10:45). This shared ministry explains Timothy's willingness to visit Thessalonica at Paul's request (1 Thess 3:2). Then there is the relationship between the missionaries and the Thessalonian Church. Timothy's report brought good news concerning faith and love in community which includes their ability to endure suffering (1 Thess 3:6-7). This suffering is modelled upon apostolic affliction (1 Thess 2:14) which in turn is modelled on the sufferings of Christ (explained in more detail, 1 Cor 4:8-13). The apostolic missionaries also cared for the community both like a nurse (1 Thess 2:7) and as a father (1 Thess 2:11). This pastoral care in turn ensured that the Thessalonian church reciprocated this generosity of spirit (1 Thess 1:6). Turning to the Christian Gospel meant that the believers were exhorted to live ethically both among themselves (e.g. 1 Thess 4:9-12) and as an example in wider civic society (e.g. 1 Thess 5:14-15; 2 Thess 3:6-12). This ethical living, however, is based upon the prior demands of theology and the Gospel. How we live is based upon what we believe. Principles and practice go hand-in-hand. For the contemporary Church, therefore, the letters to the Thessalonians offer challenges as to how we exercise the ministry, how we practise the Faith and live the Gospel as *ekklesia* (1 Thess 1:1; 2 Thess 1:1) and how our lives are to be structured morally. Such an examination will surely prove to be good news for us.

C. THE NATURE OF THE GOSPEL

I have indicated that in three places in 1 Thessalonians the argument presented returns to the basic facts of the Gospel (1:9-10; 4:14 and 5:10). This term represents one of several similar expressions which refer to the initial missionary preaching concerning the saving activity of Jesus (Stanton, *CCStP*, 173).

5:10 demonstrates God's wrath/salvation axis, salvation being obtained through the death of the Lord Jesus Christ (note the Christological emphasis) in which both the living and the departed are able to share. 4:14 contains the same pattern: thinking about the future depends on Jesus' death and resurrection and, by implication, the hope of salvation and eternal life with God. 1:9-10 contains information as to what happened when the Thessalonian citizens turned to the Gospel. It is sometimes maintained that these verses contain a summary of Gospel preaching. Rather more likely, given the stark nature of this summary, is that they indicate the topics to be considered in the Thessalonian letter(s). A study of the verbal forms used indicated how the text should be interpreted. The expression 'you turned to God from idols' indicates the conversion of Gentiles. This process would have been unnecessary for Jews given the monotheist nature of their faith. To be Christian therefore would mean alienation of Roman civic religion and thus to be viewed suspiciously by the civic community and open the possibility of persecution from them. Searching for good news means a reassessment of the idols which afflict contemporary society. What are we being told about them in terms of the Gospel? The process of turning to God means serving God both in terms of devotion and in following particular ethical mores. Then as now this serving involves 'cost', living on 'costly grace', following the implications of the Gospel as a totality in daily life. The reminder of the summary deals with particular Christological tenets implied by serving God through Jesus. One of these is waiting for the *parousia*, the explanation of which is found later at 1 Thessalonians 4:13, 5:11 and 2 Thessalonians 2:1-11. This waiting is based on God's raising of Jesus from the dead (see 1 Cor 15:4bff) and of Jesus acting, as a result, as our rescuer from the coming wrath (later 1 Thess 5:9). These Christological, Gospel 'summaries' have two functions: first, for the letters they ensure that whatever detailed pastoral issue is being considered it is always enshrined within the saving activity of Jesus' death and resurrection and secondly, for us who are considering good news for today, it provides a vital focus for our interpretation of what Paul and his fellow apostolic missionaries are wanting to communicate.

CHAPTER 2

TO THE GALATIANS

St Paul's Letter to the Galatians is one of the most personal and passionate texts in Christian literature. It is not a co-authored letter like 1 and 2 Thessalonians. Galatians deals with the fundamental issue as to how we ought to approach God (4:9) and on what terms (2:19-21). In this letter Paul is opposed totally to some of the answers given by other believers (1:6-8), usually named 'Judaizers', who demand from Gentile converts (4:8) adherence to the Mosaic Law (in Hebrew *Torah*, in Greek *nomos*, 2:16) including circumcision (5:2). The term Judaizers is the name given in contemporary scholarship to Paul's opponents here in Galatia and perhaps also in Corinth and Philippi. The term originates from Paul's question to Cephas in Galatians 2:14 as to why he is encouraging Gentile Christians to judaize (*ioudaizein*, infinitive form of the verb 'to make Jewish'). It would appear that these Jewish Christians were arguing that Gentiles could not be considered fully as 'the new people of God' unless they conformed to all the requirements of the *Torah* (a reflection of their teaching may be seen in 4:10; 5:7-12; 6:12-13). The scope of the *Torah* is greater than the usual English concept of Law and law enforcement. In Hebrew *Torah* means teaching and instruction more like 'way of life' or 'life style' in contemporary English idiomatic speech with the proviso that *Torah* represented God's teaching. The translators of the Hebrew Scriptures into Greek (known as the *Septuagint*, represented by the Roman numerals for 70, LXX) used the Greek word *nomos* to translate *Torah*. Again *nomos* has a broader meaning than our English word law. *Nomos* could mean also custom or tradition and was linked to the Greek concept of justice (*dike*) which would have been well understood by many of Paul's Gentile hearers who inhabited the Graeco-Roman cities of the eastern Mediterranean. For Jews this *Torah* is to be found in the first five books of Sacred Scripture, Genesis through to Deuteronomy, within which God's commandments were delivered to Moses on Mount Sinai (Ex 19ff). These books have been named the Pentateuch, the five fold collection. Their content is fundamental for Judaism (both in Paul's time and our own) as they represent God's covenant (*diatheke*) with his chosen people, Israel, to which adherence to *Torah* is the only proper response. Circumcision was considered a vital sign for entry into God's covenant nation (Gen 17:9-14). Practising *Torah* was Israel's way of being accepted by God. By believing in Jesus' Messianic status, however, Paul, who previously had accepted a traditional interpretation of *Torah* (1:13-14), now argued that being in the right before God is obtained on grounds of faith in Christ (2:20) and through the operation of divine grace (2:21).

Given this complexity relating to the concept and practice of law I have retained, when discussing Paul's usage, the traditional Hebraic term, *Torah*, in order to remind the reader that the discussion focuses on the interpretation offered on the first five books of the Bible. For Paul, the way in which the newly conceived covenant community was entered is of vital importance. Entry into this community, which includes both Jews and Gentiles, is to be gained through Baptism which, in turn, seals both our equality and acceptance before God (3:27-28) and our clothing (3:27) in Christ. As a result circumcision as a rite of entry can now be disregarded. At the same time, however, Paul offers a positive interpretation of *Torah* (5:14; 6:2). It is not that *Torah* is to be abolished (3:21-22) but interpreted as a result of its fulfilment in and through Christ.

It is important to understand in outline terms this Jewish based theology and practice and the background from which the concepts emerged, in order to appreciate the arguments which Paul is presenting, especially both here in Galatians and later in Romans.

SECTION 1 – STRUCTURE

A. OUTLINE

Joseph Fitzmyer (*NJBC*, 47:10) presents a structure outline which follows the rhetorical analysis of the letter of Galatians given by H.D. Betz. In my judgement this approach is both too complicated for the initial stages of study, and academically, begs too many questions relating to Paul's use of Graeco-Roman rhetoric. I suggest that on hearing the letter read aloud in English and noting the questions and emphasis in the text it is possible for us to understand three levels of operation relating to the art of persuasion.

First, there is Paul's attempt to persuade the Galatian Christians to re-examine how they have become bewitched by the Judaizers through accepting a '*Torah*-based' understanding of the Gospel. The second level relates to Paul's confrontation with the Judaizers themselves by presenting his own ideas relating to faith, grace, apostleship and ethics, in contrast to their emphasis on *Torah* observance as an entry-requirement for Gentile believers. Thirdly, from the contemporary standpoint, there is the issue as to how we might enter into this rhetorical debate and what we shall gain by this process. Thus, in place of Betz's rhetorical analysis I have divided the letter into three sections: autobiographical, theological and ethical.

1:1-10	Opening address and warning to the Galatians not to follow a 'different Gospel'.
1:11-2:21	Autobiographical: The Origin and Content of Paul's Gospel (justification by grace through faith).
3:1-5:1	Theological: *Torah*, Faith and Gospel.
5:2-6:10	Ethical: Freedom and love in the power of the Spirit.
6:11-18	Postscript and concluding greetings.

B. LINES OF ARGUMENT

Opening greeting, 1:1-10

Compared with 1 Thessalonians Paul's opening greeting in Galatians is both individual and designed to enter immediately into one of his contentions that his apostolic ministry is based upon his divine call rather than upon human appointment (1:1). Paul is clear that his apostolic ministry was given him by God. While the general custom with regard to the Graeco-Roman letter convention for the opening greeting is followed, nevertheless, Paul adapts the convention to comply with the contents of individual letters and the theological and pastoral issues which he is facing on each occasion. The Galatians are offered the grace (*charis*) and peace (*eirene*) from God and Jesus, as Lord and Christ (1:3; cf. 1 Thess 1:1). In this context Jesus' ministry of dying as a result of human sins and being raised from the dead by the action of God (1:1) is emphasised. As will be explained in the letter, faith (2:16) in this ministry of Jesus forms the foundation upon which the preached Gospel is to be based. This Gospel is centred upon Jesus' ministry of rescuing humanity from the present age which is evil (1:4) with the offer of transforming it into 'a new creation' (6:15) which is the age to come. Within this greeting Paul notes that, while the letter is written in his own hand (6:11), nevertheless a group of brethren (1:2) are with him and sharing in his ministry. Unlike 1 Thessalonians, Galatians is a circular letter written to a group of churches (1:2) and which would have been read, probably in the context of worship (doxology in 1:5), and then passed on by messenger to a neighbouring church.

Unlike other Pauline letters Galatians has no declaration of thanksgiving for the life and ministry of the particular church instead Paul expresses astonishment (1:6) that the Galatians are turning to 'a different Gospel' from that which he preached. Paul uses the powerful verb 'to desert' (*metatithemi*, 1:6, in Greek literature the verb means to change allegiance in political or philosophical terms) to describe the Galatians acceptance of the norms of the Judaizers, i.e. acceptance of Jesus as Christ must be accompanied by strict adherence to Jewish (*Torah*) law (cf. 4:10 and 5:10b). For Paul this acceptance means a denial of the Gospel of 'grace' and 'faith' and those who oppose it will be 'accursed' (*anathema*, 1:8; 1:9, a Jewish idea, Num 21:3; Deut 7:26) by God. It is important at this stage to perceive the Galatians debate, not as between Christian and Jew (cf. 1 Thess 2:14), but as being within Christianity itself. It should be noted also that in the AD 50s these terms were still somewhat fluid.

Autobiographical, 1:11-2:21

Paul's preaching and ministry came by way of the divine revelation (*apokalupsis*, 1:12, verb form in 1:16) received from Jesus Christ. This revelation meant that Paul embraced the new Messianic faith forsaking some of his earlier attitudes and practices 'in Judaism' (1:14) which included the persecution of believers in Jesus as Christ (1:13). This revelation brought with it the assurance that Jesus is God's Son (1:16), that Paul had received a prophetic call (Jer 1:5) as a result of God's grace (1:15, also 2:9) and that his particular ministry was to proclaim this Gospel to the Gentile nations (1:16). Thus, through this experience, it was confirmed that Paul had been set apart and called (*kaleo*) by God into faith and ministry. The concept of 'call' (Latin *vocare*, root word for vocation) will develop in Paul's thought (see later, 1 Cor 1:1; 1:2; 1:9) in terms of his apostolic role within the divine mission. As a result of his experience Paul saw no need to confer with the Jerusalem apostles but went to Arabia and then Damascus (1:17). The Jerusalem visit did not take place for a further three years and then for only fifteen days, Paul holding consultations with Cephas (Peter) and James, the Lord's brother (1:18 and 19).

Fourteen years later Paul visited Jerusalem accompanied by Barnabas and Titus (2:1). This visit was a private one to the leaders of the church who were 'of repute' (2:2), also called 'pillars': James (1:19), Cephas (1:18) and John. This visit was not at their command but as a result of a 'revelation' (2:2) from God on similar terms to which Paul's call and commission had been revealed to him (1:16). The purpose of the visit was for Paul to ascertain if his evangelisation of Gentiles, and what was required from them in terms of religious practice, was in accordance with God's plan for the extension of the Messianic community (2:3). Although certain Judaizers infiltrated the discussion (2:4), the Jerusalem leaders affirmed the Pauline mission to the Gentiles (2:7; 2:9), agreed that their mission should be directed to the Jews (2:7; 2:9) and there was common agreement relating to serving the poor (2:10; also 1 Cor 16:1-3; Rom 15:25-26 from Psalm 41:1) which is of crucial importance for Paul for the manifestation of the Gospel in action. Evidence of the Jerusalem leaders' good faith was that Titus, who was a Greek, was not compelled to be circumcised (2:3). The unanswered question is whether or not the Judaizers would accept this situation, given that not all the implications (see later, 2:12) of the Gentile mission had been considered. There is also the issue to which the extent of the agreement between Paul and the Jerusalem 'pillars' could be sustained given that the division of apostolic labour between Jewish and Gentile evangelisation would, in practice, be somewhat fluid.

Paul then relates how serious difficulties arose in Antioch relating to eating practices within the Messianic community (2:12). These difficulties led to a quarrel with Cephas (2:11) which involved both the representatives from James (2:12) and Barnabas (2:13). The Jewish legal mores were that the food consumed should be kosher and that this food should not be eaten in the company of Gentiles (cf. contemporary Jewish practice in the book of Jubilees 22:16). If these mores were accepted within the Messianic community, Paul argued, then the implications of the Gospel of Jesus Christ based on grace and faith, rather than on Jewish nationality and its Law, would be seriously compromised. From this pastoral situation Paul's theology of justification (2:16) by grace (2:21) through faith (2:16) is developed. Paul explains his argument as follows:

1. Both he and Cephas were born Jews. Through their acceptance of the Gospel and the practice of its ministry they have lived like Gentiles, sharing their food and fellowship (for Cephas note Acts 10:13-15). Why then is Cephas now forcing Gentiles within the Messianic community to become Jews (2:14)?

2. The way to be in the right (*dikaioo*) before God is not by practising the 'works' (2:16) of the *Torah*, but through faith in Christ (2:16, the idea is repeated in both parts of the verse).

3. This justification should not imply that believers cease to be sinners (2:17). This idea is part of Paul's 'now' but 'not-yet' of salvation. Believers receive 'rightness' before God now, the totality of which will be experienced in the future (see later 1 Cor 15:22). In order that this tension remains, Paul asks if this state of affairs means that Christ himself is a minister of sin. The reply comes in one of Paul's forceful negatives, 'certainly not' (2:17).

4. In continuing to express his theological and pastoral position Paul now uses personal statements rather than general maxims. If he returns now to practise the 'works of the law' then his 'conversion' to Christ would have been in vain. In accepting God's offer of free grace in Christ as a result of faith (2:20) Paul 'died to the law' (2:19). He has been co-crucified (2:20) with Christ who lives in him (2:20). This Christocentric faith results because of Christ's prior love and self-offering for Paul. If Paul were now to declare that 'being in the right' before God was achieved through the Mosaic *Torah* then it follows that Christ's death, which is the means of uniting to God, was in vain (2:21).

Theological, 3:1-5:1

In 3:1 Paul turns his attention to the Galatian situation. Building on his personal experience Paul questions the Galatians' readiness to accept the theory and practice of the Judaizers (1:6). These questions are based on the implications of Christ's crucifixion (3:1; 2:20) and on the relationship between their understanding of law, faith, flesh (including circumcision, 2:3; 5:2ff; 6:12-15) and 'the Spirit' (*to pneuma*, 3:2; 3:3; 3:5; 5:16ff). Of these concepts mention of 'the Spirit' forms a new element in the argument. Given that Paul's use of this term is many and various it seems that, at this point, he is referring probably to the divine life force (e.g. Ps 104:30a; Ezek 36:26) which is received at Baptism (3:28) when believers acclaimed their belief in God as Father and in the salvation achieved through the ministry of Christ (4:6). If the Spirit has been received, why should the Galatian Christians feel it necessary to accept circumcision, a 'work' (3:5) demanded in the *Torah* for entry into God's covenant community (Gen 17:9-14)?

Given that it was to Abraham that God first gave the command regarding circumcision, Paul now considers the role of Abraham both in terms of being 'the father of a multitude of nations' (Gen 17:5) and in his place in God's plan of salvation. In his first reference to Abraham (3:6) Paul begins by quoting Genesis 15:6 in order to confirm from Scripture that Abram was declared 'to be in the right' before God on the basis of Abram's belief in his supremacy over world events (Gen 13:14-17). On this basis those (in particular Gentile believers) who have faith in the saving power of Jesus the Messiah become sons of Abraham (3:7). This position is confirmed by reference to Genesis 12:3 and 18:18 where God's promise of blessing to Abraham is offered to all nations. By implication, in this context, this promise is offered to all Christian believers who have expressed their faith in Jesus Christ (3:1). This reference to Abraham in turn leads Paul to consider the grounds upon which Christ gained salvation for humanity (3:10-13). Paul's method here is to state a proposition which he confirms by a scriptural reference (e.g. *Torah* rests on faith, Leviticus 18:5). The purpose of his exposition is two fold: first, that Gentile believers in Christ will receive the blessings promised by God to Abraham and his descendents (3:14a). Secondly that, as a result of faith in this belief, the promise of the Spirit is granted (3:14b). The two clauses which form this exposition begin with 'so that' in order to demonstrate that what Christ has achieved might also be shared by believers.

Arising from this complex nexus relating to Spirit, inheritance, Law, curse and redemption, Paul now asks about the point and purpose of *Torah* in the context of God's revelation in Christ (3:19). First, Paul uses the concept of covenant agreement (3:15 and 3:17). Using covenant (*diatheke*) in the sense of a will, Paul argues that it is impossible to add a codicil after the will has been ratified. As a result God's covenant, using the term now in the sense of living agreement, made with Abraham, offers an inheritance to a single offspring (*sperma*, seed) who is Christ (3:18). Secondly, there is the historical issue that God's promise to Abraham (Gen 17:4ff) was given 430 years before the *Torah* was given to Moses on Mount Sinai (Ex 20:1ff). Yet the former promise remains valid even after Moses received the *Torah* because God is one and always acts without contradition or division (3:20). Thirdly, by its nature as law the *Torah* exposes human sin. The question now presented by Paul to the Galatians is, how can this sin, alienation from God, be removed from humanity? Paul's answer is that its removal can be obtained by faith in the redemption offered through the crucifixion of Jesus Christ. Through this action (3:22 and looking back through the argument to 3:13; 3:3 and 2:20) humanity can become 'in the right' before God (2:16). Fourthly, and as a result of the above action of Christ, the *Torah* now has a temporary role. To explain this temporality Paul uses the image of the schoolmaster (*paidagogos*, 3:24-25, cf. Stanton, *OBC*, 1160). When the student reaches maturity he needs no longer the discipline of a schoolmaster, so it follows that when faith in Christ is professed the ritual discipline of the *Torah* is no longer required. Fifthly, the two related questions now arise, who is able, and by what method, can this renewed (6:15) covenant community of Israel (6:16) be entered? The answers are: i. who – all humanity of whatever station in life, ethnic origin or gender (3:28) who have faith in the redemptive power of Jesus (3:26); ii. by what method – through the sacrament of Baptism (3:27) which makes the request for circumcision redundant (5:2).

This theme of inheritance and maturity is continued in chapter 4 with a reference to slavery. The Galatians were once slaves (*douloi*) to the 'elemental spirits' of the world (4:3) and by using a Christological confessional statement in 4:4 and 4:5 Paul illustrates how freedom through Christ can be obtained. It is possible that Paul uses the slavery metaphor on two levels: first, being largely Gentiles (4:8), and as a result of their faith in Christ, the Galatians are now free from the superstitious elements which bind humanity. Secondly, they are also free from the burden of circumcision (5:2-6). The Christological statement here has a six-fold pattern. It is important to present this pattern clearly as Paul uses similar Christological statements elsewhere in order to secure particular arguments (see later; for example, 1 Cor 15:3ff; 2 Cor 5:21; 8:9; Rom 1:3-4; 4:25; Phil 2:6-11 and Col 1:15-20). These statements, which may have been part of the liturgy of church worship or may have been proclaimed by Paul himself, are wedded always to their context. If already used liturgically their contents would not only be familiar to the worshippers but their use in a worship setting would have given them greater solemnity and authority. In each case, therefore, the pattern of the confession and the context should be understood. In Galatians 4:4 the Christological progression is:

1. But when the fullness of time came
2. God sent forth his Son,
3. having been born of a woman,
4. having been born under *Torah*,
5. in order that he might redeem those under *Torah*,
6. in order that we might receive adoption as sons.

This confession is then related to the redeemed (4:5; cf. 3:13), faith-status of the Galatians. They are granted adoption as sons as a result of Jesus' Sonship in relation to the Father (background, 2 Sam 7:14) which includes the giving of his Spirit (4:6, cf. 3:3 and 3:5). The ancient Aramaic (Mk 14:36; Rom 8:15) address to God as '*Abba*' (4:6) is maintained indicating the intimacy of relationship of the believers to God. Their status is that of sons and heirs not as slaves or minors (4:7).

At 4:8 Paul returns to the situation in the Galatian churches and of his original apostolic ministry amongst them (4:11). Having explained their faith-status and recalling how they became known by God (4:9), Paul asks why they are reverting to the observation of the Jewish Sabbath and Jewish festivals. By asking this question Paul is entering into the Galatians' dilemma. For them the acceptance of monotheism would imply entry into Judaism. Faith in Jesus' redemptive activity meant however that, according to Paul, certain elements of the *Torah*: circumcision, not eating with Gentiles, keeping the Sabbath and other festivals need not be practised or observed. At 4:12 Paul's appeal to the Galatians becomes personal. He returns to the issue of his own ministry (1:6-9) and faces the various issues as to how it might have gone wrong and why (4:12-18). Paul's tone varies between the strident (1:9 and 4:11) and the perplexed (4:20), which represents his attempt to understand fully the nature of his apostolic vocation. In doing so Paul returns to its Christological focus (1:1; 1:3; 1:12). On this occasion it is applied to Galatians by use of the metaphor of pregnancy (4:19). If only the Galatians would allow Christ to be formed (*morphoo*, note the use of the noun Christologically in Phil 2:6 and 7) in their 'womb'.

At 4:21 Paul reverts to the slavery/freedom issue (4:22), in this instance in relation to the Galatians continuing desire to live under *Torah*. To illustrate this point Paul uses elements of the Hagar-Sarah narratives found in Genesis 16-21. These narratives are used allegorically in Galatians:

Hagar = slave woman.	Sarah = free woman.
Mt Sinai = location where the *Torah* was given, represents the old covenant.	By implication Jesus' action, represents the new covenant.
Earthly Jerusalem = for where Paul's opponents emerge (2:12). SLAVERY	Heavenly Jerusalem = divine revelation of the Gospel (1:13). FREEDOM

Paul's understanding of the freedom of the heavenly Jerusalem is allied with the concept of motherhood and the use of the quotation from Isaiah 54:1 (4:27). This combination is ironical. The 'barren one' of Isaiah refers back to Sarah who, as a result of God's action gave birth to Isaac, Abraham's heir. In the same way the true faith orientated, Spirit filled believers in Galatia are able to receive the new birth of God given inheritance. But are they? Paul's opponents in Galatia are hindering this process by demanding *Torah* adherence.

Like Hagar (Gen 21:10) they should be dismissed from the Galatian churches (4:30).

5:1 probably forms the climax and conclusion to this section while preparing for the next. It should be seen, most likely, in two parts. First, there is the statement that for the sake of freedom (from *Torah* obligation) Christ has set us free (5:1a, cf. 3:13). Secondly, Paul issues an injunction to the Galatians that they are to remain loyal to the Gospel of faith and of the Spirit which Paul preached to them originally, and which they accepted at the time, and not revert, as the opponents would argue, to the practice of the *Torah*. Although we can only speculate as to how far the previously Gentile Galatian believers understood the complexity of Paul's scriptural arguments, in the end a clear choice lay before them: a faith of slavery or freedom represented by adherence either to Paul or the Judaizers.

Ethical, 5:2-6:18

For Paul ethics, in the sense of codes of behaviour, are always governed by theology, thus the various sections of Galatians overlap with each other and their categorisation is merely a useful way of following Paul's lines of argument. We can speculate that, for the Judaizers, if Gentiles are not required to adhere to the *Torah* within Judaism what then becomes of the ethical framework for living?

In response to this position Paul summarises his argument thus far in terms of how freedom in Christ is to be understood (5:2-12). He maintains that, in this context, circumcision is of no value (5:1) and that submission to circumcision means that the injunctions of the *Torah* as a whole must be kept (5:3). 5:4 and 5:5, returning to the argument of 2:15-21, balances the negative and the positive aspects of the debate. On one hand justification through *Torah* means that grace is abandoned as is redemption through Christ; on the other, faith is given through the Spirit (cf. 3:3) and, as a result, the hope of righteousness is assured. Within this dichotomy the moral demands of Christ are clear, circumcision is of no value ethically only faith working through love. 5:7 returns to the issue of the behaviour of the Galatians (from 1:6-9) who, in accepting the practices of the Judaizers, have thereby abandoned the teaching of Paul. In this regard he uses an athletic metaphor (5:7a) to describe the Galatians' conduct and a culinary one (5:9) to describe that of the Judaizers. Paul, not only believes that they will be subject to the Lord's judgement (5:10b), but also wishes that those who demand circumcision would castrate themselves (5:12). In addition to the antitheses between circumcision and Baptism and *Torah* and Spirit there now reappears the dichotomy between the ministry of Paul and that of the Judaizers. Their ministry leads to deception and slavery while the faith-centred (5:5 cf. 2:16), cross-proclaiming ministry (5:11a cf. 2:20a) of Paul leads to freedom. In this context he asks why he remains a victim of persecution (5:11b cf. 4:29, with its allusion to Gen 21:9, and 4:16-17).

5:13-26 both renews the analysis of the freedom theme of 5:1, with its scriptural background example of 4:2-31, and discusses the ethical implications of freedom in a context where the *Torah* as a means of justification is no longer required. 5:13 both prepares the hearer for the Spirit (*pneuma*) flesh (*sarx*) discussion of 5:16-26 and indicates the need for internal harmony (5:15 for the dangers of division) and the basis of love (*agape*) upon which mutual service within the Galatian community should be based. In 5:14 the concept of *Torah* is used in a positive sense (cf. 4:21). The quotation from Leviticus 19:18 indicates the moral foundation on which affairs are to be conducted amongst the believers (later at 6:10) and the way in which *Torah* has been fulfilled through the ministry of Christ.

In this context believers are to 'walk' (5:16, Hebraic ethical terminology) by the Spirit which is the life-force on which their filial relationship with God is based (4:6). This living by the Spirit is contrasted with gratifying the desires of the flesh (5:16). For Paul flesh (*sarx*) represents earthly, material existence without reference to the moral demands of God. For the Galatians the issue is set clearly before them: on what basis do they conduct their lives: Spirit or flesh, and how are these qualities manifested by the various types of human conduct? If the Galatians use the Spirit as their moral guide then they need not be concerned with the authority of *Torah* (5:18). Then follows a list of the various vices and virtues which result from living by either the flesh or the Spirit. These lists were a familiar feature of both Greek and Jewish literature; for Paul, however, their context is Christological, the crucifixion of Christ, having destroyed 'the flesh' (5:24), provides a new Spirit-based ethic (5:25) constructed on love (5:6 and 5:14) and mutual respect (5:26). 6:1-10 offers a series of general ethical imperatives. The basis of their interpretation both in terms of thought and practice is to be found in the phrase 'and so you will fulfil the law of Christ' (6:2b). The wisdom sayings of 6:1-10 are thus given new meaning as a result of the ministry and salvation offered by Christ. The 'so then' which begins 6:10 marks the conclusion of the ethical section. The injunction is two-fold. First, given the differences in both theological perception and social consciousness within the Galatian churches outlined in the letter, the believers are to strive for a spirit of unity (cf. 3:28). Secondly, they are to reflect the virtue of goodness to society as a whole.

The postscript and concluding greetings (6:11-18), as is usual in Pauline letters, summarise the contents. Paul's insistence on writing in large letters in his own hand (6:11) in this section of Galatians emphasises the personal importance that he places on the statements which the letter contains. The theological position relating to Christ's crucifixion, the uselessness of circumcision, Paul's own ministry (6:14) and the believing community in terms of being 'a new creation' (6:15) and the reconstituted 'Israel of God' (6:16). Unlike some other Pauline letters (e.g. 1 Cor 16:15-20) Galatians concludes with no personal greetings. Instead, first, Paul requests to be left alone (6:17a, and not to be subjected to the abuse of the Judaizers, 5:11?) and secondly, he wants the Galatians to know that on his body are to be found the marks (*stigmata*) of Jesus (6:17b). This fact links intrinsically the sufferings experienced by Paul in his apostolic ministry to those of the crucified Jesus. The letter ends Christologically with the grace formula (6:18 cf. 1:3) and with the Semitic 'Amen' (so be it) which affirms the contents of the letter and brings it full circle (5:17 cf. 1:10).

SECTION 2 – CONTEXT

A. THE ENVIRONMENT

The difficulty of finding a precise environment for the letter to the Galatians stems from the problem of knowing where 'the churches of Galatia' (1:2) are to be located, and is intimately connected with the question of the ethnic identity of the Galatians (3:1). In the 50s AD the Roman province of Galatia occupied the central section of what is now modern Turkey and stretched from its boundary with Pontus in the north to Pamphylia on the Mediterranean sea coast in the south. Thus 'the churches of Galatia' could have been situated in the north of the province (around modern Ankara) where the native Galatians (3:1) lived who were descended ethnically from the Indo-Aryan Celts or Gauls who had settled in this region in the third century BC. Alternatively, 'the churches of Galatia' could have been situated in the south of the province which encompassed the cities of (Pisidian) Antioch, Iconium, Lystra and Derbe (cf. *BSGT,* 152-161).

When Luke came to narrate Paul's missionary activity he found considerable information related to his ministry in the southern cities (Acts 13:1-14:28, see Map 2) but Luke's references to Paul's subsequent missionary activity in Galatia as a whole are somewhat vague (Acts 16:6-7, 'Phrygia and Galatia... opposite Mysia' and Acts 18:23, 'the region of Galatia and Phrygia', see Map 3). This uncertainty of locating the Galatian churches has lead to a division in contemporary Pauline scholarship between those who argue for a north Galatian destination and those who believe that the letter was written to the cities in the south to which Luke later refers in detail (Brown, *INT,* 474-476). Although this division of opinion does not affect the basic interpretation of the letter it does have implications, however, for any discussion relating to the chronological development of early Christianity and of Paul's role within that development, the extent to which the Galatian believers were either Jews or had knowledge of Judaism (Luke notes the presence of synagogues in Antioch, Acts 13:14 and Iconium, 14:1) and for the dating of the

Galatian letter. Finally, if the north Galatian destination is accepted, it is difficult to see why Paul is evangelising in what appears to be a political backwater away from major highways, in sharp contrast to his usual choice of prominent, accessible urban centres.

B. THE GALATIAN CHURCHES WITHIN PAUL'S MISSIONARY ACTIVITY

The difficulty of placing the Galatian letter within Paul's missionary activity is further complicated by attempts to relate Paul's chronology to that of Luke: which of Luke's apostolic conferences is being referred to in Galatians 2:1-10, that of Acts 11:29-30 or 15:1-29 and why does not Paul refer to the so called 'apostolic decree' of Acts 15:20; 15:29 and 21:25? Galatians could have precipitated the Acts 15 conference, in which case Paul's letter predated the apostolic decrees recounted in Acts 15:20ff, or it could have been written after it, in which case Paul presumably chose not to discuss the recent decrees. These alternatives account for the variety of dates offered (between 50 and 55) for the composition of Galatians.

This historical difficulty of placing Galatians precisely within Paul's missionary activity should not deter us from perceiving the theological and pastoral clarity with which Paul is tackling his major point of disagreement with the Judaizers (and perhaps with even the Jerusalem pillars, Galatians 2:6 and 2:9?): namely, what 'shape' is this Christological movement within Judaism to take? How are Gentiles to be received into it and what entry rituals should be required of them? Whatever differences there are between Paul's understanding and Luke's interpretation of him, nevertheless questions relating to Gentile entry and the requirements demanded of them as a result of their entry were matters of major 'internal pluralism' within Christianity from c. AD 35-65.

SECTION 3 – THEOLOGICAL, PASTORAL AND HERMENEUTICAL ISSUES

I highlight three particular areas for consideration of Paul's message in terms of 'Good News for Today'.

1. Grace and Law

One of the challenges in presenting Galatians hermeneutically in the contemporary age is that the original context of the letter, the issue of Christian believers being expected to adhere to Jewish mores is now not applicable, while the theological perceptions which the letter enshrines are, in my judgement, as relevant and powerful as ever. No one today would even contemplate that converts to Christianity should embrace also the facets of Judaism such as circumcision, kosher food laws and, more generally, practise that Paul calls 'works of the law' (2:16). Yet Paul's theological ideas relating to Christian initiation: justification, faith, grace, which receive public recognition through Baptism (3:27-28), form the bedrock of contemporary Christian Theology. In this context 'works of the law' might be interpreted as those religious actions which are undertaken mechanically without reason, thought or heart. Paul helps us to perceive that other attitudes and vocabulary are needed for the journey into Church membership: Spirit, grace, faith and freedom.

At the centre of Christian initiation, and to explain the process by which it is achieved, Paul employs the concept of justification (2:21; 3:6, a quotation; 3:21; 5:5), of being declared to be 'in the right' before God (2:16; 2:17; 3:8; 3:11; 3:24; 5:4). These terms are not easy to explain given the difficulty of translating, both in form of concept and language, from their Greek original into English. The nearest we have are the ideas of justice and righteousness. In this context it should be noted that the Greek *dikaio* words from which these terms originated formed the basic structure of the Greek social and political order as found in the concept of *dike*. In Jewish thought they referred also to the way in which Israel should live theologically and ethically in the way God requires: 'to do justice, and to love kindness, and to walk humbly...' (Micah 6:8). Given these antecedents it can be seen that these terms, as used by Paul, are metaphors from the realm of judges, political assemblies and law courts. They are metaphors which Paul's Galatian hearers would have understood easily on account of their social and political activity. Paul, however, interprets them, in the sphere of his missionary activity, theologically and Christologically. God is the perfect judge because he is perfectly righteous. We are sinners. We have 'missed the mark' of righteousness (2:15). Thus, in terms of God's power we should be declared 'guilty'. Instead, through the redemptive action of Christ Jesus (3:13) we are justified, acquitted in the sight of God and, as a result, are able to inherit the blessing once offered to Abraham (3:14).

Within this idea of justification two other terms need to be considered: faith (*pistis*) and grace (*charis*). The term 'faith' occurs twenty times in Galatians where Paul uses the term to illustrate a dual truth: first, that we recognise ourselves as sinful and unable to enter the newly established covenant community as a result of personal merit by practising 'works of the law'. Secondly that we profess our belief in Christ Jesus in order that God's salvation might be received (2:16). Faith is our trustful response to God's revelation in Christ. It can be demonstrated by Paul's own response to 'a revelation of Jesus Christ' (1:12) that he received and to which he responded by accepting the commission to be a preacher 'among the Gentiles' (1:16).

Grace is God's favour towards undeserving humanity. This concept is used as a greeting (1:3; 6:18), it is a characteristic of a loving God (2:21); the way of receiving the Gospel of God's gift of salvation in Christ (1:6) and the means by which Paul's commission for ministry is given (1:15) and sustained (2:9). It is possible to fall away from grace (5:4) as the Galatians have done by accepting the teaching of the Judaizers. Although these terms have a wide variety of meaning nevertheless their basic focus in Galatians is to demonstrate the character of God, the Christological foundation for salvation and the proper attitudes needed for initiation both into Christ, and into his redeemed community. For Gentile converts initiation into the 'right' (Paul's) interpretation of Jewish theology would also be required, in particular in relation to monotheism and ethics.

The concepts of justification, faith and grace are symbolised, and given visible reality, through the rite of Baptism. In Galatians this rite is explained in terms of 'being clothed' in Christ (3:27). The consequences of Baptism are manifested in the universalisation of the community. In it boundaries of ethnicity (Jew/Gentile), social status (slave/freeman) and gender (male/female) disappear because, ideally, in the new community '...are all one in Christ Jesus' (3:28).

2. Paul's apostleship

Fundamental to Paul's self understanding of his call from God is the concept of apostleship. The concept is an ambassadorial metaphor, being sent as an agent of some higher authority. Paul is clear that he is an ambassador 'through Jesus Christ and God the Father' (1:1). In Galatians Paul emphasises that this office is exercised as a result of divine calling, for the evangelisation of the Gentiles, and not as a result of any human agency (1:12-16). It is likely that Paul envisages his apostleship as both conferring a 'status' or 'office' within God's plan of salvation through Christ with a particular commission. However Paul's apostolic status is to be interpreted, it is clear that he believes that it confers divine authority both to preach and uphold the Gospel (1:6) concerning justification before God in terms of faith and grace. He aims to be identified totally with the message which he is proclaiming and with the mission to which he has been commissioned. This identification is expressed in terms of apostleship. It is likely that, first the Judaizers, and later the Galatians, questioned both Paul's apostolic status and the way he exercises the apostleship, which would explain the extent to which, in Galatians 1 and 2, he is prepared to present, in autobiographical terms, the nature of his apostolic calling.

The other two uses of apostle in this letter refer to the Jerusalem apostles, in particular Cephas and James the Lord's brother (1:17 and 1:19) whom Paul visited after three (1:18) and fourteen years (2:1) of ministry respectively. Although it is sometimes claimed that early Christianity was divided between the 'Pauline group' and the 'Petrine, Jerusalem apostles' group, I imagine that in reality the situation was more subtle and complex. I suspect that Paul's own understanding of his position was more ambivalent than he would like to suggest. On one hand he wished to emphasise his personal, divine call and commission to apostleship, on the other hand he wished to consult, and perhaps even gain the approval of, those who were 'apostles before him' (1:17). In this desire Paul was unable to avoid Jerusalem in his reflection upon the origin of Christianity. First, because it was the historical venue for Jesus' crucifixion and resurrection together with the resonances of it being David's city (2 Sam 5:7 and the sonship motif, Ps 2:7). Secondly, Cephas and John were called to apostleship by the earthly Jesus and James was a member of his family. Their historical and authoritative 'pride of place' seem to have been recognised by Paul in 1:17. Hermeneutically Paul's ambivalence in this regard is understandable given the tension often felt between centralised ecclesiastical bureaucracy and the local churches.

If we are to detect within Paul's concept of apostleship both external opposition and internal ambivalence then we should note another designation which accompanies it that of being a slave of Christ (1:10, also later at Rom 1:1 where apostle and slave are found together; see also Phil 2:7, where Christ assumes the form of a slave). The institution of slavery was all pervading in the Graeco-Roman world. For Paul it meant that, like a slave was dependent totally on his master, so he is dependent totally on Christ, having no 'rights' apart from him. In this regard Paul fully identifies his ministry with Christ's crucifixion. Paul has been crucified with Christ (2:19); his bodily ailment identifies Paul with Christ's sufferings (4:13); Paul does not glory in anything except Christ's cross (6:14) and the marks that he bears for Jesus are like those branded on the skin of slaves (6:17). Paul know that his ministry was dependent on Christ's crucifixion for redemption (3:13) and for delivering from 'sins' (1:4). Christ's offering in this regard meant; first, that Paul's ministry was not based on 'saying the right things' in order to persuade (1:10), but in order to proclaim the Gospel relating to Jesus Christ's work of salvation, the entry into which was based on justification, faith and grace available to all humanity. Secondly, Christ's redemptive work offers freedom from the bondage of evil under which humanity is labouring (1:4). Ironically, it is only when the crucifixion of Christ is experienced that freedom can be known (5:1). Was it the failure to perceive this irony that proved to be the weakest point of the Judaizers' otherwise apparently persuasive argument (5:4 and 5:8)?

In the attempt to understand Paul's position hermeneutically I should argue that it is essential that, in terms of contemporary ministry, in particular but not exclusively ordained ministry, we wrestle with Paul's categories and relate them to our own contexts. As our 'dialogue' with Paul's ministry emerges through the study of his letters, the categories of mission and Gospel, apostleship and servant-hood, together with our identification with Christ's ministry revealed through his death and resurrection, will both inform and renew our ministry in its contemporary setting.

3. Ethics

Paul's Galatian hearers would have been well aware of *ethikos* (although Paul does not use the term) of the appropriate behaviour expected within society. Aristotle had argued that living ethically ought to result in virtuous conduct given that virtue (*arete*) was the highest goal for humanity to obtain (see the opening sentence of *Nicomachean Ethics*, 1094a). In our attempt to relate contemporary ethical issues with those of Paul and his historical and intellectual antecedents, how should ethics be defined? Ethics is concerned with the making of moral choices, to consider the values which lie behind these choices and the principles on which they are based. Ethics is also concerned with character, both the character of the community and its striving for justice, and the character of the individual and of the relationship between them. Aristotle's basic question is: what is the best way for humanity to live? In Galatians Paul helps us to reflect upon these issues and, in particular, on the principles on which they are based. Thus Galatians assists us more with ethical principles rather than with specific ethical issues (although particular vices are mentioned in 5:19-21), such as marriage (see later 1 Cor 7).

As with theology, Paul confronts and expounds issues as they arise in the particular churches and not for their own sake. The major principles in Galatians on which ethical matters are based are: first, the concept of law (*nomos*). Like *ethikos* the Galatians would have well understood *nomos* as a principle. It is well expressed by Pericles in his Funeral Oration, 431/430 BC, '...when it is a question of settling private disputes, everybody is equal before the law (*nomos*)... in public affairs we keep to the law... for we render obedience to those in authority and to the laws (*nomoi*) and especially to those laws, although unwritten, which are desired to protect the oppressed...' (Thucydides, *History of the Peloponnesian War*, Book 2:37, my general translation). In this speech law (*nomos*) is interweaved with justice (*dike*) for the good ordering of the city (*polis*), and serves as an example of the civic context in which the Galatian believers would have associated such concepts.

The Galatians would have also been introduced to another concept of *nomos* that of the Jewish *Torah*. The question now arises as to the value of *Torah* within an ethical framework. Paul speaks of 'the law of love' (5:14) and 'the law of Christ' (6:2). It would appear that Paul is arguing for the continuing value of *Torah* ethically so long as it is interpreted through Christ's saving action and mission. In this context social *ethikos* is governed by *Torah* interpreted Christologically.

The second concept which Paul utilises is that of Spirit (*pneuma*). For Paul, the Spirit is the operation of God's love which imparts life, a life which belongs to Christ and as such is superior to *nomos* (5:18b) because *nomos* is now interpreted as a result of the Spirit's work (5:18a). The manifestation of the Spirit indicates the arrival of God's new, eschatological, age. One of the features of it would be the moral behaviour of those who accept it (5:25a). They must 'walk by the Spirit' (5:16 and 5:25b). This ethic probably emerged as a result of Paul's reflection upon Jewish prophetic texts relating to the Spirit, for example, Ezekiel 36:27. Living and walking by the Spirit is manifested negatively by the avoidance of vice (5:19-21), as activities by which the kingdom of God cannot be inherited (5:21b) but also positively by practising 'the fruit of the Spirit' (5:22). The metaphor of fruit indicates both that these virtues are offered as a gift from the Spirit but also with the obligation they must be visible ethically in the lives of the believers who operate under the grace of the Spirit.

Thirdly, Paul utilises the concept of freedom. 5:1 is an example as to how the indicative and the imperative function ethically in this regard:

5:1a   Indicative statement, 'For freedom Christ has set us free'.

5:1b   Imperative command (how to act ethically on the basis of the statement): 'Stand fast therefore, and do not submit again to a yoke of slavery'.

Like the other principles, the Galatian believers would have been aware of the background to these concepts of freedom and slavery both in theory and practice. Paul builds upon this knowledge to expound them in a particular way. First, any claim to freedom must be based upon Christ's saving power. Secondly, there can be no freedom ethically without recourse to obligation and responsibility, manifested by the avoidance of vice and serving the brethren 'through love' (5:13). From Paul's perspective his moral maxims/ethical imperatives are based on the theological indicative manifested by God's offer of salvation through Christ in the power of the Spirit. In this context it is Paul's concern that believers live ethically in accordance with the values that they have been offered through their acceptance of the salvation which they have received through Christ. Ethical issues, therefore, are to be discussed, and the ethical life experienced, on the basis of God's grace (1:3 and 6:18).

Galatians forms an excellent basis for reflection on the good news which Paul offers, both in the context of its original composition, and in his subsequent ministry, as many of the themes stated within the letter are utilised later. Galatians serves also as an example how concepts already known to the believers: justice, law, freedom and slavery, for example, are given new meaning by Paul as a result of his Christian missionary theology and of his reflections on the ethical behavioural patterns of those who accepted this theology.

CHAPTER 3

TO THE CORINTHIANS

Paul engaged in a prolonged correspondence with the communities in Corinth, subsequent to his foundation of the Corinthian church in 51-52 AD, at various times between c. 54-57 AD. Portions of this extensive correspondence are preserved in the canonical letters, 1 and 2 Corinthians, whilst reference is made to additional letters which are no longer extant (e.g. a 'previous letter', 1 Corinthians 1:9, in which the Corinthians are warned not to associate with immoral people).

The precise extent of Paul's correspondence with the Corinthians is complicated by queries surrounding the order and integrity of the documents that have been preserved, in particular 2 Corinthians. Is it possible that 2 Corinthians is comprised of two (or more) originally independent letter fragments that have been combined in its present canonical form? One influential theory, as outlined, for example, by Jerome Murphy-O'Connor, divides 2 Corinthians into two originally distinct letters:

Letter A
2 Cor 1-9
Letter B
2 Cor 10-13

The principal reason for this proposed division is a perceived shift in tone that takes place in 2 Corinthians chapter 10, leading Jerome Murphy O'Connor to conclude that: 'it is psychologically impossible that Paul should switch from warm, generous celebration of reconciliation with the Corinthians (ch 1-9) to savage reproach and sarcastic self-vindication (ch 10-13)' (*CCStP*, 83-84, cf. also MacDonald, *OBC*, 1134). (For a further range of alternative reconstructions of multiple letter fragments in 2 Corinthians consult H.D. Betz's article in the *Anchor Bible Dictionary*, I, 1148-54).

The literary integrity of Paul's correspondence with the

Corinthians is intimately bound up with broader historical reconstructions of Paul's missionary involvement with the city (both periods of extended residency in the city and briefer visits) mentioned both within these letters and as described in a more schematic fashion in Acts (cf. 2 Cor 2:1; 12:14; 13:1; Acts 18:1, 20:2).

Within this historical and literary complex there arises the issue how best to study the Corinthian correspondence. The proposed method of this study is to begin with the surviving texts in their canonical order (1 Corinthians, 2 Corinthians). It is preferable to begin with the 'final form' of this corpus, as preserved in the earliest manuscript witnesses (e.g. P46), in order to consider carefully the content, structure and tone of this correspondence in its preserved form. Once readers are familiar with the content and flow of these letters they will then be in a stronger position critically to evaluate various compositional theories of the original order and integrity of these letters (especially 2 Corinthians) outlined in the scholarly literature referred to above.

SECTION 1 – STRUCTURE

A. OUTLINE – 1 CORINTHIANS

1:1-9	Opening greeting and thanksgiving
1:10-4:21	Divisions within the church community with the exercise of the apostolic ministry.
5:1-6:20	Divisions within the church community relating to unethical behaviour of members.
7:1-40	Answers to the questions the Corinthians asked, marriage and social status.
8:1-11:1	Answers to questions, living in the city, Paul's apostolic authority.
11:2-34	Answers to questions, within the worshipping assembly.
12:1-14:40	Answers to questions, Spiritual gifts, love and worship.
15:1-58	The Gospel and the resurrection.

2 CORINTHIANS

B. LINES OF ARGUMENT

1 CORINTHIANS

Opening Greeting, 1:1-9

Paul's opening greeting in 1 Corinthians follows a similar structure to that found already in 1 and 2 Thessalonians and Galatians but with some interesting features brought about because of the particular Corinthian context. First, Paul utilises the language of 'call' (Greek *kaleo*). He refers to his personal call (1 Cor 1:1) to apostolic ministry in the name of 'Christ Jesus'. The Corinthians are called to be God's holy ones (1 Cor 1:2) because, in company with believers everywhere, they call upon (1 Cor 1:2) the name of the Lord Jesus Christ in worship. Paul uses these 'call words' to illustrate how his apostolic ministry (1 Cor 15:9) and the Corinthians' call to Christian discipleship (1 Cor 1:9) are intrinsically linked. The combination, however, will manifest itself in the tensions which arose (at many levels) between Paul and the Corinthian church.

Secondly, Paul associates Sosthenes with the writing of the letter (1 Cor 1:1). It is likely that he is the same person mentioned by Luke as 'the ruler of the synagogue' (Acts 18:17) and it can be inferred that he was converted as a result of Paul's Corinthian mission in AD 51-52. Yet he cannot be classified as a 'co-author' as Silvanus and Timothy were in 1 Thessalonians 1:1. This is because throughout 1 Corinthians Paul writes in the first person singular thus making the letter his personal literary statement, with Sosthenes, as also with Chloe, Stephanas, Fortunatus and Achaicus, pictured as faithful disciples who live by its injunctions and so act as an example to others.

Thirdly, Paul enlarges the scope of the letter by uniting the Corinthians' sanctification (1 Cor 1:2) 'in Christ Jesus' with those who call upon him 'in every place' (1 Cor 1:2). Paul is here emphasising the basic unity and communion which exists between all Christian believers (thus the collection, 1 Cor 16:1-9), a theme which will become increasingly important in many ways in his theological understanding (e.g. Rom 15:17-20; Col 1:3-8; Eph 2:11-22). In the thanksgiving section (1 Cor 1:4-9) Paul highlights some of the issues with which he will be dealing in the body of the letter. These issues are focussed through his use of key words and the themes which lie behind them: speech, in the sense of the proclamation of the Gospel (*logos*); knowledge (*gnosis*); grace and gift, in the sense of spiritual graces and gifts from God (*charis*) and communion (fellowship, *koinonia*).

Divisions within the church community connected with the Apostolic ministry, 1:10-4:21

The first six chapters deal with the reality of the Corinthians' failure to live as their calling in Christ demands. The issues are twofold: (i) they concern divisions connected with the exercise of the apostolic ministry (1 Cor 1:10-4:21) and (ii) they relate to problems caused by the unethical behaviour practised by some members of the church (1 Cor 5:1-6:20).

Paul begins by demanding that the Corinthians end the divisions (1 Cor 1:10) which exist amongst church members and to strive for unity of mind and opinion. These divisions are due to allegiance to various groups connected with

Christian leaders and their 'theology': Apollos, Cephas and Paul. According to Luke, Apollos was a converted Jew from Alexandria (Acts 18:24-28). The extent to which he opposed Paul with his spiritual and wisdom-based teaching is difficult to determine. There could have been also a 'spiritual group' who maintained that they pledged allegiance only to Christ (1 Cor 1:12) and who regarded themselves too 'superior' spiritually to identify directly with other groups who formed around established Christian teachers. In response to this divisive situation Paul asks three rhetorical questions (1 Cor 1:13), relating to Christology, crucifixion and Baptism. From the questions emerge the following: (i) that Paul's apostolic authority to preach the Gospel is related directly to the cross of Christ (cf. Gal 6:14). (ii) Paul undertook a limited baptismal ministry in Corinth. Through hindsight he is pleased with this approach as, it can be implied, many Corinthians have subsequently proved themselves spiritually and ethically unworthy to share in God's new covenant community (cf. Gal 3:26-28 and 6:15). (iii) There is a reminder that Paul's original message was delivered on the basis of the 'folly' of the cross and not through 'the speech of wisdom' (1 Cor 1:17). In this phrase another of Paul's word themes is introduced, that of wisdom (*sophia*) which is used on twenty six occasions in 1 Corinthians 1-4 and with it the tension between human rhetoric and divine disclosure. This reliance on Graeco-Roman rhetoric seems to have had a divisive effect upon the Christian community in particularly with regard to their understanding of wisdom (*sophia*). Paul's understanding of wisdom is biblical, having its basis in the wisdom traditions of ancient Israel which contain a rich use of metaphor, poetry and proverbial sayings.

1 Corinthians 1:18-2:5 enlarges upon this theme on the basis of the theological exposition relating to the 'word of the cross'. This exposition is developed by means of contrasts, tensions and ironies. It begins with the contrast between folly and power which, in turn, is linked to the theology of salvation. Salvation is contrasted with perishing, the state of those who do not believe that Christ's saving work is to be perceived through his crucifixion, for them the cross is folly.

Building upon the testimony of Scripture, Isaiah 29:14 (1 Cor 1:19) numerous questions are asked and propositions made to further the exposition. These questions and propositions relate to the nature of Christ's crucifixion and the power of God, ironically, being manifested through this weakness. Both Jews and Gentiles have misunderstood this irony. The Jews seek supernatural nature declarations of God's power while Gentiles depend on human wisdom as evidence on which reality might be based (1 Cor 1:22). For Paul reality is to be found in the irony of the total loss of identity as demonstrated by the crucifixion which, in turn, manifests God's power and wisdom. The profundity of this argument, therefore, is demonstrated by subtle 'word-play' and 'concept reversal'. Folly and wisdom are capable of opposite meanings both positive and negative illustrated, for example, by the contrast between the wisdom of the world and the wisdom of God. In this context the believers are called into a Christological relationship as Christ is seen as both the power and wisdom of God (1 Cor 1:24).

In the light of this theological exposition the Corinthian Christians are requested to consider (reconsider?) their call. In this reconsideration the social divisions which exist amongst them are revealed. This theme is an on-going one through the letter (1 Cor 1:26b; later, 11:17-22). From it some most important issues emerge: in what sense does Christian belief effect or should change the perception of the different levels of social stratification within the Christian assembly? There is a certain ambiguity in Paul's evidence that 'not many' of the community are worldly-wise, powerful or of noble birth (1 Cor 1:26), triggering scholarly debate as to the social status of some of the named individuals (cf. 1 Cor 11:21). Of fundamental importance for Paul, however, is the impact that Christology has on social status.

In this regard Paul argues that reversals in social status take place because the rejected crucified Christ becomes 'the Lord of glory' (1 Cor 2:8). On this basis the 'despised brethren' become 'pillars of strength'. The question remains as to how this theological perception can become reality in pastoral practice. Again Christology abounds and with it soteriology: Christ Jesus is wisdom, righteousness, sanctification and redemption for believers (1 Cor 1:30). Their self-confidence therefore can be based only on Christ who by his ministry renders reliance upon human wisdom redundant (1 Cor 1:31, quotation from Jer 9:24, cf. 1 Cor 1:17).

In 1 Corinthians 2:1-5 Paul returns to the question of the nature of his evangelistic ministry. Again he places emphasis both on his personal weakness and on the power of God. The nature and meaning of God's wisdom which Paul preached is again discussed (cf. 1 Cor 1:18-25). On this occasion, however, with reference to God's hidden plan, of the refusal of the political rulers to perceive it, and that what is beyond human comprehension has been revealed by God in Christ (1 Cor 2:9 with quotations from Isa 64:4 and 65:17). In this context it is the Spirit's role to search and reveal the things of God: twin activities which assist, in those open to receive them, the understanding of the Gospel.

In 1 Corinthians 3:1ff. Paul describes his initial ministry with the Corinthians in terms of their infancy and immaturity. Although they may have perceived themselves as wise they have, on the contrary, demonstrated insufficient maturity to understand both the totality and implications of the Gospel. This immaturity is manifested through their disunity and rival allegiances to various Christian leaders (1 Cor 3:4 cf. 1:12). In the presentation of these arguments it is likely that Paul is utilising, and reserving, the terminology used by those teachers whom he regards as opponents. In 1 Corinthians 3:5-4:5 Paul explores further the nature of Christian leadership in terms of a series of metaphors: horticulture (1 Cor 3:6-8); building (1 Cor 3:10) and stewardship (1 Cor 4:1). The purpose of these metaphors is to provide the basis for understanding Christian leadership in terms of Christology (e.g. 1 Cor 3:11) and with it the wisdom/folly dualism (1 Cor 3:19) which Paul has employed already. The basis of this exposition is scriptural (Job 5:13 in 1 Cor 3:19; Ps 94:11 in 1 Cor 3:20). These scriptural references form an illustration as to the demonstration of the revelation of God's hidden wisdom (cf. 1 Cor 2:7) manifested through Paul's exercising of the Christian ministry on these terms. Any judgement upon him depends, therefore, not on any human assessment but on the Lord (1 Cor 4:4b).

On these grounds Paul compares his ministry to the aspirations, expectations and attitudes of the Corinthians. Again the language is contrasting and ironic: the true apostle is a condemned man (1 Cor 4:9) while the Corinthians act like worldly rulers (1 Cor 4:8), thus contrasting total weakness with political power. Christian ministry, therefore, because it is based on the crucifixion of Christ, must manifest vulnerability and insecurity. Ironically these states of life are the source of its power and effectiveness. Yet within this irony there is a certain ambivalence in Paul's approach to the Corinthians. On one hand he can be disparaging and sarcastic towards them (e.g. 1 Cor 4:3); on the other, he can be paternal, acting as *pater familias* having continuing spiritual authority over them, thus addressing them as his 'beloved children' (1 Cor 4:14; compare 1 Cor 4:17 refering to Timothy). This paternalistic approach is continued by Paul as he describes his role as father and guide, qualities which have their origin in his particular status as the founder of the church, thus making him a more significant guide than other teachers. This position should encourage the Corinthians to be more ready to heed his guidance and follow his direction. As with the Thessalonian community Paul sent (or intends to send?) Timothy as his special envoy with the promise that, at a later date, Paul will come in person (1 Cor 4:19). The question is, with what attitude should he undertake such a visit: with a view to punishment or gentleness and to what degree? In the event the visit proved to be more difficult than he imagined (2 Cor 2:1-2). In 1 Corinthians 1-4 therefore Paul counters the divisions within the Corinthian Christian community by stressing their unity in Christ and his paternal authority over them. Furthermore, he reverses the rhetorical arguments of his opponents by demonstrating that true wisdom can be found only through sharing in 'the word of the cross' (1 Cor 1:18).

Divisions within the church relating to ethical matters, 5:1-6:20

On the basis of Paul's fathering the Corinthians in the ways of the Gospel and the divine wisdom which is offered through the Gospel he now turns to ethical issues. These issues relate to the problems of living the Christian life within Corinthian, urban, society. The first issue relates to a relationship between a man and his stepmother which Paul (and perhaps even Corinthian custom?) regards as incest and therefore as immoral (1 Cor 5:1; background, Lev 18:8; details, *DPL,* 600). Envisaging that one of the activities of the church community is to act as a court, Paul demands and declares the man's expulsion in which the Lord Jesus is seen as the ultimate judge (1 Cor 5:4-5). This demand reflects the eschatological position of the community and is related to Jesus' role as Lord and eschatological judge. From this particular case Paul then addresses the question of morality in general. In doing so he uses a series of Passover purity images in order to highlight the Corinthians' laxity in controlling ethical matters, a subject which formed the basis of Paul's first letter (no longer extant, cf. 1 Cor 5:9) and which the Corinthians appeared to have partly ignored. In this context two particular points should be noted: first, that in a largely Gentile context Paul utilises Jewish images and mores as the basis for ethical discussion (leaven/unleavened bread, 1 Cor 5:6-8; Ex 12:15-20; Deut 16:3-4; also Mt 13:33). Secondly, the Corinthians are exhorted to imitate Christ ethically as the true Passover Lamb (1 Cor 5:7b; Ex 12:5), an image which Paul will utilise later in connection with the Lord's Supper (1 Cor 11:17-34).

Paul then turns to the issue of the Corinthian Christians settling their differences through the civil courts (1 Cor 6:6). By the use of rhetorical questions it is clear that he is against this practice probably for three reasons. First, the existing social divisions within the church are exacerbated as a result of expensive law suits, thus justice is made available only to those who can afford it. Secondly, the witness of the church in society is not well suited by this method of seeking civic legislation. Thirdly, disputes amongst the Christian brethren should be settled within the Christian assembly. This situation leads Paul to make general comments regarding those unrighteous people who by their actions demonstrate that they will not inherit the kingdom of God (1 Cor 6:9-10). For believers such immoral behaviour lies in the past. As a result of Baptism, sanctification and justification they have become united with 'the Lord Jesus Christ' (1 Cor 6:11 cf. 1 Cor 1:30). By this statement Christology, soteriology and ethics are united. It is the Spirit of God (1 Cor 6:11 cf. 1 Cor 2:10 and 13) who produces this newly created life within the believers both corporately and individually.

In 1 Corinthians 6:12-20 Paul discuss the sanctity of the body (*soma*, note the multiple uses of this term actually and symbolically: the human body, the body of Christ received in the Eucharist, the Church as a body and the civic body of the city state); in relation to immorality and prostitution. As a result of Christian initiation (1 Cor 6:11) the human body is incorporated into Christ (1 Cor 6:13b) and thus becomes the means through which God might be glorified (1 Cor 6:20b) because the body is thereby 'the temple of the Holy Spirit' (1 Cor 6:19). 1 Corinthians 6:12 uses the expression:

> 'all things are lawful for me, but not all things are beneficial'
> 'all things are lawful for me, but I will not be enslaved by anything'.

Later, at 1 Corinthians 10:23 Paul uses similar phraseology:

> 'all things are lawful, but not all things are beneficial',
> 'all things are lawful, but not all things are edifying'.

As these verses are difficult to interpret and can appear misleading I shall discuss them given their importance for Paul's theological and ethical arguments. By using the expression 'all things are lawful' he is probably repeating a phrase which the Corinthians themselves are using. In what sense therefore does 'freedom in the Spirit' offer an ethical framework for Christian living? Can Christians continue to behave according to their own maxims? In reply to these questions Paul argues that nothing can erode his freedom in the Gospel particularly not the slavery of sin. This position is produced by the contrast offered between 'lawful' and 'enslaved'. Ethical conduct, therefore, should be governed by the things which Christ has shown will benefit both the community and individuals in the Christian life and witness and which, in turn, will also edify the believers (cf. 1 Cor 8:1). In 1 Corinthians 6:12 Paul adds the phrase 'for me'. In doing so he erects a tension between his behaviour and that of the Corinthians. This tension is explored in 1 Corinthians 6:13-20. These verses form a fitting conclusion to his discussion in chapters 5 and 6. In pursuing virtue the Corinthians must act Christologically, being aware of the ethical implications for them of Christ's ministry (e.g. 1 Cor 6:20a). By guiding them in this direction Paul is uniting his discussion in chapters 1 to 4 concerning his apostolic preaching and ministry relating to unity to his instructions relating to how, and on what basis, they should live ethically.

Answers to Questions (Marriage, Apostolic Authority, Worship, Spiritual Gifts), 7:1-14:40

1 Corinthians 7 marks a change in two respects: first, Paul is replying to questions which the Corinthians have asked of him (1 Cor 7:1a) and secondly, the issues to be discussed move from ones concerning ethical licence ('all things are lawful', 1 Cor 6:12) to those which apparently demand asceticism ('...good for a man not to touch, [i.e., not to have sexual relations with], a woman/wife', 1 Cor 7:1b, both phrases are those which the Corinthians are using). Within this scenario four possible circumstances seem to be involved: (i) married partners who are avoiding sexual relations within their marriage (1 Cor 7:1-6); (ii) those who are married but who are seeking a divorce especially if one partner is not a believer (1 Cor 7:10-16); (iii) whether or not single people should be urged to avoid marriage (1 Cor 7:8-9) and (iv) whether or not engaged couples should proceed with marriage (1 Cor 7:36-38).

Two particular problems arise in the interpretation of this chapter: first, why are the Corinthians taking these ascetic attitudes towards marriage and secondly, how should we unravel Paul's advice to them? Especially seen within 1 Corinthians as a whole the first problem is difficult to understand. It might be connected with the perceptions of some of the Corinthians with regard to the receiving of the Spirit which meant that, as a result, they argued sexual relationships within marriage could be denied and that to remain single was the best option (1 Cor 7:34?).

Paul's advice is coloured by two maxims: first, he is single (1 Cor 7:8) and thus able to spend more time in serving 'the Lord' (1 Cor 7:32 compare, 1 Cor 9:5?) which meant being free to be engaged in itinerant evangelistic ministry. This celibate ministry Paul regards as a gift from God not given to every believer. Secondly, Paul, like many others of his age, believed that there would be a time of trial and distress before God concluded the present world order (1 Cor 7:26 and 31b) and that this time would be approaching shortly (1 Cor 7:29). Given this circumstance Paul is anxious to affirm the single life in order to avoid unnecessary anxiety during this period of eschatological turmoil for those with spouses and children (1 Cor 7:32).

Given these considerations Paul's advice can be related to the particular circumstances mentioned above. Regarding (i) Paul realises that sexual activity within marriage should be permitted, which he regards as a 'concession' (1 Cor 7:6). Abstinence could lead to prostitution and immoral living (1 Cor 6:16 and 7:2) and should be practised only by the unmarried (1 Cor 7:8-9). Relationships between husband and wife should be reciprocal (1 Cor 7:3, not so in church, see later, 1 Cor 14:35). Regarding (ii) separation or divorce (1 Cor 7:10-11) Paul appears to be mindful of Jesus' ruling on the subject of divorce (Mk 10:2-12; Mt 19:3-12). Paul, however, is acting on his own authority by extending Jesus' provision to include all marriages where one partner is a believer, the other an unbeliever. Two reasons are given for this extension: first, the presence of one Christian partner sanctifies the marriage and the children born from the marriage (1 Cor 7:14). Secondly, the unbelieving partner may convert to Christianity as a result of the witness of the believing partner and so enter into salvation. The onus for separation, therefore, is placed upon the unbeliever (1 Cor 7:15), a position known subsequently as 'the Pauline privilege'.

In 1 Corinthians 7:17-24 Paul broadens his particular arguments about marriage to include circumcision (Jewish converts) and slavery (social status). Given the eschatological perspective mentioned above Paul's advice is to remain in the state of life in which they were called originally by God into the Christian life (1 Cor 7:24). Regarding (iii) virginity (1 Cor 7:25) Paul returns to his argument in 1 Corinthians 7:8 which continues the 'remain in the state you are' proposition of 1 Corinthians 7:24. He is aware that Jesus gave no specific commands on being unmarried but Paul believes that the advice he is offering represents sound spiritual wisdom in the light of God's approaching eschatological judgement (1 Cor 7:26). In the light of this scenario there is the question of engaged couples (iv). It appears that he is retaining his 'remain as you are', 'be like me' (1 Cor 7:8) arguments but with the proviso that, if powerful sexual passions dictate, marriage is the best option (1 Cor 7:9; 7:36b) although celibacy is a better one (1 Cor 7:38). In this discussion Paul is again employing the concept, prominent in Graeco-Roman education, of imitation (*mimesis*), following the example of the teacher. Paul uses this concept in numerous ways, in this instance it concerns the Corinthians following his celibate state (1 Cor 7:7a), if that course of action is possible (1 Cor 7:7b). The same 'remain as you are' arguments apply also to widows (1 Cor 7:39-40a). Paul concludes the section with the declaration of the wisdom of the advice offered on the grounds that he possesses the 'Spirit of God' (*pneuma Theou*, 1 Cor 7:40b). In Section 3 I shall endeavour to deal with some of the pastoral and hermeneutical issues which these ethical issues raise for contemporary discussion.

To understand the issue of food offered to idols with which Paul is concerned in 1 Corinthians 8 it is necessary to be aware of the general religious culture which existed in the Graeco-Roman world. As will be demonstrated in Section 2 the city of Corinth contained numerous temples and altars dedicated to Graeco-Roman gods (*BSGT,* 58). It was the custom that

73

animal sacrifices were made to these gods. In reality only a small part of the animal was consumed, the remainder could be eaten by the family and friends of the donor either, at home, or in the particular temple in which the sacrifice was offered (the restaurants of the ancient world). Alternatively the meat could be resold in the city's meat market. The Jews would take no part in these activities, either in the actual eating or in the social gathering which accompanied it, as their monotheistic faith and practice, the eating of kosher meat, forbade it. They coined the term *eidolothyta*, idolatrous sacrifices, the offering of which was forbidden by the *Torah*, as it represented the worship of an alien god (Ex 20:3-5). The issue with which Paul was faced concerned the behaviour of Gentile Christians in these circumstances. Paul begins his argument by referring to knowledge (*gnosis*, 1 Cor 8:1-3). This term seems to have been another of the Corinthians' watchwords. Paul uses the concept in two, contrasting, ways: first, to illustrate the frailty of human knowledge (the Corinthians thought their knowledge was superior) and secondly, to demonstrate that the knowledge of God is obtained by (humbly) loving him (also, Gal 4:8-9a). Paul then proceeds to state the basic theological proposition that, despite the fact that numerous gods exist, for believers there is one God, the Father, who has revealed himself through 'the one Lord, Jesus Christ' (1 Cor 8:6). In this carefully constructed parallel confession Paul shows how Jesus shares with the Father in the work of creation and salvation (but note 'from' the Father and 'through' the Christ). With this conjunction Jewish monotheism (the *Shema* of Deut 6:4, 'Hear, Israel, the Lord our God is one Lord') and the Christian confession of Jesus' Messiahship as Lord and Christ are united.

While Paul adheres totally to this theological confession the initial problem of 1 Corinthians 8:1 remains as an issue of pastoral sensitivity with regard to the 'weaker brethren' (1 Cor 8:9), in this instance Gentile believers. This 'weakness' could refer, therefore, both to a 'weakness' resulting from social standing or ethical weakness. In this situation Paul returns to 'the love principle' which is offered in the context of Christian community solidarity (1 Cor 8:1). This principle is superior to all others, (later, 1 Cor 13, in terms of the virtues) certainly to knowledge. Not all the Gentile members of the church have reached a sufficient standard in terms of knowledge to be able to withdraw from *eidolothyta* given the social and political connotations of the practice (1 Cor 8:10). In this situation Paul asks about the importance of this issue in the order of things (1 Cor 8:8) to which he replies that the salvation offered to all humanity (both Jews and Gentiles) through the death of Christ is of paramount significance. In this context it would be sinful for the 'strong' to wound the 'weak'. If food be the reason for one of the brethren to leave the Christian community Paul would rather be a vegetarian (1 Cor 8:13).

In 1 Corinthians 9 Paul returns to the theme of his apostolic ministry (cf. 1 Cor 4:9). As a result of four rhetorical questions (1 Cor 9:1) he is able to state his claims to apostolic ministry, his freedom in proclaiming the Gospel, the way in which he is supported financially and his relationship with the Corinthian church. In the matter of material and financial support Paul compares what he and Barnabas are doing in supporting themselves (1 Cor 8:12; Acts 18:3) to the support given to Cephas and the other apostles (1 Cor 9:5). By not receiving such support, does this fact render Paul unapostolic? To counter this claim Paul uses both examples from secular life, Scripture and Jesus' own teaching (compare Mt 10:10, Lk 10:7). The setting aside of this right (1 Cor 9:15) is for two reasons. First, that the accepting of financial support would place Paul under obligation to some of the wealthier members of the church and thus limit his freedom. This position reflects the patron-client relationship which formed an important role in the social structure in which he was operating. Secondly, Paul recognises the operation of God's grace in his apostolic work (later, 1 Cor 15:10). This grace means that his own self-confidence (1 Cor 9:15-16) rests upon his commission, given by the Risen Christ (later, 1 Cor 15:8) to preach the Gospel. With this commission Paul uses the idea of reward (1 Cor 9:17 and 18a) ironically. Doing his own will, accepting payment as is his right, will bring an earthly reward but delivering the Gospel without charge will bring, a far greater, heavenly reward. Paul then describes his ministry with the paradox of freedom and slavery (used in a different way in Gal 4:31 and 5:13). Being free from financial obligation enables him to become slave to all groups in the service of the Gospel and for their salvation (1 Cor 9:19). Three groups are mentioned: Jews (1 Cor 9:20), Gentiles (1 Cor 9:21) and the 'weak' (1 Cor 9:22). Paul's approach represents an 'incarnational model' for ministry: identification with each section of Corinthian society in order that, in their own way, they might perceive the blessings being offered through the proclamation of Christ's Gospel of salvation (1 Cor 9:23 and later, 1 Cor 15:3-11). Paul concludes this part of his argument by using the metaphor of the games to describe his apostolic ministry. Earthly victors receive a laurel wreath but Paul has the hope of an eternal crown (1 Cor 9:25 and later, 1 Cor 15:54-58).

In 1 Corinthians 10 Paul's tone changes from 'all things to all people' (1 Cor 9:22) to a solemn warning about idolatry. It could have been that his 'understanding' approach to *eidolothyta* in 1 Corinthians 8:7-13 had led, ironically, to a negligent attitude amongst the Corinthians with regard to Christian thinking and practice. Perhaps surprisingly in a Gentile context Paul turns to the Exodus narrative of Israel's (called 'our fathers', 1 Cor 10:1) journey through the Red Sea and into the wilderness of Sinai (Ex 13-17) in order to offer a parallel to the Corinthians as to how their actions could result in them experiencing the same fate as Israel (1 Cor 10:1-5). The events in which Israel shared were sacred and spiritual (1 Cor 10:3-4). They represented God's gracious action at the Red Sea, in the cloud for direction, the manna and water from the rock. These events are reinterpreted by Paul Christologically and sacramentally. This reinterpretation offers to the Corinthians an insight into the reality of their contemporary Christian experience seen in relation to a particular period in Israel's past. The narration of Israel's subsequent activity in the wilderness represents examples ('types', 1 Cor 10:6) of behaviour that the Corinthians are exhorted not to follow in relation to: the worship of idols (1 Cor 10:7 where reference is made to the golden calf narrative, Ex 32:6); immorality (1 Cor 10:8, reference to Num 25:1 and 9); tempting (1 Cor 10:9, reference to Num 25:5-6) and complaining against God (1 Cor 10:10, reference to Num. 16:41 and 49). Paul reinterprets these events to relate to the eschatological age in which he believed he was living and to God's coming judgement (1 Cor 10:11-12). Yet God is faithful and gracious and will not allow temptation (1 Cor 10:13) beyond human strength and endurance. In this context, however, the injunction to shun idol worship is repeated (1 Cor 10:14 cf. 1 Cor 10:7 and the failure of Israel in this regard).

Paul then offers a specific example: that of the Christian Eucharist. The key concept in this regard is communion or participation (*koinonia*, 1 Cor 10:16). Paul asks if sharing in the Christian Eucharist is not also a sharing in Christ's sacrificial offering for the salvation of humanity. The two questions of 1 Corinthians 10:16 lead to the statement that the Eucharist represents the reality of unity: unity both in Christ's offering and in the church (note use of *soma*, 1 Cor 10:17). This statement reminds the hearer/reader that the theme of unity was the first issue to be addressed in this letter (1 Cor 1:10), the implications of which will be exposed in the following chapters. In the development of the theme in chapter 10 Paul returns to consider and interpret what occurred in the life of Israel (1 Cor 10:18a, reference to Lev 7:6, cf. 1 Cor 10:1-5) regarding the priests eating of the animal sacrifices. This question leads to another relating to their issue of food offered to idols (1 Cor 10:19, cf. 1 Cor 8:1). For worshippers, food offered to idols is now considered by Paul to be offered to demons (1 Cor 10:20) and not to God, and thus the worshippers become in partnership (*koinonia*, 1 Cor 10:20) with demons. Sharing both in the cup of the Eucharist and the wine drunk in the temples is rendered impossible (1 Cor 10:21).

Paul concludes the section with some general ethical principles: first, that every activity must be done to glorify God (1 Cor 10:31); secondly, that every action of Christians should be evangelistic, aiming for the salvation of unbelievers (1 Cor 10:33) and thirdly, the Corinthians should imitate Paul's example in the same way as he imitates that of Christ (1 Cor 11:1). In section 3 I shall consider some issues raised by this advice in a contemporary context.

Paul now turns to examine the ordering of worship within the Christian *ekklesia* (cf. 1 Cor 1:2, the assembly where Paul's letters were read). He begins this discussion by referring to the traditions on this subject which he delivered to them. In 1 Corinthians 11-15 Paul uses the language of tradition in the sense of transmission (Greek *paradidomi*) on three occasions: (i) here, at 11:2, '…maintain the traditions as I delivered them to you'; (ii) at 11:23, 'For I received from the Lord what I also delivered you…'; (iii) at 15:3, 'For I delivered to you as of first importance what I also received …'

This concept of transmission, which Paul has inherited from Judaism, involves both sacred concepts (in each case, creation, Eucharist, Gospel) and sacred customs (at worship, at the Eucharist). In 1 Corinthians 11:2 Paul's use of holding fast to or maintaining meant that these concepts and customs must be adhered to continuously in the Corinthian church (1 Cor 11:16). The sacred concept involved in 1 Corinthians 11:2-16 concerns theological relationships within the order of creation: woman to man to Christ to God. These relationships are held together by the concept of headship (the head, *kephale* found in the three parts of 1 Cor 11:3 and, for man and woman based on Gen 2:21-23), 'head' being used metaphorically to describe hierarchy. Arising from this sacred concept come particular sacred customs. When assembling for worship; first, men and women come together and secondly, the traditional custom should be observed that men worship with uncovered heads while the women must have their heads covered with the veil. Paradoxically it was the veil which gave women authority (note the use of *exousia* 'authority' for veil or hood in 1 Cor 11:10, authors of later manuscripts not understanding this connection used the word veil, *kalumma*). Exactly as to how this 'authority' was exercised in Corinthian church worship is difficult to ascertain (note later, 1 Cor 14:34 but be aware of textual problems here). Another related issue was men who had long hair (1 Cor 11:14). Was this custom 'natural' (1 Cor 11:14) and, what kind of signal was being sent out to Corinthian society by the Christian assembly in which men had long hair and women had unveiled heads? For contemporary readers Paul's arguments may appear complex, strange and irrelevant. As we shall see in section 3, however, they must first be placed in their original context and then their inner meaning might be applied to today's setting.

Paul's discussion of the Eucharist (noun, *eucharistia*; verb, *eucharisteo*, thanksgiving and to give thanks, 1 Cor 11:17-33) begins with the problem of social divisions (cf. 1 Cor 1:10) relating to the sharing of food in the Eucharistic meal, specifically the neglecting of the poor members of the community. As he does frequently, when pastoral matters arise, Paul returns to the first principles of the Gospel and, in this case, the Eucharistic celebration which enshrines the Gospel. As a result Paul returns to narrate the historical circumstances which occurred in Jerusalem on the night before Jesus suffered death by crucifixion when he instituted the sacred meal of the Eucharist (1 Cor 11:23-26; note 1 Cor 10:16-17; also Mk 14:22-24; Mt 26:26-28; Lk 22:17-20, but note textual difficulties here). This meal is to be seen in the context of the Passover (cf. 1 Cor 5:6-8). On this occasion emphasis is placed on the theme of memory (1 Cor 11:25, *anamnesis*, Lk 22:19b cf. Ex 12:14), the act of recalling the past into the present and of giving the past a present reality and significance. In the context of the Eucharist, therefore, the past actions of 'the Lord Jesus' (1 Cor 11:23) become powerfully relevant in the context of the Corinthian church (1 Cor 11:26). Thus the Eucharist becomes deeply symbolic in three ways: first, as the ritual proclamation of the Gospel of Jesus' death, burial, resurrection and living presence. Secondly, as being representative of God's renewed covenant agreement (*diatheke*, fulfilling Jer 31:31) with humanity through the action of Christ and thirdly, as symbolically anticipating the Lord's return (1 Cor 11:26, cf. 1 Cor 7:26 and 31 in relation to marriage and later, 1 Cor 16:22 in the *Maranatha* prayer). It is this dimension which gives the Eucharistic meal eschatological significance. The proviso for sharing in this sacred meal is ethical living in accordance with the demands of the Gospel (1 Cor 11:17-32). As Paul has shown in previous chapters, some members of the Corinthian church have fallen short in this regard. The discussion concludes with, first, the point where it began, the dangers highlighted by social and material divisions in the church (1 Cor 11:34a cf. 1 Cor 11:18-22) and, secondly, the promise of further directions on this and other issues when Paul next visits Corinth (1 Cor 11:34b, later 2 Cor 2:1).

Paul now offers advice relating to spiritual matters (1 Cor 12:1, *pneumatikoi* can relate to either things or people), particular gifts of the Holy Spirit which are given to the believers (Gal 5:22-23) or particular spiritual people to whom the gifts are given. This discussion occurs as a result of the particular context in which Gentile converts have found themselves in relation to the worship of idols (1 Cor 12:2, cf. 1 Cor 8:46). As such the hearers are reminded of Paul's earlier discussion of the Spirit in 1 Cor 2:4 and 6-16 and to 3:1 where he says that he is unable to address them as 'spiritual people'. In 1 Cor 12:1-3 Paul returns to first principles by maintaining that it is the Holy Spirit working within the human soul that allows the confession of faith that 'Lord (is) Jesus' to be uttered (1 Cor 12:3b, *Kurios Iesous*, later 2 Cor 4:5). The declaration 'Anathema (is) Jesus' (1 Cor 12:3a, *Anathema Iesous*), can never be attributed to the Spirit because such action would be against the Spirit's nature and the purpose of his activity. The precise context of this dualism between 'Anathema Jesus' and 'Lord Jesus' is difficult to determine, but one possibility is that the believers were being asked by the civic authorities to curse Jesus because the confession of Jesus' Lordship conflicted with the lordship of Caesar. Whatever may have been the case 'Lord (is) Jesus' formed the basic Christian confession, one utilised by Paul because it applied to Jesus the Lordship of God (cf. 1 Cor 8:5-6; other examples, Rom 10:9; Phil 2:11).

Paul continues to use the notion of the Spirit (1 Cor 12:3) to relate to the spiritual gifts (*charismata*, 1 Cor 12:4) which are offered to the community. The emphasis is placed upon diversity in unity which links intrinsically the many gifts offered with the unity found in God: 1. Spirit, 2. Lord = Jesus, 3. God. This relationship is demonstrated in 1 Corinthians 12:4-6:

1. 'But there are diversities of gifts (*charismata*) but the same Spirit (*pneuma*),

2. and there are diversities of ministries but the same Lord (*Kurios*),

3. and there are diversities of workings but the same God (*Theos*)....'

Paul then lists the diversity of gifts available: 'a word of wisdom'; 'a word of knowledge'; faith; healing powers; prophecy; speaking in tongues; their interpretation and discerning between spirits (1 Cor 12:8-10). From this list some important theological and pastoral points emerge: First, the gifts offered are divinely given, they are apportioned by the Spirit as he wills (1 Cor 12:11). Secondly, in particular with regard to wisdom and knowledge, they are to be perceived and are given in a different way from which some Corinthians understood. Thus, words of wisdom (note 1 Cor 1:17; 2:1; 3:19) and knowledge (note 1 Cor 8:1 and later, 1 Cor 13:2 and 8; 14:6) must be seen in terms of 'the word of the cross' (1 Cor 1:18) which was the prime feature of Paul's original preaching (1 Cor 1:17). Thirdly, the purpose of these gifts is 'for the common good' (1 Cor 12:7), the up-building of the ministry within the church and for its mission to the wider Corinthian society. On these grounds the gifts are available to every believer (1 Cor 12:6).

In order to reinforce these arguments Paul returns to the metaphor of the body (*soma*, cf. 1 Cor 10:16-17) to describe the relationships which the Corinthian Christians ought to have with each other but primarily with Christ (1 Cor 12:27). This particular 'body relationship' is secured; first, as a result of participation in the baptismal rite which transcends ethnic origin or social status (Gal 3:26-28) and which gives the Spirit (1 Cor 12:13) and second, by receiving the body of Jesus in the Eucharistic celebration (1 Cor 11:18-24). In this way the tension is created between entering the body through the once-for-all sacrament of Baptism and being sustained within the body through participating regularly in the Eucharist. The analogy of linking the diversity of spiritual gifts found within the 'body' of the church to the limbs of a human body (1 Cor 12:14-26) may have been used by Paul because it was a way for political philosophers to explain the inter-relationships and the necessary contribution of each citizen of the body politic of a Graeco-Roman city state and therefore familiar, in particular, to the politically active Corinthians (1 Cor 1:26). In the context of their newly found Christian faith, however, this 'body language' is both Christological (1 Cor 12:12 and 27) and ethnically and socially egalitarian (1 Cor 12:13).

Paul then applies the same arguments which he has used above to the variety of ministries appointed by God within the church (1 Cor 12:28). A series of rhetorical questions follow to illustrate both the 'diversity in unity' principle and the fact that not every member of the body can claim the same ministry, as these ministries must work in coordination with each other. Maybe mindful of the difficulties encountered by Paul in his own claim to apostleship (e.g. 1 Cor 9:1; 2 Cor 12:12) he argues that God did not call every church member to be an apostle. These thoughts then lead Paul to discuss the 'still more excellent way' (1 Cor 12:31) of love (*agape*, 1 Cor 13:1; cf. 1 Cor 8:1).

The purpose of 1 Corinthians 13 is to offer a reflection on the subject of what he considers to be the greatest virtue, that of love. It could be that Paul was utilising existing essays on the subject as, at face value, the chapter is not a theological statement in the sense of analysing God's love for humanity manifested in Christ. Yet an examination of the various phrases in the chapter illustrate the importance of the theme to the Corinthian context. Love was precisely the virtue that some of them lacked, as illustrated by their conduct towards Paul (e.g. 1 Cor 9:3) and each other (e.g. 1 Cor 11:18-19). Love stands as the greatest virtue, even above faith and hope (1 Cor 13:13), and as such forms an important bridge chapter between the discussion of spiritual gifts and the exercising of them within the church as found in 1 Corinthians 12 and 14. The question of speaking in tongues, for example, to which much attention is given in chapter 14, is heralded in 1 Corinthians 13:1 by the statement that even speech 'in the tongues of men and of angels' is merely a series of useless sounds if unaccompanied by love (*agape*). 1 Corinthians 13, therefore, allows the discussion of church membership and ministry to be given its proper perspective in the context of the exercise of the greatest virtue of love (1 Cor 14:1) which never ends (1 Cor 13:8).

In 1 Corinthians 14:1-25 Paul discusses the superiority of prophecy over speaking in tongues (*glossalalia*). The purpose of affirming this superiority is in order that church worship might be edified (literally 'built up', cf. 1 Cor 8:1, 12:4, 14:3, 12). To the idea of edification Paul adds the concepts of encouragement and consolation which affirm the prophetically based church in its mission and ministry (1 Cor 14:3). The concept of prophecy has its foundation in the prophetic movement of ancient Israel. The basis of this prophetic action is the Spirit, a reminder that Israel's prophets spoke in the power of the Spirit (e.g. 1 Sam 10:10). On occasions Paul both refers to (e.g. 1 Thess 2:15; Rom 1:2; 3:21; 11:3) and quotes from (e.g. Isa 29:14 quoted in 1 Cor 1:19) Israel's prophets but it is clear that he also envisages a ministry of prophecy within Christianity based on these earlier models, evident particularly in the Corinthian correspondence. The phenomenon of *glossalalia* relates to addressing God in unintelligible speech (1 Cor 14:2a) which he hears but which is indecipherable to humans without interpretation (1 Cor 14:13, contrast Acts 2:17 referring to a diversity of human languages). In Corinth Paul is not forbidding the use of *glossalalia* (1 Cor 14:39, cf. 12:10) rather he wishes to place the gift in its proper context so that Christian worship in Corinth might be done decently and in the right order (1 Cor 14:40). Given that *glossalalia* could lead to spiritual arrogance (1 Cor 14:12a?) the Corinthian worshippers were no doubt reminded of Paul's earlier injunction relating to 'the word of the cross' (1 Cor 1:18) and preaching only 'Jesus Christ and him crucified' (1 Cor 2:2). Christian worship, therefore, was to manifest and to be regulated by the basic principles of the Gospel (1 Cor 14:26).

1 Corinthians 14:34-35, which relates to the role of women in the worship assembly, are verses which are difficult to interpret. First, the injunction to women to remain silent appears to contradict what Paul has said already in 11:5. Secondly, some manuscripts omit them altogether or alternatively, others place them after 14:40. It could be (but

is by no means certain) that they are a later scribal addition in order to link Paul's injunctions to the Corinthians with the later thoughts on the subject expressed in 1 Timothy 2:11-12. Alternatively, Paul is either being inconsistent in his directions or a particular issue had arisen in Corinth relating to women interrupting the discourse of the (male) prophets (cf. Rom 16:1-2, Phil 4:2, Rev 2:20-23). The concluding verses of chapter 14 summarise the whole of Paul's arguments: although prophecy is superior to *glossalalia* this latter gift should not be forbidden (1 Cor 14:39, cf. 14:1-5); worship concerns the nature of God (1 Cor 14:40, cf. 14:33a) and that the individuals who believe that they have been given particular gifts for ministry should follow Paul's instructions because they have been given to him by Jesus, the Lord (1 Cor 14:37-38, cf. 11:23 and 12:3-11).

The Gospel and the resurrection, 15:1-58

For Paul, pastoral and spiritual concerns, in this case the offering of worship, must be anchored always in the basic principles of the Gospel and it is these principles to which he returns in chapter 15 (1 Cor 15:1-2). 1 Cor 15:3-8 embodies an existing Christian confession of faith which Paul received (1 Cor 15:3a, cf. 11:23 'received from the Lord') and passed on to the Corinthians in the context of the delivery and reception of the Christian message. The structure of the confession is as follows:

1. 'that Christ died for our sins in accordance with the scriptures' (15:3b);

2. 'and that he was buried' (15:4a);

3. 'and that he was raised on the third day in accordance with the scriptures' (15:4b);

4. 'and that he was seen by Cephas, then by the Twelve' (15:5);

5. 'afterward he was seen by more than five hundred brethren at one time...' (15:6);

6. 'afterward he was seen by James, then by all the apostles' (15:7);

7. 'last of all, as to one untimely born (lit. by an abortion), he was seen also by me' (15:8).

By appealing to early liturgical traditions Paul returns the Corinthians to 'first principles', namely what God did/is doing through Christ towards humanity (note the passive form of the verb 'was raised', i.e. by God). Into an existing schema of early Christian witnesses to the resurrection, Paul becomes a partner (1 Cor 15:8). It is likely that the inherited tradition concluded at 15:7 and, in the verses that follow, Paul includes himself (15:8-11). This inclusion, however, both differentiates Paul from, but also equalises him with, the existing apostles. How then was this tension to be understood? On one level continuity is maintained by Paul using the verb 'appeared' for himself (15:8) as he has done for the earlier brethren (15:5; 15:6; 15:7) yet, on the other hand it was known that the risen Christ appeared to Paul in a different context (cf. Gal 1:15-16 and compare Luke's later accounts, Lk 24:36-42 and Acts 9:3-6). For the Jerusalem faithful it was in the form of Christ's physically recognisable risen body; for Paul, Christ appeared by way of 'visions and revelations' (2 Cor 12:1; also, Gal 1:13-14; Phil 3:8-11). In these circumstances Paul describes his feelings in terms of being 'untimely born' (15:8), in that he was a persecutor of the faithful, therefore unworthy to receive grace. Yet at the same time this appearance of Christ to Paul means that he shares the same 'status' as the other, earlier, apostles. Paul is commissioned by Christ and empowered for mission in the same way as they have been. Thus, any in Corinth who doubted (the 'spiritual party'?) Paul's apostolic claims could see that, paradoxically, 'the least of the apostles' (15:8) has become equal to the earlier apostles (15:5-7, including Cephas and James, Gal 1:18-19 and 2:9-10). Thus, the statement relating to the basic principles of the Gospel (15:1-8) relates back to the discussion concerning the conduct of worship (14:26-40) and forward to the hope of eternal resurrection for all believers.

This resurrection (1 Cor 15:12; 15:13; 15; 21; 15:42) is impossible to achieve without the historical and theological fact of, and the belief in, the resurrection of Jesus which results from God's mighty action towards him. By the use of conditional clauses ('if' is used six times in 1 Cor 15:12-19) the inter-connection between the resurrection of Christ and that of the faithful is explored. In the light of this connection Paul asks why some members of the Corinthian church are denying the prospect of the resurrection of the dead (1 Cor 15:12b). In this context it is difficult to ascertain precisely what aspect of resurrection faith is being denied: is it the fact of resurrection *per se*, is it the belief that resurrection has occurred already as a result of a 'spiritual union' with Christ or is it that the concept of the resurrection of the body is denied in favour of that of the immortality of the soul? Some or all of these suggestions are possible; perhaps these varying ideas were held by the rival church groups in Corinth who identified themselves with the teaching of the different personalities? (1 Cor 1:12; 3:22?). These denials relating to resurrection, however, do not represent merely a variety of opinion concerning the after-life, rather they challenge the heart of the Gospel which Paul preached to them (1 Cor 15:14). They place in jeopardy the whole experience of salvation to be found in Christ, sin remains unconquered (1 Cor 15:17, cf. 15:3) and the dead are denied immortality (1 Cor 15:18). The purpose of Paul's heightened language is to challenge the Corinthians to rethink their objections to resurrection and to realise the consequences of failure to appreciate that the raising of Christ's body from death anticipates and refigures the bodily resurrection of the believers.

The conditional clauses of 1 Corinthians 15:12-19 give way both to statements relating to the objective reality of Christ's resurrection (1 Cor 15:20-22) and a forecast by Paul as to how the future kingdom will be inaugurated (1 Cor 15:23-28). By these statements God is portrayed as the Lord of history with Christ as the central focus of that history in terms of salvation for the cosmos, including all humanity. Paul's explanation of this scheme is to offer a series of parallel statements as follows:

1. 15:20: (a) Christ has been raised. By implication this resurrection is a foretaste of the future resurrection for believers. This anticipation is explained (b) by the metaphor of the offering of the first fruits of the harvest (Deut 26:2). This harvest metaphor is now reinterpreted. Christ is the first fruit (note singular, *aparche*) who gives resurrection to all believers, whereas originally the term (in the plural) referred to the ingathering of produce in the land of Israel.

2. 15:21: (a) A man brought death (to all humanity). (b) Another man brought resurrection to the dead.

3. 15:22: The general observation of 15:21 is now made specific: (a) The man who brings death (note present tense) to all is Adam (Gen 3:17-19); (b) The man who will bring life (note future tense) to all is Christ.

These parallel statements lead forward (1 Cor 15:23-28) to the theme of order (in the sense of military rank, 15:23). The Corinthians have been confronted already by Paul's desire for order (14:40) in earthly worship now this concept is transferred, prophetically, to the age to come although technically the age began with the resurrection of Christ (1 Cor 15:4). The resulting order, therefore, is as follows:

1. Christ's resurrection is portrayed as 'first fruit'.

2. Christ's return (note the use of the concept of *parousia*, cf. 1 Thessalonians 2:19; 3:13; 4:15; 5:23 and background to be found there) is to be accompanied by the resurrection of the faithful (1 Cor 15:23).

3. The end (*to telos*) will then arrive when Christ, who has destroyed every earthly power, delivers the kingdom to God his Father (1 Cor 15:24). In these verses the concepts of *parousia*, *telos* and resurrection are combined.

Death is seen, therefore, as the last enemy to be destroyed (1 Cor 15:26). In return for Christ's action the Father subjects all things to him. The scriptural evidence for such a claim is to be found in the allusion to Psalm 110:1 in 1 Corinthians 15:25 and the quotation from Psalm 8:6 in 1 Corinthians

15:27. In portraying God's scheme of salvation through Christ in this way Paul is utilising the Jewish apocalyptic vision of death being succeeded by life for the faithful. In the case of 1 Corinthians, however, this vision is Christological as well as being theological.

1 Corinthians 15:35-50 deal with the question of the resurrection body. In this context two particular points are of importance: first, to perceive the question in relationship to the concept of the immortality of the soul which may have been one of the points of issue in Paul's disagreements with the Corinthians regarding the resurrection. Secondly, the concept of body (*soma*) used here should be related to the other ways in which the term is used earlier in the letter (e.g. 1 Cor 6:13; 7:34; 11:24; 12:12). In this discussion Paul uses both the analogy of the seed (1 Cor 15:37-38) and ideas from ancient medicine and cosmology (1 Cor 15:39-41) to illustrate both the variety and the development of the human body in life and after death. These images are then applied to the original question raised in 15:35 as to the kind of resurrection body at issue (1 Cor 15:42a). In developing this issue Paul walks a tightrope. On one hand he needs to demonstrate continuity between earthly and heavenly existence. This continuity is achieved by utilising the 'body' concept. On the other hand he needs to demonstrate discontinuity between sinful, earthly life and the perfection to be found in the heavenly resurrection life but without denigrating earthly existence. To achieve this balance Paul makes a dichotomy between the physical and the spiritual body together with the resultant implications of this dichotomy relating to physical and spiritual; weakness and power; dishonour and glory and perishable and imperishable (1 Cor 15:42b-44).

In 1 Corinthians 15:45-49 Paul returns to the Adam/ Christ tension of 15:21 and 22. Humanity, represented by Adam, has been created in God's likeness (Gen 2:7) but humanity shares in Adam's disobedience towards God (Gen 3:17-19) therefore the body is perishable. In Christ, the last Adam, the man from heaven, humanity is given the possibility of a renewed spiritual, eternal body which is brought out as a result of Christ's resurrection. The transforming process from earth to heaven, from one stage of existence to another (1 Cor 15:50), is confirmed by the resurrection which 'gives us', the believers, God's victory over sin and death 'through our Lord Jesus Christ' (1 Cor 15:57).

The description of this climax, however, cannot be achieved without the use of metaphor: sleep for death (1 Cor 15:51) and the trumpet of victory (1 Cor 15:52, cf. 1 Thess 4:16). These metaphors, like the language of transformation described above, are features to be found in Jewish apocalyptic literature. Because the future resurrection and the transformation of believers after death depends on faith, hope and love (1 Cor 13:13), the accounting of the expectation of them remains a mystery (*musterion*, 1 Cor 15:51). It is this mystery, however, that provides contemporary Christian experience with its framework and purpose in the light of the changes: perishable to imperishable, mortal to immortality, which will occur in the future (1 Cor 15:53-54). The certainty of death, resulting in human decay and defeat, will be transformed, paradoxically, into bodily renewal and victory. This position is confirmed by reference to Scripture, (Isa 25:8, Hosea 13:14). 1 Corinthians 15:55 implies that the 'sting' of death has been removed by Christ's saving death which abolished sin (1 Cor 15:3 and later 2 Cor 5:21) and, as a result of his resurrection, immortality and eternal blessedness are assured. The chapter concludes from where it began with the injunction to steadfastness (1 Cor 15:58 cf. 15:2) with the proviso that if its theological contents are accepted the possibility of believing in vain (15:2) is removed because their labouring for the Lord will demonstrate beyond doubt the truthfulness and effectiveness of God's Gospel seen through the action of Christ (1 Cor 15:58).

What next?, 16:1-18

1 Corinthians 16 contains reference to a series of projects linked to what Paul intends to do next in terms of his ministry in relation to the church of Corinth. The first project concerns the collection for the poverty-stricken church of Jerusalem (1 Cor 16:1-4, note also Gal 2:10 and Acts 11:27-30). The

way that Paul suggests that this ministry is undertaken is that a special collection is made during the Lord's day worship (now on Sunday because of the resurrection of Christ). Then specially selected ministers are appointed with the responsibility of taking the collection to Jerusalem, a group to which Paul might join as their leader (1 Cor 16:4).

Secondly, in 1 Corinthians 16:5-9, Paul reveals his missionary travelling intentions, presumably for the purpose of encouraging the churches, Thessalonica and Philippi, for example, in their mission and ministry. Thus, these plans include a visit first to Macedonia, and then back to Corinth. Paul, however, seems to be ambivalent as to the length of the Corinthian visit (1 Cor 16:6-7) maybe he is mindful of the earlier criticism lodged by the Corinthians that he was unwilling to make a personal visit to them (cf. 1 Cor 4:18-19). Paul, however, is ever aware of the challenges being presented to him in the work of the Gospel; as a result, he intends to remain in Ephesus until Pentecost. The reasons for this extended visit are two-fold: first, because of the opportunities offered for ministry there and secondly, because of the opponents to this work which he is encountering (1 Cor 16:8-9, also Luke's account of Paul's Ephesian ministry, Acts 19:1-20:1). Thirdly, Paul speaks of two others who are involved with him in the Corinthian ministry; Timothy (1 Cor 16:10-11) and Apollos (1 Cor 16:12). Paul is worried that Timothy's ministry might be rejected either because of his youth (1 Tim 4:12) or because of his close links with Paul. Paul's connection with Apollos seems to be of a different kind (cf. 1 Cor 1:12; 3:4-6; 3:22; 4:6 and Acts 18:24; 19:1). The reason why Paul wished Apollos to visit Corinth is uncertain. It could have been that Paul wished to demonstrate the partnership and unity between them. Whatever the reason Apollos seems unwilling to make the visit at this time but will reconsider at a later date (1 Cor 16:12).

In 1 Corinthians 16:13-14 Paul offers a series of injunctions which sum up some of the arguments presented in the letter; for example, the Corinthian Christians are to be steadfast in the faith (cf. 1 Cor 15:58) and to ensure that all their actions are undertaken in love (*agape*, cf. 8:1; 13:1; 13:13;

14:1). A similar procedure is demonstrated by reference to the household of Stephanas (1 Cor 16:15 and 17, cf. 1:16). This household is praised by Paul for their ministry and he exalts the Corinthians to be subject to them. Stephanas, Fortunatus and Achaicus have been valuable sources of information for Paul regarding the position of the church. The Corinthians are to recognise and act upon their authority, as they appear to have Paul's countenance to act in a ministerial role with him.

Concluding greeting and blessing, 1 Cor 16:19-24

Paul's conclusion to 1 Cor falls into two parts. First, he offers greetings from the churches of Asia (the Roman province of Asia, see Map 5) of which Ephesus is the principal centre. This greeting is personalised through Aquila and Prisca (Priscilla) who have established a house church in Ephesus but who were Paul's original contacts at the beginning of his Corinthian ministry (cf. Acts 18:2-3). As is usual in liturgical gatherings Christians are to greet each other 'with a holy kiss' (1 Cor 16:20, cf. 1 Thess 5:26).

Secondly, in his concluding blessing, Paul emphasises that the greeting has been written with his own hand (1 Cor 16:21), thus providing its contents with his personal, apostolic authority (1 Cor 15:9-11). Three liturgical elements now follow (1 Cor 16:22-23): (i) an *anathema* which excludes those theologically and ethically unsuitable from participation in the worshipping assembly (cf. 1 Cor 5:12-13 also Rev 22:15); (ii) an ancient Aramaic prayer for the return of the Lord, *Maranatha*, and (iii) the grace (*charis*) prayer for the presence of the Lord Jesus to be with them. The final phrase is Paul's own greeting of love (*agape*, 1 Cor 16:24) to be with all the believers.

2 CORINTHIANS

Opening greeting and thanksgiving, 2 Cor 1:1-11

Paul begins, in what is known as his second letter to the Corinthians, with an opening greeting in a way similar to his other letters. Compared with 1 Cor 1:1-3 there are both similarities and differences. In 2 Corinthians 1:1-2 he repeats the point that his apostolic authority is grounded in 'Christ Jesus' as a result of God's will. Paul addresses the Corinthian churches as 'saints' (2 Cor 1:1) and offers the same grace (*charis*) and peace (*eirene*) from God and Jesus which Paul does in 1 Cor 1:3 (2 Cor 1:2). Yet first in 2 Corinthians there is a return to Timothy's co-authorship (2 Cor 1:1, cf. 1 Thess 1:1 and 2 Thess 1:1). Timothy had an important mediatorial role to perform between Paul and the Corinthians (cf. 1 Cor 4:17; 16:10-11; later, 2 Cor 1:19 and Acts 19:22). Secondly, the scope of the letter is broadened to include all the believers living in the Roman province of Achaia of which Corinth is the capital. Is this Paul's method at this stage in his missionary activity of perceiving his letters as being written, not merely to a precisely defined local church, but rather to churches within a particular province? This development certainly became a feature of some later Christian letters (e.g. 1 Pet 1:1). Alternatively, it could be that Paul is referring to the Corinthian satellite churches (e.g. Cenchreae, Rom 16:1). Whatever explanation is accepted the result is that the context of this letter is broadened in order to embrace a wider audience.

The thanksgiving section which follows divides into two parts. First, there is a series of statements relating to the theme of God's encouragement to believers in times of tribulation (2 Cor 1:3-7). Divine consolation is delivered when tribulation occurs (1:4, cf. 1 Thess 1:6; 3:3; 3:7; 2 Thess 1:4; 1:6). In 2 Corinthians 1:3-7 consolation is both an attribute (1:3) and an activity (1:4) of God. It is also an activity connected with the apostolic ministry in relationship to believers (1:4) and it is an attribute of Christ seen, in particular, in his death. This variety of meaning is held together by conditional phrases; if we (Paul and his apostolic followers) suffer, then in turn the strengthening and salvation of the believers is manifest. In this way God, Christ, Paul and his supporting apostles and the Christians of Achaia are brought together in the closest possible theological and spiritual relationship. The whole section is then bound together by offering blessing (*eulogetos*, 2 Cor 1:3) to God in a Christological context. This form of theological blessing was a feature in Jewish worship and, in Christianity, became a feature of later letters (Eph 1:3; 1 Pet 1:3).

Secondly, this relationship is given practical demonstration as a result of Paul's apostolic afflictions in Asia (2 Cor 1:8-11), identifying his apostolic ministry with the sufferings of Christ. The theme of thanksgiving is finally referred to in 1:11. Note that here Paul is giving thanks for a particular church, but the believers are giving thanks for the endurance shown and the blessings received in the exercise of the apostolic ministry. It is in this context that the prayers of the Achaian Christians are important for the sustaining of this ministry.

Paul's plans, trials and ministry, 1:12-2:13

Much of the section, 2 Corinthians 1:12-2:13, forms a personal defence by Paul of the conduct of his apostolic ministry. That is why much of the narrative is written in the first person singular. The first issue in this defence relates to Paul's self-confidence (2 Cor 1:12, cf. 1 Cor 1:31). In this context Paul raises again the dichotomy between worldly wisdom and reliance upon God, with the affirmation that the totality of Paul's evangelistic ministry has been based on God's demands and not his own. In this situation Paul believes that he will be affirmed on the coming eschatological 'day of the Lord Jesus' (2 Cor 1:14, cf. 1 Cor 16:22b) when the common mutuality between the apostle and the apostolic congregation will also be affirmed. It could have been that Paul's critics were arguing that he manifested overconfidence in his claims and in the attitudes that he was taking.

With 2 Corinthians 1:15ff. Paul confronts practical details. The point here concerns the non-fulfilment of Paul's travel plans (2 Cor 1:16, cf. 1 Cor 16:5-9); was this lack of achievement due to serious pastoral issues relating to the Ephesian church or because he was vacillating in visiting Corinth? Did the 'Yes', I am coming or the 'No', I am not, indicate Paul's worldliness and self-interest? Was he denying the Corinthians their 'double pleasure' (or favour of a double visit)? In all these circumstances Paul maintains that he was always straightforward (2 Cor 1:18). The evidence for this assertion is to be found in the way that the Gospel was preached in Corinth (cf. 1 Cor 2:1-5) which demonstrated how God's promises were being fulfilled, illustrating how the divine 'Yes' is at work (2 Cor 1:18-20).

In 2 Corinthians 1:23 it is revealed that Paul consciously changed his plans regarding a further visit to Corinth now he justifies this change. The reason for this decision was to spare the Corinthians the further pain (2 Cor 1:23 and 2:2) of personal contact in the deteriorating relationships between the apostle and the church. Instead Paul wrote to them, presumably setting out the differences between them (2 Cor 2:3 and 2:4). In this context Paul is demonstrating both affliction at their behaviour and, at the same time, expressing love (*agape*, 2 Cor 2:4, cf. 1 Cor 13:7) for the believers.

Both in 2 Corinthians 2:5, and later in 7:12, Paul refers to some wrongdoing committed by an individual (2 Cor 2:5) within the Corinthian church. Dealing with the pastoral implications of sin and forgiveness these verses (2:5-11) interrupt the narration of Paul's missionary travel plans. Under the guise of his apostolic authority Paul declares that the man's punishment (temporary expulsion?) has been sufficient. This man should be forgiven, loved and presumably allowed back into the worshipping community (2 Cor 2:6-8; cf. 1 Cor 5:13). From the Corinthians Paul, as their founding apostle, expects obedience (2 Cor 2:9, cf. 1 Cor 4:15) in order that he might share in this mutual forgiveness (2 Cor 2:10). Despite the presence of Christ in the Church's pastoral mission, be that mission connected with forgiveness or Paul's travels, Satan is ever at work, thus all believers should be aware of his designs (2 Cor 2:11). With 2 Corinthians 2:12-13 Paul returns directly to the justification of his missionary travel plans. These plans give reality to what Paul actually did following the proposals which he made in 1 Corinthians 16:5-9. He went to Troas (see Acts 16:8-11 and 20:6-11) because opportunities for evangelisation were there opened to him 'by the Lord'. Despite these opportunities Paul did not find contentment as Titus (cf. Gal 2:1 and 2:3) was not present. As a result Paul journeyed into Macedonia, the narrative of which, including the reconciliation of Titus, is continued later in 7:5ff. With these circumstances in mind Paul constructs, in the following section, 2:14-6:10, his theology of missionary ministry and his apostolic vocation within it.

Why Paul's Apostolic work is authentic, 2:14-6:10

The foundation of Paul's apostolic vocation is both theological and Christological, which validates its authenticity. First Paul returns to first principles by placing this vocation and ministry within the context of the dynamic progression of God's Gospel in Christ throughout the eastern Mediterranean world and perhaps beyond. To illustrate this dynamic progression two metaphors, familiar at the time, are utilised; first, from the Roman political world. The Gospel is seen in terms of a triumphal procession in a way similar to the processions which the Romans employed to demonstrate their superiority over the nations conquered by them. The irony apparent in this metaphor shows that, for the Romans, their triumphs indicated power and subjection while the Christian Gospel brought peace and freedom, which would indicate a fundamental difference between the *Pax Romana* and Christian evangelisation and its ecclesial life. The second metaphor is religious. The sweet aroma of incense rising from the sacrifices offered in Graeco-Roman Temples becomes symbolic for the fragrance of the Gospel which permeates everywhere (2 Cor 2:14; see also Rev 8:3). Again the metaphor is ironic (2 Cor 2:15-16a). Paul has written already about 'idols', 'lords' and 'gods' which achieve nothing, whereas God's Gospel concerns creation and Christ's Lordship (cf. 1 Cor 8:4-6). The objectivity of this demonstration of the Gospel in these terms effects both believers and unbelievers alike. The choice between death and life is thus presented to all (2 Cor 2:16a).

In the context of the triumph of the Gospel Paul raises the question of sufficiency or competence (2 Cor 2:16b). The question leads to the statement in 2:17 that the apostles are not peddlers of God's word like the philosophical teachers of the time but are sincere in their claims because they have received the divine commission from God in Christ. This statement represents both a personal claim on Paul's behalf (cf. Gal 1:10-12 and in 1 Cor reaching its climax in 15:8-9) and also for the others in his circle, including probably Titus, Timothy and Silvanus.

On this basis Paul asks if this claim is not another form of self-aggrandisement? Is a letter of recommendation needed (from the 'superlative apostles', 11:5? or from the Corinthians themselves?) to prove the authenticity of this claim? (2 Cor 3:1). At this point Paul offers a piece of evidence which he has used from the beginning of his ministry (cf. 1 Thess 2:19) that the believers (you, 2 Cor 3:2) themselves and the apostolic churches to which they belong, symbolise the authenticity of Paul's claim. The metaphor of the letter is now used to describe those who have accepted, and thereby received, the salvation offered by Christ as preached to them by Paul and his colleagues (2 Cor 3:2). This process represents the work of the Spirit who has 'written' metaphorically the message on their hearts (2 Cor 3:3).

2 Corinthians 3:6 contains the new idea that Paul and his colleagues are 'ministers of a new covenant'. Three points can be made about this idea in relation to the apostolic ministry. First, the language of covenant has been used already in connection with Jesus' saying over the cup at the Lord's Supper with regard to its contents as being 'the new covenant in my blood', traditional liturgical language which Paul has utilised in 1 Corinthians 11. This connection means that the apostolic ministry is identified with Christ's sacrifice which is demonstrated symbolically in the Eucharist. Secondly, Paul and his fellow apostles share in the new agreement which God has made with humanity through Jesus. Thirdly, the idea of the 'new covenant' is a reminder of that 'new covenant' which God made with Israel in connection with the prophetic work of Jeremiah (Jer 31:31-34). Here, in this new Christological context, the apostolic ministry is also seen to be prophetic in that the word of God (2 Cor 2:17) is being proclaimed. As with Jeremiah, so with Paul, this new covenant is to be 'written' upon the hearts of humanity (2 Cor 3:3 is based on Jer 31:33). Inherent in this concept, however, is the dichotomy created by the new in relation to the old: the 'old law' brings

death while the 'new law' gives life through the Spirit. This dichotomy prepares the reader for the series of contrasts which Paul will use later in 4:16-5:10.

This dichotomy is explained and defended in 2 Corinthians 3:7-18 by reference to Paul's biblical interpretation of Exodus 34:29-35; first, in relation to glory (*doxa*, 3:7-11 based on Exodus 34:29-30) and secondly, and emerging from it, to the concept of permanence (3:11-18 based on Exodus 34:33-35). Glory was symbolic of the presence and splendour of God with his people Israel both in the wilderness and later in the Jerusalem Temple. Paul argues that 'the ministers of a new covenant' (3:6a) share in a greater glory than the glory which accompanied Moses when he descended from Mount Sinai with the tablets containing the *Torah*. This greater glory established the ministry of Paul and his colleagues in the new order as having a superior ministry to that of Moses in the old order. This dichotomy can be represented diagrammatically as follows:

NEW COVENANT	OLD COVENANT
Jesus	Moses
Christian believers	Israel
Spirit – righteousness	*Torah* – condemnation
permanent	temporary
= superior ministry	= inferior ministry

In 2 Corinthians 3:13 Paul reflects on the veil (*kalumma*) worn by Moses (Ex 34:33-35). This reflection has a dual function. First, it attempts to interpret the text of Exodus in terms of what happened at that time: the purpose of the veil was that the Israelites might not see the fading glory on the face of Moses. Secondly, in c.56 AD (this day, 3:14), the text can be applied to the Jews who, on hearing their scriptures read in the synagogue, have their minds veiled in that they are unable to turn to Jesus and acknowledge him as God's Christ and Lord (2 Cor 3:15, cf. the grace greeting in 2 Cor 1:2). This interpretation reflects one angle of Paul's ambivalence towards his 'former life in Judaism' (Gal 1:13) upon which comment will be made later (cf. 1 Thess 2:13-14 and Rom 11:1-2).

It is the Israelite hardness of heart which unites this dual interpretation of the text (Ps 95:8). Despite this hardness when Jews turn to Christ this veil is removed and clarity of vision is restored (2 Cor 3:14b and 3:16). At the Tent of Meeting the purpose of the veil is to 'shield' God (Num 4:5) whereas Christ reveals the totality of God's presence.

With 2 Corinthians 3:17 the Christological perspective is reiterated by Paul in which he presents a new factor in the equation relating to Christ's Lordship (cf. 1:2) that 'the Lord is the Spirit' (3:17a). The implication of this equation is that where the Spirit is present freedom is to be found (3:17b). The concept of freedom has been used already by Paul in Galatians (4:21 for the analogy; 5:1 for the statement). In this case it represents freedom from *Torah* and its implications for Christian living, in particular, the requirement demanded by the Judaizers of circumcision for Gentile converts in addition to Baptism. In 2 Corinthians 3:17 freedom is given by the Spirit of Christ who allows believers to enter into the freedom of God's new covenant (cf. 3:6). Christian belief allows for the permanent removal of the veil because Christ the Lord manifests the totality of God's glory. As a result, through the ministry of the Spirit, believers can be transformed in order that they may obtain continually the new existence of both the meaning and the living of his glory (*doxa*, 2 Cor 3:18).

In 2 Corinthians 4:1-6 Paul both summarises and develops his theme of the apostolic ministry in which he, and his colleagues share (note the use of the first person plural; cf. 3:6) and which should be seen in terms of enlarging upon the perceptions revealed already in 2:14 onwards. This ministry operates as a result of God's mercy (4:1). It is a ministry which they offer with sincerity (2 Cor 4:2 cf. 2:17). The 'veiling' of the Gospel (cf. 3:13ff) results from unbelief (2 Cor 4:3-4), a failure to perceive that Christ is the likeness ('image', *eikon*) of God. Their ministry is thus concerned with their role as 'slaves' (*douloi*, 2 Cor 4:5) of Jesus whom they proclaim as Christ and Lord. The Gospel message is concerned with God as creator (Gen 1:3) and who through Christ offers salvation which gives light out of darkness (2 Cor 4:6 quoting Isa 9:2). The apostles have responded positively to this light which brings with it knowledge. This knowledge concerns the glory of God as seen in the face of Christ (cf. Moses' face, 3:13). The purpose of this knowledge is that in order that all who hear and respond positively to the Gospel message will receive the eschatological glory of salvation and the eternal life which God is offering. In view of the implications of this theology for the apostolic ministry Paul is able to declare that, even in the face of opposition and suffering, they do not lose heart (2 Cor 4:1).

In addition, this 'knowledge' (2 Cor 4:6) brought with it a new Christological way of interpreting the Jewish scriptures (e.g. Jer 31:31; Ex 34:29-35; Gen 1:3); which, with this method of interpretation, brought not merely the Word of God, but the Word of God in Christ. It was the Spirit which empowered this newly discovered knowledge of biblical interpretation.

In 2 Corinthians 4:7 Paul utilises a new metaphor to describe the apostolic ministry, that of the earthenware jar. These jars would have been a familiar feature of the domestic life of the ancient world. Being fragile in themselves they might yet contain family treasure. Although the apostles may be feeble in body (Paul, later 2 Cor 10:10b) nevertheless, by their actions, they proclaim the Gospel of Christ. This fact illustrates yet again that their ministry is of divine origin, offered as a result of the divine command (2 Cor 4:7, cf. 2:17b) and reflects the excellence of the divine power. Paul then explains the situation of the apostolic ministry by using gladiatorial imagery:

afflicted	not	crushed,
perplexed	not	driven to despair,
persecuted	not	forsaken,
struck down	not	destroyed (2 Cor 4:8-9)

But how can this imagery be explained in terms of the apostolic ministry? In doing so a new idea is introduced: that of the apostles carrying within (note the use of body, *soma*, language) themselves the death (*nekrosis*, lit. corpse, 2 Cor 4:10) of Jesus in order that his life might be manifest through the way that they exercise their ministry. It is this paradox that lies at the heart both of the totality of Paul's missionary activity in Corinth but also with regard to Christian evangelisation in general (2 Cor 4:10-11). At this point, by using the name 'Jesus' without qualification, Paul is returning to the historical reality and the theological implications of Jesus' death in Jerusalem, c.AD 30 (cf. 1 Cor 15:3-4a) in a way that he has done already in relation to the Last Supper (1 Cor 11:23-26) and to the resurrection (1 Cor 15:4b -7). Thus, to identify with Jesus' death means to identify with: (i) the fact of his death; (ii) the way in which he died, by the Roman punishment of crucifixion (e.g. Gal 2:20; 1 Cor 2:2) and (iii) the circumstances which led to his death (e.g. 1 Thess 2:15). Although this concept of dying which is manifested through the apostolic preaching and living (cf. Paul's personal statements, 1 Cor 2:1-5; 9:15-18), the results are shown by those, including the Corinthians, who have responded to the message and way of life presented by the Gospel (2 Cor 4:13 quoting Ps 116:10). Thus, Christian believers are filled with the new and eternal life offered by God in Christ (2 Cor 4:12). This situation represents the heart of resurrection theology. At this stage it is to be recognised that the Gospel message is dynamic: more and more people are accepting it, for which all must be thankful and give the credit for this dynamism where it belongs, to God (2 Cor 4:15).

Returning to the principle of not losing heart (2 Cor 4:16a cf. 4:1b) Paul then presents another tension, this time between the outer nature (the body) and the inner nature (the spirit): a tension which involves the wasting away of the outer nature and the continual renewal of the inner spirit (2 Cor 4:16b). This tension is extended further to include the earthly (things that can be seen) and the temporary contrasted with the heavenly (the unseen) and the eternal (2 Cor 4:18). This tension has been explored already by Paul in terms of the resurrection of the dead and the comparison between 'a physical body' and 'a spiritual body' (1 Cor 15:44).

In 2 Corinthians 5:1-5 these arguments are continued and enlarged on the basis of what is known already (For we know, 2 Cor 5:1) in terms of 'the tent' and the 'building' (cf. 1 Cor

3:9 and 14:12). Alongside these metaphors there is included that of clothing (2 Cor 5:2-5) and of dressing and undressing. The context of the passage is Paul's awareness of the frailty of all human existence (building upon 4:16ff) and maybe of his own situation of facing death. Despite the complexity of the argumentation the contrast being made is clear: between the temporary nature of the earthly tent, accompanied by anxiety of living, and the permanence of the eternal, heavenly building and of everlasting life with God. Nevertheless the issue remains as to the nature of being in God's final, eschatological, heavenly age. In this context the clothing metaphor is relevant (5:2-4). Paul is confident that in the heavenly realms he will be clothed (maybe in the white robes of resurrection and purity found in apocalyptic literature, e.g. Rev 6:11; 7:9; 7:13 and the angelic figures of Acts 1:10) in a spiritual body (1 Cor 15:44). Paul's confidence in this matter can be attributed to his sure hope in the approaching eternal life with God, a life which is guaranteed by the gift of the first instalment of the Spirit (2 Cor 5:5, cf. 2:22). This hope then presents the tension between the desire for this heavenly existence and the continuation of earthly life with all its opportunities for mission and ministry. This tension is described metaphorically by the image of being at home compared with being away from home (2 Cor 5:6 and 5:9). In the end all must be subject to the judgement of Christ, a judgement which will be made on ethical grounds between the good or evil done in life (2 Cor 5:10). Given this judgement the apostles walk by heavenly faith and not by earthly sight (5:7) and, as a result, they remain in good heart.

In 2 Corinthians 5:11-13 Paul applies these arguments to his major theme, that of his explanation and justification of the apostolic ministry. As with 5:1 he begins with the idea of knowing, on this occasion in 5:11 the idea of 'knowing the fear of the Lord'. It is only on this basis that the apostles can use persuasive rhetoric because the sincerity of their ministry is known to God (cf. 2:17b). There is no question of the apostolic missionaries again recommending themselves (2 Cor 5:11, cf. 3:1). The purpose of this declaration, however, is in order that the believers might be proud of them and be able to defend them to the apostles' opponents (2 Cor 5:12). In this context the purpose of the apostles' mystical experiences (Paul, later in 2 Cor 12:1-4) is to glorify God; on the other hand, the demonstration of their rationality was designed to convince the believers regarding their preaching and living the Gospel (2 Cor 5:13). Then follows a series of Christological statements beginning with the declaration of the all controlling power of Christ's love (2 Cor 5:12, how the believers should live themselves, 1 Cor 8:3 and 13:1). On this basis Paul demonstrates that this love is manifested through Christ's saving actions: his death and resurrection for all humanity. The purpose of these actions is in order that all humanity might turn and live for Christ (2 Cor 5:14-15).

In 2 Corinthians 5:16-21 there are further Christological statements which continue to interweave the ministry of Christ with that of the apostles. The contents of the passage has two principal features; first, it is argued that the human way of understanding Christ no longer applies (5:16). It would be a mistake, I should argue, to interpret the phrase 'if also we knew Christ according to the flesh' to mean that Paul knew Jesus before his crucifixion; rather the phrase concerns knowing Christ according to spiritual encounter rather than on the basis of personal acquaintance. Secondly, while many of the traditional Pauline themes can be detected such as 'new creation' (Gal 6:15b), 'sin' (1 Cor 15:3, used in the plural) and righteousness (e.g. 1 Cor 1:30), these themes are being utilised in the context of the new theme of 'reconciliation' (used five times in 2 Cor 5:18-20). The source of this metaphor is military and political as it evokes the restoration of peace after conflict. In 2 Corinthians 5 Paul uses the metaphor in a particular way. God is the subject and initiator of reconciliation (5:18). Not that he is hostile like an angry monarch, rather it is out of love that he wishes sinful (trespasses, 5:19) humanity to return and be part of his own new creation order. In this order the relationship between God and humanity is restored. This reconciliation is achieved through the ministry of Christ (5:18, cf. 5:15), and continued by the evangelistic ministry of Paul and his fellow missionaries, as ambassadors on Christ's behalf (5:20).

In 2 Corinthians 6:1-10 Paul both concludes his general perceptions with regard to the apostolic ministry which was begun in 2:14 and prepares for the direct appeal to the Corinthian church to be made in 6:11 and 7:2. Reference to 'grace' (*charis*, cf. 1 Cor 15:10 and 2 Cor 1:12) and preaching 'in vain' is a reminder of the vulnerability of the relationship between the Corinthians and the apostolic partners. Paul attempts a further justification of the character of his own apostleship, and that of his colleagues, in order to demonstrate that the way in which they exercise the ministry is in conformity with that of Christ.

How Paul's Apostolic ministry is related to the Corinthians, 6-11-7:16

It is at 2 Corinthians 6:11-13 that the first appeal is made to the Corinthians on the basis of the theology of the apostolic ministry as outlined above. Two points need to be made in this context. First, it is possible that there has been some dislocation of the text. 6:11-13 seems to be more directly linked to the second appeal in 7:2-4. In literary terms is 7:2-4 a repetition of 6:11-13 or does the second appeal refer to a later occasion linked with Titus (7:6)? The intervening material in 6:14-7:1 is concerned with another subject: that of the dangers faced by Christian believers when in social intercourse with unbelievers. From a literary perspective, however, the final-form of the text needs to be considered in order to appreciate the flow of the argument as the text now stands. I present the structure as follows:

A1. 6:11-13, First claim: Open attitude of the apostles towards the Corinthians, [implication: the Corinthians are reluctant].

B. 6:4-7:1, Second claim: Open attitude of the Corinthians to unbelievers.

A2. 7:2-4, Appeal: Corinthians asked to open themselves to the apostles, [implication: open to us rather than to unbelievers – we are God's agents, they are unclean, 6:17].

The second appeal to the Corinthians in 2 Corinthians 7:2-4 which Paul makes is characterised by his confidence in them as a church and prepares for the new, cordial relationship which Titus has engineered and which continues the narrative (in 7:5ff) from 2:12-13 where Paul is placed in Macedonia. Paul and Titus are portrayed as having a close partnership in the work of the Gospel (see later in 8:23). It appears that Titus' role is as Paul's envoy, the effectiveness of which is demonstrated by the Corinthians' favourable response to him (7:15). Two particular issues conclude this period of activity between Paul and the Corinthian church. First, there is a return to the 'encouragement language' found in 2 Corinthians 1:3-7. Again it is God who is described as 'the comforting one' (7:6), encouragement being a feature of his nature. The precise occasion for this encouragement (7:13) is the arrival of Titus (7:6 and 7:13) in Macedonia with news of the Corinthians' repentance (7:10) and of their high regard for Paul's ministry (7:7). Secondly, reference is made to Paul's (sorrowful?) letter (7:8, and 7:12, cf. 2:3-4). It appears that this letter has had its desired effect. As a result Paul renews his confidence in them as proper representatives of Christ.

Supporting the Jerusalem church with financial aid, 8:1-9:15

On the basis of this renewed relationship Paul is able to advance the issue of the collection for the Jerusalem church which he suggested first in 1 Corinthians 16:1-4. It could have been that the Corinthians were slow (possible hints in 2 Cor 8:10 and 9:2) in enacting Paul's suggestions as proposed there. The literary relationship between 2 Corinthians 8 and 9 remains a matter of debate. Although these chapters cover the same theme: that of the collection and the principles on which it should be based and the reasons why the Corinthians should embrace it, chapter 9 seems to represent a more formal, even bureaucratic approach. The collection for the Jerusalem church was, for Paul, of both practical and symbolic significance. Clearly he wished to support this church financially but symbolically the acceptance of the collection would confirm that the Jerusalem community, the birth-place of the Christian movement (cf. Acts 1:8), endorsed Paul's missionary activity and the churches which he had founded (Gal 1:18 and 2:1; Rom 15:26-29). Although previously Paul did not wish to accept the support of the Corinthian church for his own ministry (cf. 1 Cor 9:15), now he makes every effort to encourage them to support the Jerusalem church.

2 Corinthians 8:1-5 offers the Corinthians the example of the churches of Macedonia whose generosity the Corinthians ought to follow. Titus is introduced again (from 7:6; 7:13; 7:14) as a source of encouragement for them to be engaged in this particular ministry. As the Corinthians excel in faith (*pistis*, cf. 1 Cor 2:5 and 16:3), speech (*logos*, cf. 1 Cor 2:1; 12:8) and knowledge (*gnosis*, cf. 1 Cor 8:1; 12:8), language already well known to them, so now on this basis they ought to support the initiative of the collection.

In the context of the collection both Paul's concept of apostolic authority and his literary techniques are demonstrated. First, Paul does not impose his apostolic status as their 'founding father' on the Corinthian church but he suggests rather that, being engaged in the collection, will show that their love is a reality (2 Cor 8:8). Secondly, in dealing with pastoral situations, Paul returns to Christology, the need to follow the example of 'our Lord Jesus Christ' (2 Cor 8:9). In following this example Paul uses the riches/poverty paradox, Christ reversing his status in order that believers might become rich (for a similar framework see later, Phil 2:6-11). On the basis of this Christology Paul advances the principle of equality (2 Cor 8:14): the common sharing of resources which should be the hallmark of Christians. This principle is demonstrated by reference to scripture, Exodus 16:18 being quoted in support of the argument.

In 2 Corinthians 8:16-23 Paul describes the ministerial arrangements with regard to the collection. Titus (8:16, 8:23) and two other brother apostles are to be engaged in this work. There are two features that should be noted in this context. First, their ministry is corporate and universalised, being 'appointed by the churches' (8:19 and 8:23) for the proclamation and living of the Gospel. Secondly, the purpose of their ministry is to demonstrate the glory (*doxa*, 8:23; cf. 3:9-11) of Christ. Finally, Paul gives the Corinthians the injunction to be an example to the other churches in their attitude to the collection and to prove the confidence (8:24; cf. 1 Cor 1:31) which Paul has placed in them.

In 2 Corinthians 9:1-5 the Corinthians are encouraged by Paul to continue their resolve with regard to the collection by his suggestion that Macedonian Christians might accompany him to Achaia (cf. 1:1b) in order to stir the Corinthians into action. This action, however, would bring shame to them (9:4), instead Paul reminds them that the gift is a voluntary one and should not be seen in terms of extortion (9:5; a vice word, Rom 1:29). 2 Corinthians 9:6-10 justifies this position by reference to scripture (Prov 11:24, 22:8-9, Isa 55:10, Hosea 10:12).

In 2 Corinthians 9:11 Paul returns to the particular situation in Corinth by considering the theological and ethical implications of their hoped for generous gifting. Both in general terms, and with particular reference to the Jerusalem collection, generosity produces thanksgiving to God (9:11 and 12; note same theme being used in connection with evangelisation, 4:15). This theme is now placed within the context of the Gospel, the ministry and discipleship. Generosity is a proof (9:13) of the sincerity of the ministry which, in turn, is seen in terms of obedience to the Gospel of Christ, the purpose of which is to glorify God. The effect of these perceptions is to demonstrate that giving to those in need lies at the heart of the Gospel. As a result the churches who receive the gift will see the surpassing grace of God working within the Corinthian Christians. Paul concludes the section in 9:15 with the declaration of thanks to God for the inexpressible gift (*dorea*). In this context 'gift' must be seen in a broader setting than the Jerusalem collection, rather it refers to the total action of God in Christ towards humanity in all its aspects.

Paul's personal defence of his apostolic ministry, 2 Cor 10:1-13:10

Whatever their sequence in Paul's relationship with the Corinthian Christians the purpose of these chapters is to prepare them for his impending visit (2 Cor 12:14 and 13:1). Their contents are personal in the sense that they are written as Paul's defence of himself and as an appeal (2 Cor 10:1) to them. Their tone is often harsh and sometimes sarcastic. 2 Corinthians 10:1-6 states the consequences of their disobedience in terms of his apostolic authority (2 Cor 10:6). As a result they are exhorted to follow 'the meekness and gentleness of Christ' which Paul himself manifests (2 Cor 10:1) by the way he exercises the Christian ministry. It appears that he is being accused of living according to worldly standards (2 Cor 10:2), a charge which he has denied earlier (cf. 2 Cor 1:17). In this context the language of siege warfare is used to further apostolic arguments (Prov 21:22; 2 Cor 10:3-4), the 'I' now becoming the 'we' of the corporate apostolic proclamation.

2 Corinthians 10:7-18 restates the grounds on which Paul's apostolic authority is based and the objections raised by the Corinthians against him are challenged. There is a golden thread running through both the accusations and the defence. It is that Paul's apostolic status is manifested through his personal weakness which is, ironically, the source of his strength and which paradox is based, in turn, on the weakness-strength of the crucified but risen Christ. Paul cites the example of his letters (2 Cor 10:9). These letters, the Corinthians apparently declare, are 'weighty and strong' while their author is both physically weak and lacking in rhetorical skill (2 Cor 10:10). This opinion, however, ignores the purpose of the letters which for Paul is to declare in writing what he would say if he was actually present; thus, personal appearance is of no avail. The only qualification necessary is to have been called by God to perform a particular ministry and to live in conformity with Christ. In 2 Corinthians 10:12 Paul confronts the ambiguity of comparison. On one hand he refuses to compare himself with his rivals who are commending themselves through the use

of 'letters of recommendation' (cf. 2 Cor 3:1-3); on the other hand, such a comparison would demonstrate that his rivals are without understanding. The comparison motif continues in 2 Corinthians 10:13-18. The self-confidence of Paul's rivals is based on worldly premises (10:18), whereas Paul (like the prophet Jeremiah, Jer 9:23-24 is quoted) finds his confidence 'in the Lord' (10:17; also, 1Cor 3:13). On this basis Paul is able to 'justify' the nature and the direction of this missionary activity in relation to Corinth. This mission is based on divine authority (2 Cor 10:14). It was based originally on the premise that Paul did not evangelise in places where the Christian Gospel had been preached already (2 Cor 10:16; later, Rom 15:20). This fact demonstrated that Paul understood the boundaries and responsibilities of his evangelistic work both in terms of not interfering with the missionary and pastoral work of other apostles and, as the founder of the Corinthian church, was able to claim continuing spiritual fatherhood over the community (cf. 1 Cor 4:14-16). At the same time the Corinthians must appreciate that the conceptual and geographical boundaries of the Pauline mission are developing. Corinth can never be the only place meriting his spiritual and pastoral attention (2 Cor 10:15). In this regard it could have been the case that the Corinthian Christians expected Paul to be ever-present within the community and thought that spiritual pastoring by the means of letters to be unsatisfactory. To fill this apparent vacuum other apostles were invited into the community. This situation demonstrates, however, that the Corinthians misunderstood the itinerant nature of Paul's missionary ministry and the theological concepts on which it was based.

2 Corinthians 11:1-12:13 encapsulates what has been known as Paul's 'fool's speech'. This description of the contents of these chapters needs to be understood carefully; first, the idea of 'speech': (i) In this context 'speech' would refer to the reading of Paul's correspondence within the worship of the Corinthian church (cf. 1 Cor 14:26). This worship was also deeply eschatological in that, by using the liturgical declaration *Maranatha* (Aramaic form of 'Our Lord come', 1 Cor 16:22), the reading of Paul's texts (including their contents) was

placed within the orbit of prayer for the eschatological return of Christ. (ii) Given the references to 'fool' or 'foolishness': 'fool' (*aphron*), 2 Corinthians 11:16; 11:19; 12:6; 12:11 and 'foolishness' (*aphrosune*), 2 Corinthians 11:1; 11:17; 11:21; questions arise as to the cultural background of these terms and why Paul felt the need to use them here within this powerful first person singular narrative.

In contemporary speech 'fool' is used to describe what is considered to be stupid characteristics or actions but for Paul and his Corinthian readers 'fool' had wider, cultural connotations. It could be used in politics to describe political *naïveté*; in education to describe a lack of reasoned understanding or to denote a character in the theatre. Fools played a part in comedy (like the later court jester), they often came from the 'lower orders' and would appear as eccentric and ugly. At the same time, however, despite being portrayed as weak and humiliated, they were capable of serious moral points about the action of the play and its principal characters. The extent to which Paul was using this cultural background is difficult to assess. The point is that resonances in the lives of the Corinthians were being touched in a way that would be unfamiliar to us and that are helpful to note in order that we can comprehend the various layers of meaning which the 'speech' conveys.

It is clear also that Paul is utilising Graeco-Roman rhetorical norms given that the 'speech' is full of parody and irony. Its purpose is to expose both the foolishness of Paul's apostolic opponents with whom he is disagreeing profoundly and, at the same time, reveals his 'philosophy' of apostolic ministry both with regard to the Corinthians, as well as offering the general precepts on which his ministry is based. Within Paul's 'foolishness', however, the Corinthian Christians are expected to discern God's will working in Paul's ministry.

In this dimension 2 Corinthians 11:1-12:13 ought to be read in the light of, and as a continuation of, what Paul has written already in 1 Corinthians 1:10-4:21 in terms of folly and wisdom. With this observation, however, it should be noted that, in the latter passage, Paul uses the word *moros*, for 'fool' (also meaning dull or stupid) and, utilising a different structure, constrasting *moros* with *sophia* (wisdom, 1 Cor 1:25). In 2 Corinthians 11:1-12:13 little of this antithetical parallelism occurs. It is the Corinthians who seem to be claiming wisdom (2 Cor 11:19; note also, 1 Cor 4:10) while God is seen as having the power of knowing (2 Cor 11:11; 11:31; 12:2 and 12:3), Paul claiming knowledge only on one occasion in the 'speech' (2 Cor 11:6).

First, though, in 2 Corinthians 11, Paul feels the need to place the 'speech' within his particular 'philosophy' regarding his relationship with the Corinthian Christians. For this purpose he utilises the ancient Hebraic marriage metaphor which describes God's relationship with Israel (portrayed ideally in eschatological terms, Hos 2:19-20). Opposite to God's command to Hosea (Hos 1:2 and 3:1) Paul perceived the Corinthians in terms of a 'pure bride' whom he betrothed to Christ which gave their thinking and living a single, Christological focus in terms of having 'one husband' (2 Cor 11:2). This experience of 'paradise' was soon corrupted by the arrival within the Corinthian community, of missionaries who were opponents of Paul. These missionaries Paul describes by the use of the biblical narrative which narrates the corruption of Eve by the serpent (2 Cor 11:3 based upon Gen 3:1-6; 14-20). According to Paul, in language familiar to that which he has used already in Galatians 1:6-7, these rival teachers preached 'another Jesus' and a 'different Gospel' in a 'different spirit' from that proclaimed by him. Apparently the Corinthians accept readily this variant interpretation of the Gospel (2 Cor 11:4). It is not clear as to what this 'different Gospel' represents. It is likely to be at variance with Paul's 'theology of the cross' as outlined in 1 Corinthians 1:17-2:5 and which forms the basis for his interpretation of his apostolic ministry in 1 Corinthians 4:8-13. It could have been that Paul's opponents are preaching a message of wisdom and power rather than one of humility and suffering, and are stressing the importance of the visionary experiences which *they* have received. The difference is that these other apostles are skilled in rhetorical speech, possessing the gift of oratory in a way that Paul says that he does not (2 Cor 11:6). Again this position would relate to his earlier claim that he preached the 'theology of the cross' not in 'lofty words or wisdom' (cf. 1 Cor 2:1-5). Yet Paul is able to claim one attribute which the other apostles do not possess: knowledge (*gnosis*, 2 Cor 11:6). This knowledge, however, is concerned with the knowledge of God manifest through the suffering of Christ and which, by implication, unites Paul's apostolic affliction (2 Cor 1:8-9) with Christ's death. In this sense Paul can claim a 'superior knowledge' to that of his apostolic rivals.

The identity of Paul's opponents in his 'fool's speech' (and indeed throughout the Corinthian correspondence) is a matter of considerable debate, especially as he seems to be recognising two groups: the 'super apostles' (2 Cor 11:5 and later 12:11) and the 'false apostles' (2 Cor 11:13); groups who have apparently arrived in Corinth after Paul's departure from the city. On one hand, he seems to feel some equity of status to the 'super apostles' which has led to speculation that they may have been the Jerusalem apostles (Gal 2:9); whereas the 'false apostles' are deceitful workers pretending to be good men (2 Cor 11:13 and 11:16) who, like Satan (2 Cor 11:14; cf. 11:3), can appear as 'angels of light'. Yet the difference between the 'super apostles' and the 'false apostles' may be more apparent than real. The Corinthians could have been offered two perspectives on *one* group. In this case the Jerusalem apostles might not have been directly involved and the two designations about their apostleship relate to one group who have entered (or were asked to enter) the Corinthian church in order to (or felt it necessary to) discuss/question/oppose Paul's interpretation of the Gospel. It is likely that they prized highly their own ecclesiological influence and were well regarded by many of the Corinthian Christians.

Whatever may have been the case Paul feels the need, in 2 Corinthians 11:7-11, to 'justify' his exercise of the apostolic ministry to the Corinthians. First he 'justifies' further the fact that he did not accept financial support for his ministry (1 Cor 9:12 and 9:15-18; later at 2 Cor 12:14). Instead he 'robbed' other churches (2 Cor 11:8) and continued to support himself by working manually (2 Cor 11:9; cf. 1 Cor 4:12). Secondly, there was no contradiction in accepting financial support from the Macedonian churches (note later, Phil 4:10-20).

Paul's purpose was not to burden the Corinthians financially. Perhaps he did not wish to be dependent on the city's wealthy patrons? Yet in all this activity Paul's over-riding concern was to demonstrate love (use of the verb, *agapao*, 2 Cor 11:11) towards the Corinthian believers and with the knowledge of the Gospel as properly understood.

The 'foolishness theme' is renewed at 2 Corinthians 11:16 and, with it, the related issue of self-confidence, together with the question of Paul's credibility as a person and as an apostle. The Corinthians are challenged (in an atmosphere of strained relationships – recall the marriage metaphor in 11:2) to reflect upon these themes in connection with Paul, the other apostles mentioned, and themselves. This triangle of relationship is portrayed (explicitly and implicitly) by a variety of terms, often used by Paul ironically: foolishness, wisdom, slavery, freedom, weakness, knowledge and power and, with them, the question as to where they are to be found and how they are to be demonstrated in terms of the Gospel of God and manifested through the saving activity of Jesus, the Christ. This question leads to a further issue as to how the apostolic ministry should be exercised in the light of them (2 Cor 11:19-21a).

With 2 Corinthians 11:21b-12:10 Paul lists the events in his apostolic ministry which demonstrate both, the authenticity of that ministry and, through them, how he has manifested 'the signs of a true apostle' (2 Cor 12:12). Again, like other places within the Corinthian correspondence, this passage is full of irony, utilising Paul's own particular form of rhetoric. He says that he is writing like a 'fool' (2 Cor 11:21b) and a 'madman' (2 Cor 11:23) yet, through this 'speech', and implicit within it, the knowledge of God is being declared in so far as Paul can match any claim which his opponents are making. In the early fifth century St Augustine used 2 Corinthians as an example in order to demonstrate Paul's rhetoric skill. In this attempt Augustine was illustrating how biblical study (and preaching) ought to be situated in the context of Roman learning, including the all-embracing educational culture (inherited from the Greeks) of rhetoric, the art of persuasion. If this is how 2 Corinthians 10-13 ought to be interpreted, the question arises as to whether Paul was 'successful' and who is persuaded by his 'case'?

In this context three (rhetorical) questions are raised by Paul which relate to his Jewish heritage (later, Phil 3:5): being a Hebrew, an Israelite and a descendent of Abraham (2 Cor 11:22-23); thus, in terms of 'Jewishness', he is well equal to his opponents. More seriously perhaps in the present context is his claim to be a minister (*diakonos*) of Christ (2 Cor 11:23a). In this regard Paul is superior to his opponents, the evidence for this position being provided by the sufferings which he has endured for the sake of Christ (2 Cor 11:23b -28). These sufferings include corporal punishment at the hands of both Jews (thirty-nine lashes, 2 Cor 11:24 on the basis of Deut 25:1-3) and Romans (beaten with rods; see Acts 16:22 and 16:37, technically illegal for Roman citizens but sometimes ignored). Other sufferings include those endured through travel (2 Cor 11:25-26); persecution (2 Cor 11:23-26) and as a result of the conflicts both in relation to opponents (2 Cor 11:26), and in relation to the churches (2 Cor 11:28). The purpose of this list is now clear: to demonstrate Paul's weakness and humiliation which identify him with the ministry of Christ showing that he is a 'true apostle' unlike others who are deceitful apostles.

This paradox is continued in 2 Corinthians 11:30-12:4 which reveal how, despite suffering and weakness, God's blessing has been working through Paul's life. In this regard he cites two different incidences; first, his escape from Damascus.

This is the sole event recorded in the Pauline literature where an incident in Paul's life is linked to an event in Roman history. Aretas was king (probably technically governor) of the Nabatean people from AD 9-39 and whose territory extended from the Red Sea to the north of Damascus (he was given control of this city by the Emperor Caligula in 37) with his capital at Petra. Why Aretas wished to detain Paul is not clear, perhaps it was in order to satisfy the Jews after Paul had preached Jesus as Messiah in the synagogues of Damascus? (2 Cor 11:32-33; note also the later account in Acts 9:23-25). The date of this event was c.AD 38/9. In 2 Corinthians

11 Paul considers his escape, and the circumstances of it, as illustrating God's protective care over him and of God's will that Paul should continue to exercise the apostolic ministry (in terms of Gal 1:16?).

Secondly, out of the numerous 'visions' and 'revelations' which Paul received (2 Cor 12:1) from Christ he gives an account of a particular mystical experience which he received 'fourteen years ago' (note the chronological precision, 2 Cor 12:2). By definition such an experience cannot be communicated (2 Cor 12:4) but, given the antecedents in the Jewish tradition relating to Moses, Isaiah, Enoch, Daniel and Levi where bodily transformation is received and the experience of paradise given, Paul is able to relate his experience. As a result he places himself within this Jewish tradition whereby God's will is revealed and the ministry of those who receive the vision is confirmed in relation to Israel or at least to the 'righteous group' within the Israelite tradition. Paul's commission, however, is deeper and broader as it identifies the fact that Jesus is Christ and Lord to all nations, a message of 'good news' which Paul was commissioned to proclaim. If his opponents can claim that their ministry is based on revelations of the supernatural he can go further. Not only is Paul placed within the Jewish mystical tradition and accordingly situated on the same level as the 'heroes' of Judaism but, at the same time, is commissioned to go beyond them (note Paul having a superior ministry to Moses, 2 Cor 3:12-16) as a result of the vision which he received from Christ.

In relating such an experience both Paul's commission and his ministry enter dangerous waters in so far as he could be tempted to indulge in the same religious superiority (2 Cor 12:6b) which his opponents are demonstrating and, at the same time, to forget the basis of his own ministry: knowing nothing except Jesus Christ crucified (1 Cor 2:2). Instead 'a thorn in the flesh' was given to him which he sees as being 'a messenger of Satan' (2 Cor 12:7), an indication that the 'thorn' was some kind of temptation for him to be untruthful and deceitful (cf. 2 Cor 11:3). It is uncertain as to what the metaphor of the thorn relates, suggestions include either a physical ailment or an external opponent. Whatever may have been the case Paul makes a three-fold request 'to the Lord' for its removal. The precision of this three-fold request seems to indicate actual occasions of which the Corinthians may have been aware. The reply from the Lord, however, is offered in terms of two maxims: (i) the maxim relating to Paul's ministry and (ii) a general maxim which applies to all circumstances.

(i)   'My grace (*charis*) is sufficient for you (Paul)'. As a result,

(ii) 'for the/my power (*dunamis*) is perfected in weakness' (2 Cor 12:9a).

It is only on this basis that both Paul's ministry and that of all true apostles is secure. It is in conformity with the death of Christ, therefore, that Paul accepts persecution (cf. 2 Cor 11:23-28) thus, with this humiliation, he is paradoxically powerful (2 Cor 12:9b-10), because he has identified with the pattern set by Christ in his saving activity with regard to humanity.

Interestingly the 'speech' is not concluded with 2 Corinthians 12:10. Instead, three more verses are added which provide a finale to the 'speech' by returning to, and offering a summary of, the 'fool theme': Although he experiences humiliation (2 Cor 12:11; cf. 11:21b -30 and 1 Cor 4:8-13) he is not inferior to the 'super apostles' for the reasons stated above (cf. 2 Cor 10:7-11). On the contrary he manifests, through the character of his ministry, the 'signs of a true apostle' (note 2 Cor 12: 1-4). On these grounds he asks why the Corinthians should be complaining that he has favoured other churches in comparison to them. Was it because he refused to accept their offer of financial support? If so, and in a tone of bitter sarcasm and irony, he asks for their forgiveness (2 Cor 12:13).

With 2 Corinthians 12:14 (and also 13:1) Paul returns to the question of making a third visit to Corinth and with it the renewal of the issue of financial support for his ministry. This issue now exposes the divide between what Paul believes belongs to the Corinthians and the ministry being offered to them (without charge) for their sake (2 Cor 12:14). In seeking to bring them his continuing ministry Paul restates the parental metaphor to describe his commitment to them (2 Cor 12:14-15; cf. 1 Cor 4:14-15). Yet is this expression of pastoral care and love mere deceit on Paul's part? Against such accusation he defends himself by repeating the claim that he is not a burden to them and how, in addition, he sent Titus and another brother to them as his representatives. In so doing did these representatives take advantage of the Corinthians? Were they a burden to them (2 Cor 12:18)? Such a scenario raises literary and historical questions concerning the link between 2 Corinthians 12:14-18 and the information relating to the collection from the churches of Macedonia and Achaia for the Jerusalem church recorded in 2 Corinthians 8:1-9:15. Was Paul being accused of financial irregularity by the Corinthians? If so, Paul (with Titus) declares his innocence (2 Cor 12:18).

In 2 Corinthians 12:19-21 Paul addresses the question as to why he is 'justifying' his ministry. Is this justification merely for the purpose of defending himself and his apostolic representatives? On the contrary Paul maintains that all his efforts have been for the sake of the Corinthian church and for its 'upbuilding' (2 Cor 12:19; cf. 1 Cor 14:3, Rom 14:19). Yet such a third visit by Paul may prove to be disappointing. Paul and the Corinthian church may have grown apart and some of its members may be indulging in vices (2 Cor 12:20; see also, 1 Cor 5:1-5; 6:15-16 and Gal 5:20). When he arrives on his visit maybe Paul is fearing further alienation from the church manifested by their humiliation of him which will indicate, in turn, that the pastoral and spiritual relationship between them is dead and, thus for Paul, will be a cause for mourning the 'departed' (2 Cor 12:21).

The link between 2 Corinthians 13:1 and the contents of 12:14-21 is provided by the projected third visit. If the Corinthians are displeased with Paul they are to follow the ancient Jewish tradition by examining him before two or three witnesses (2 Cor 13:1b; based upon Deut 19:15-21, see also Mt 18:16 regarding 'church order'). Given this possibility Paul goes on the offensive: he will, as he has done before, write and speak firmly to 'those who have sinned' (2 Cor 13:2) within the community and, in so speaking, he will be declaring the authority of Christ. It is the judgement of Christ which is important and, with it, the paradox of weakness and power (2 Cor 13:3-4).

On this basis Paul is able to declare the purpose for which his letter(s?) have been written. It is in order that the Corinthians may 'test' themselves in order to be sure that they are living in conformity with Jesus Christ (2 Cor 13:5) and in tune with the ethical implications of this conformity (2 Cor 13:7), that they live in the truth (2 Cor 13:8) and understand the fundamental paradox between weakness and strength (2 Cor 13:9) which Paul has outlined both in his initial preaching and in his subsequent communications with them. The mourning metaphor of 2 Corinthians 12:21 is, in 13:9, left aside for the more positive concept of prayer for their restoration, Paul's final hope is that his letter may serve this purpose and that his proposed third visit to Corinth may be a fruitful one, not for severity but for the continuing edification (2 Cor 13:10; cf. 12:19) of the church.

Concluding greeting and blessing, 2 Cor 13:11-14

2 Cor 13:14 concludes the letter with a 'Trinitarian' structure which is more complex than the Blessings found in Paul's earlier letters (but cf. Eph 6:23-24). It organises God's blessing around: the Lord Jesus Christ and grace (*charis*); God and love (*agape*); and the Holy Spirit and communion (*koinonia*). No one English translation (communion/fellowship/participation) can do justice to the profundity represented here by *koinonia*, which implies both the relationships which exist at the heart of Godhead, those which ought to be recognised within the Christian community and the 'communion' which the believers share as a result of the saving activity of God in Christ through the workings of the Holy Spirit. Despite all the many difficulties which existed between Paul and the Corinthian church this concluding blessing offers a vision of how Christians can, and should, respond to God and each other.

SECTION 2 – CONTEXT

A. THE ENVIRONMENT

Corinth was an ancient city believed to have been founded around 4000 BC by Corinthus, held to be a son of Zeus. Corinth, however, reached the height of its influence during the sixth century BC but was then overshadowed by its most powerful neighbour, Athens and was weakened as a result of the almost continuous warfare between city states, in particular Athens and Sparta. In 338 BC Philip of Macedon, who had conquered the area, established Corinth as the centre for his grouping of city states, the Hellenic League. This positioning, together with Corinth's geographical position, ensured its development as a place of trade and commerce. The soil to the west of the city was particular fertile which meant that its agricultural potential could be developed. Corinth also became a centre for tourism because of the establishment of the Isthmian games in the city from the sixth century onwards. They were regarded as one of the four great Hellenic festivals, ranking below the Olympic games but above those held in Delphi and Nemea. These games occurred biannually and were held in the spring. They were not merely an athletic festival (imagery used by Paul, 1 Cor 9:24-27) but were accompanied by a complex combination of sport, religion, politics and culture. Even after the destruction of the city in 146 BC, when the games were transferred to neighbouring Sicyon, their connection with Corinth was not lost and they returned to the city between 7 BC and AD 3 (around Paul's time they were celebrated in AD 49 and 51, *BSGT,* 54, and also presumably in AD 53, 55 and 57).

Following the conquest of Greece by the Romans at the beginning of the second century BC cities were allowed a degree of independence and given the capacity to form alliances with each other. Corinth became a member of the Achaean League of cities. The Roman authorities, however, became concerned as to the strength of these new political structures and demanded that the League be disbanded. Corinth refused to comply and, as a result, the Roman general,

Lucius Mummius, destroyed the city in 146 BC, executing the male residents and selling the remainder of the citizens into slavery. The city, however, was not deserted entirely and some forms of Greek religious and political life were reinstated gradually.

For the purpose of cementing his power-base in the eastern Mediterranean Julius Caesar began rebuilding Corinth in 46 BC with the intention of creating a Roman colony in the city. He also planned a canal to be constructed through the isthmus of Corinth. The purpose was two-fold. First, to provide a supply route for future military operations in the eastern Mediterranean and beyond and, secondly, to foster trade in the area. Although in the Imperial era several attempts were made to construct such a canal it was not operational until 1893. The Emperor Augustus, followed by Tiberius and Claudius, continued Caesar's aspirations for Corinth by building a huge Roman city (estimated 300,000 inhabitants in the second century and twice as large as Athens) in which were settled a large numbers of freedmen and slaves, together with veterans from the army. Corinth became the capital of the Roman province of Achaea as well as recovering its former confidence as a centre for commerce and trade. Thus, a new Roman city (in which Latin became the official language) was constructed upon the foundations, and with the history and culture of the old Greek city. An investigation of the ruins of ancient Corinth (*BSGT,* 57-65), therefore, can re-create both the environment and the atmosphere which Paul encountered when he first visited the city as a Christian missionary in AD 51.

Emerging from the historical and cultural development of Corinth is the question of the social structure of the Corinthian church and the social position of its members. This issue arises because of (i) Paul's comment that the earliest Christian converts were from the lower social orders (1 Cor 1:26) and (ii) that there were social divisions within the Corinthian church (1 Cor 11:17-22). It is clear that some members came from the educated and political elite. Gaius, for example, is mentioned (1 Cor 1:14; Rom 16:23 – written from Corinth) as being able to accommodate a church in his house which presupposes a residence of some size. Erastus is named as the city's treasurer in Romans 16:23 (note also 2 Tim 4:20). Whether or not this is the same Erastus who is named in an inscription to be found between the theatre and the north market, which records his personal donation of the paved area linking them on account of his promotion to the aedileship (chief city official), is difficult to say. It would appear then that the Corinthian church contained residents from across the social and political spectrum of the city with some important civic leaders controlling its mission and ministry. The central question is, however, what difference did Christian belief and practice make to both their social positioning and their respective role within wider Corinthian society?

B. THE CORINTHIAN CHURCH WITHIN PAUL'S MISSIONARY ACTIVITY

The period of Paul's involvement with Corinth in terms of both his missionary and literary activity, c.51-57 AD, was of vital importance in Paul's life and intellectual and pastoral development. As our study illustrates, major issues were being confronted: Christology, ecclesiology, apostolic ministry and ethics: the way Christians ought to live within the multi-cultural and multi-ethnic context of urban Corinth. This confrontation generated disagreements in particular in relation to ministry. Paul is forced to challenge his opponents and they him. In this period also some of the major tensions and paradoxes of the Pauline position emerged; for example, how, theologically, power can be obtained only as a result of weakness (e.g. 2 Cor 12:9).

Luke mentions a single visit to Corinth by Paul in Acts 18:1-18. Luke's interpretation of Paul's Corinthian ministry contains some interesting features not immediately recognisable from the Corinthian letters. First, Luke places Paul's ministry in the wider context of Jewish/Roman civic relationships. The Jewish couple, Aquila (originally from Pontus) and Priscilla, arrive from Rome having been expelled, with other (all?) Jews from Rome, as a result of an edict issued by the Emperor Claudius. I consider this edict and the evidence provided for it by the second century historical biographer, Suetonius, when the development of the church of Rome is considered in chapter 4. In the meanwhile the importance of Aquila and Priscilla religiously and pastorally in the development of the church in both Rome and Corinth should be recognised (1 Cor 16:19; Rom 16:3; 2 Tim 4:19 and Acts 18:2-18, 18:26). Secondly, Luke places emphasis on Paul's ministry to Jews (Acts 18:4; 18:5). Evidence for the presence of a synagogue(s) in Corinth is provided by the discovery of a lintel stone which bears the inscription 'Synagogue of the Hebrews' (*BSGT,* 50). Paul's synagogue ministry was two-edged. On one hand, both prominent Jews (Acts 18:8, Crispus and his household, Acts 18:17, Sosthenes, also 1 Cor 1:1) and God-fearers (Acts 18:7, Titius Justus) were converted to Christianity; on the other some Jews forced Paul to attend the tribunal over which the Roman proconsul of Achaia, Gallio, had authority (Acts 18:12). In the fashion often employed by Roman officials in Acts Gallio dismissed the case as being a matter of internal Jewish religious disagreement which had little relevance for civic order (Acts 18:16). The Gallio 'tribunal incident' in Corinth has been used by historians as a way of cementing a focal point in the reconstruction of Paul's missionary activity. This cementing is made possible by the discovery at Delphi of an inscription of a declaration from the Emperor Claudius to 'Junius Gallio my friend, and proconsul of Achaea' (text to be found in C.K. Barrett, *The New Testament: Selected Documents*, revised edition, London, SPCK, 1987, 51-52), dated 'year 12, acclaimed Emperor for the twenty-sixth time,...'. On this basis it is likely that Gallio arrived in Corinth in 50 or 51 and held office for two years, thus the date calculated from the above data being between January and August 52, the conclusion of Gallio's term of office. Paul must have been brought before him during this period (see Acts 18:12-17).

SECTION 3 – THEOLOGICAL, PASTORAL AND HERMENEUTICAL ISSUES

Given the enormous range of issues which emerge from the Corinthian correspondence I have decided to highlight three significant areas for consideration in terms of Paul's message as 'Good News for Today'.

A. THEOLOGY AND CHRISTOLOGY

In my judgement it is in this area that Paul makes advances and offers challenges to our contemporary understanding. Speaking of the Corinthian correspondence in these terms in no way negates the rich theological patterns to be found, and which I have discussed, in the Thessalonian letters or in the letter to the churches of Galatia; rather it is the particular cultural and philosophical circumstances found in Corinth which makes Paul's discussion both interesting and innovative. Given that the theological patterns and their background is varied, perhaps due both to the urban environment and the meeting of Jewish and Greek thought, I have chosen to reflect on two passages, 1 Corinthians 15:3-8 and 2 Corinthians 5:14-21 discussed in more detail in Section 1, to be viewed metaphorically as the digging of two shafts into a rich gold-mine. In any discussion of 'Paul as Good News for Today', Theology and Christology are of fundamental importance. Entry into contemporary religious debate is to enter into the discussion concerning God's action in the world. To understand Christianity we need to reflect upon both the nature of Christ and how this nature and his activity is to be explained to contemporary audiences.

In 1 Corinthians 15:3-8 Paul returns the Corinthians to 'first principles', the foundations on which the 'Good News' is preached, namely what God did/is doing through Christ towards humanity. Paul adopts a pre-existing liturgical tradition, that Christ died in accordance with the scriptures on behalf of our (Jews' and Gentiles') sins, and adds his own testimony to the resurrection alongside an existing 'cloud of witnesses'. 2 Cor 5:14-21 modifies familiar language (e.g. Christ dying on behalf of sinful humanity), utilizing Jewish sacrificial terminology, supplemented with new metaphors (e.g. of reconciliation) to describe God's action in Christ.

I consider that the ways in which Paul has developed his Christological understanding from 1 Corinthians to 2 Corinthians are twofold. First, attributes of God are now shared by Christ; for example, in addition to the love of God there is the love of Christ (2 Cor 5:14). Secondly, utilising Israel's wisdom tradition (e.g. Wis 7:25-26), Christ becomes the perfect image of God's glory and likeness (2 Cor 4:4 and 4:6). It can now be seen how Paul used different metaphors (e.g. reconciliation, 2 Cor 5:18-20; riches/poverty, 2 Cor 8:9) to explain similar Christological ideas, metaphors which are dependent on the particular context in which he is ministering.

B. CHURCH AND APOSTOLIC MINISTRY

In every section of the Christian Church there are anxieties, debates and controversies relating to its ordained ministry. These issues relate both to ministerial identity and to practice in the context of the Church's mission in the modern world.

In my concluding reflections I shall attempt to summarise some of these issues both in terms of contemporary understanding and in relation to the understanding of ministry within Paul and the Pauline tradition. In that context I shall argue that it is necessary for twenty-first-century ministers to return to this tradition for guidance in order to enable us to understand and practise the ministry with which we have been entrusted. To construct such a hermeneutical 'bridge' is not easy. There are numerous different doctrinal and ecclesial structures in which the Church's ministry is exercised together with a multiplicity of social and political contexts in which the ministerial office is undertaken. Yet, in my judgement, Paul provides a focus: the way in which his apostolic ministry, and by implication the ministry of other 'true' apostles, is rooted in Christ's ministry in which the fundamentals of God's saving Gospel are revealed. Before Paul's ministerial focus (and the issues arising from it) are discussed, two points need to be made. First, Paul's understanding of ministry forms part of the triangular relationship between Christ, the churches and the apostolic ministry. As a result, Christology, ecclesiology and ministry are inter-related. There can be no discussion of ministry without that of the Church, given that apostolic ministers are 'called' (1 Cor 1:1) by God from the body (1 Cor 12:12; 12:27) of the faithful into various forms of Spirit-filled ministry (1 Cor 12:4-11; 28-31) in order that Christ may be proclaimed (2 Cor 4:5-6). Secondly, the Pauline literature is rich with insights and reflections about every aspect of the ministerial life. In the Corinthian correspondence these insights relate to: (i) the exercise of ministry in an urban environment (1 Corinthians); (ii) the internal debates and opposition to which Paul is subjected and to which he replies vigorously (2 Cor 10-13) and (iii) the basis upon which a 'theology of ministry' might be constructed (e.g. 2 Cor 1:36:10). As a result, these insights can be utilised in contemporary discussion given that almost every area of contemporary debate about the ordained ministry which the Church and its mission to society exercised in the name of Christ can find its roots within the Corinthian literature. Although the roots of this discussion are found in the early Pauline letters nevertheless various lines of development can be perceived when the ideas about the exercise of the ministry in 1 Timothy and Titus is compared to that portrayed in 1 Corinthians. As well as considering individual letters it is necessary to gain a panoramic picture as can be obtained by visiting the totality of the Pauline tradition.

With regard to the Corinthian correspondence, amongst the numerous points which it is possible to discuss, I propose to select three issues. First, in 2 Corinthians 3:7-18, Paul makes three references to Moses (3:7; 3:13; 3:15). Paul's purpose is to demonstrate how his ministry is both superior to that of Moses and, unlike his temporary ministry, Paul's ministry is permanent. At the same time it must be recognised that both ministries, in their different contexts, originate from the same source: God's self revelation. For Moses this revelation is given in the context of the reception of God's divine Law (*Torah*) on

Mt. Sinai; for Paul, it is given in the context of the offer of the apostolic ministry personalised in Christ who is Lord (2 Cor 3:4; 3:14 and 3:17; see also Mt 17:1-8 and how this theology forms part of Jesus' transfiguration experience). This visionary ministry is now communicated to the believers ('and we all', 3:18). 'We all' are being transformed into the image of the Risen Lord and, as a result, are able to behold the presence of God through Christ with 'unveiled faces' (3:16). This process is possible because of our spirit-interpretation of Scripture (see Moses and Sinai above) and our vision of the Risen Christ which, in turn, demonstrate the purpose of the apostolic ministry in its totality: to offer 'the light of the knowledge of the glory of God in the face of Christ' (4:6b). Thus, the first question with regard to contemporary ministry is asked: how are the Church and its ministers to communicate effectively the divine vision in the way that Paul has outlined, in order that the faithful also might communicate this divine vision?

Secondly, in 1 Corinthians 4:16 and 11:1 Paul invites the Corinthian believers to imitate (*mimesis*; note also 1 Thess 1:6) him. In 11:1 the statement is qualified: 'imitate me as I imitate Christ'. The idea of 'imitation' has its roots in Graeco-Roman education: students imitating their teachers in terms of following both their instruction and their personal example. Thus the Corinthians would have been also familiar with the idea that characters from Graeco-Roman history were to be 'imitated'; for example, Thucydides as a historian, Cicero as a speaker. Imitation in this classical sense, however, is not blindly following a teacher; the teacher himself must be worthy by his/her manner of knowledge and conduct to receive such a following. The concept of 'imitation' is not easy to communicate in a contemporary context, the best explanation known to me is to describe the concept in terms of a 'good role-model' whose example can be followed.

It is necessary, however, to return to the ancient world and to the general background provided by its context in order that the injunction to the Corinthians to imitate Paul can be interpreted accurately. At its heart the 'imitation command' is Christological: imitate Paul because he imitates Christ. This 'imitation' finds its focus and meaning in Philippians 2:5-11 with its injunction for the Philippian community to identify themselves with the pattern set by Christ. In 1 Corinthians 7:7 Paul expresses the desire that, regarding marriage, the Corinthians should be 'as I myself am'. Paul's fellow workers from the household of Stephanas also are shown to be examples which the Corinthians ought to 'imitate' (1 Cor 16:16) given that, for Paul, the unity of the church depends on the believers being subject to them. Negatively, Paul provides the example of the Israelites in the wilderness whose idolatry the Corinthians are bidden not to imitate (1 Cor 10:5-7). Thus, the second question is: in what circumstances should the believing faithful 'imitate' their ministers and why? How should the Church in its mission and ministry best 'imitate' Christ? And how should contemporary apostolic ministers understand their role as figures to be imitated?

Thirdly, one of the issues behind the discussion of Paul's apostleship in 1 Corinthians 9:1-18 is the nature of the patron/client relationship which existed in the ancient world. Is one of the reasons why Paul (given his apostolic 'rights') wished to exercise his ministry in the Gospel 'free of charge' (1 Cor 9:18) because he did not desire to be dependent for financial support on wealthy patrons? Certainly difficulties existed within the social structure of the Corinthian church (1 Cor 11:17-22) relating to riches and poverty. Paul's answer is to offer the 'Eucharistic model' (1 Cor 11:23-26) and the 'ministerial model' (1 Cor 12:12) to illustrate social equality within the body of Christ even if this equality does not exist in the civic sphere. Thus, the third question is: how should social and educational differences be handled within the contemporary Church and its ministry? To what extent should we be dependent upon wealthy or powerful lay patrons? What do these varying social positions say about our preaching and living the Gospel?

The Corinthian correspondence, therefore, raises for us serious questions for the pastoral and social organisation of the contemporary Church. At the heart of this questioning, however, lies the fundamental issue as to how the Gospel of Christ should be perceived (e.g. 1 Cor 15:3-11) proclaimed (e.g. 1 Cor 9:12) and lived (e.g. 1 Cor 5:6-8).

C. LIVING THE CHRISTIAN LIFE IN AN URBAN ENVIRONMENT

Every Christian community needs to understand the social setting in which it exists and, coupled with this understanding, the need to minister to society and to be an 'incarnational presence' but also to be apart from society and to act as its critic in the ways of God. In this regard 1 Corinthians offers important insights as to the mission of the church in an ancient urban environment. At the base of this issue is the question of ethical living. Paul is aware of the dangers of either identifying with, or not renouncing sufficiently, the mores of Corinthian civic culture (1 Cor 6:9-10). He also expresses anxiety as to Christians settling their differences in the civic courts (1 Cor 6:4). There is also the issue of identifying civic religion with the question of eating food offered to idols (1 Cor 8:1). What should be the proper Christian response to this issue (1 Cor 8:7)? In the contemporary urban environment similar issues might be raised: urban alienation and its resulting violence and the social dysfunction which that unrest generates. Issues and circumstances change, each needing careful analysis and a measured response. The role of 1 Corinthians in this context, I believe, is to offer the fundamentals upon which Christian mission and ministry might operate. In the conduct of this mission Paul reminds us that we have been washed, sanctified and justified 'in the name of the Lord Jesus Christ and in the Spirit of our God' (1 Cor 6:11). In this way the 'contemporary agenda' is set: the priority of the search for justice, together with the cleansing and up-building of the social and civic community. Paul, therefore, provides the principles for living as a 'holy people' within society: neither completely conforming to it nor isolated from it. The aim is to impact upon the urban environment in order to transform it into a new creation.

CHAPTER 4

TO THE ROMANS

As I shall attempt to illustrate in section 2B when I shall discuss the Letter to the Romans in the context of Paul's missionary activity, to understand this letter it is important to relate it: (i) to the conclusion of Paul's evangelistic ministry around the Aegean Sea (Rom 15:23a); (ii) his desire to deliver the money collected from the churches there to the poverty stricken church of Jerusalem (Rom 16:25, cf. 1 Cor 16:1-4; 2 Cor 8 and 9) and (iii) his intention to initiate new areas of missionary activity which includes a desire for future evangelistic work in Spain of which Rome forms a crucial stage in his itinerary (Rom 15:24; 15:28-29). It is likely that the letter was written in Corinth and may have been sent to Rome in the beginning of AD 57 through the agency of Phoebe, a deaconess from the church of Cenchreae, who had agreed to support Paul's evangelistic intentions (Rom 16:1-3; Jewett, *CCStP*, 91) financially.

Three features arise immediately from this scenario. First, to attempt a visit to the Roman church on whatever pretext was contrary to Paul's stated missionary policy in that he did not visit churches whose participants had been evangelised by others (Rom 15:20). The proposed Roman visit, therefore, had to be justified from scripture (Isa 52:15 is quoted in Rom 15:21).

How the Roman church was founded remains obscure and a matter for speculation but it seems that Christianity was established by c. 49(?) as Luke records that, along with other Jews, Aquila and Priscilla had been expelled from the city as a result of an edict pronounced by the Emperor Claudius (Acts 18:2). Suetonius, writing in the early second century AD, records that this expulsion occurred because 'the Jews at Rome caused continuous disturbances at the instigation of Chrestus' (recorded in Suetonius' *Life of Claudius*, 25:4). There is endless discussion both over the date when the expulsion occurred, the number of Jews involved and the precise meaning of Suetonius' Latin phrase, *Iudaeos impulsore Chresto*. Does Chresto/Chrestus refer to Christ and/or Christian teachings and were the disturbances the result of inter-rivalry between (as Suetonius perceived it) different groups within Roman Jewry? Whatever may have been the case it is likely that Aquila and Priscilla had, by AD 57 (the Emperor Nero, whose reign began in 54, may have relaxed Claudius' edict?), returned to the city (Rom 16:3-4). From this information, therefore, it might be argued that a Judaeo-Christian congregation was present in Rome prior to AD 49, for a while it was largely Gentile but, after 54, the Jewish Christian element returned. Like the numerous theories expounded to describe the development of the Roman church this theory represents one among many. We should beware of being over-dogmatic, given both the partial and complex nature of the evidence both from the New Testament and ancient classical sources. We can be clear, however, that Paul's desire to visit the Roman church, should not be seen as mere convenience on his way to Spain; rather it represented a genuine desire to share with the Roman Christians some of the riches of Christianity which both Paul and the Romans shared (Rom 1:11-13; 15:23b). Whenever, therefore, Paul discusses the state of the Roman church (e.g. Rom 12:1-2; 14:10-23) he does so as a result of hearsay rather than from personal knowledge. Yet, his judgements come from a reliable source, the information imparted by Prisca and Aquila.

Secondly, Rome was the capital of the Empire and, as a result, its historical, political and social status was of paramount significance. It is not surprising that Paul wished to visit the city for its own sake let alone to make contact with the church. Rome was literally, in terms of political perception, the centre of the world. Romans must be interpreted against both the political perspectives and Paul's theological and missionary understanding as they existed at the time of the letter's composition, c. AD 57.

Thirdly, to the contemporary reader, there are difficulties in understanding the contents of the letter in terms of Paul's stated intentions in Romans 1 and 15. Why should Paul have included so much carefully argued, detailed, theological material in order to commend his Spanish mission to the Romans? In addition, to whom in the Roman church would such complex theological argumentation be of interest – non Jews, Jews or both; intellectuals or those without education 'the weak' (Rom 15:1) perhaps? It is these issues, together with the way that Romans has been interpreted down the centuries, which has made it such a powerful and controversial theological and pastoral statement.

The question arises as to how best to proceed in these circumstances? I would argue that, first, it is necessary to understand the contents of the letter. Robert Jewett (*CCStP*, 91, 93, 95, 99, 102) summaries these contents in terms of four proofs (1. 1:18-4:25; 2. 5:1-8:39; 3. 9:1-11:36; 4. 12:1-15:13). I believe that 'proof' is a difficult and probably misleading concept in this regard. Rather, we should speak of Paul's lines of arguments, stages of progression or stated propositions since, as I should argue, it was Paul's intention to impart (Rom 1:11) rather than to prove. We should see the contents of Romans as Paul's means (given that he had not met the church members) of commending ways of re-visiting and renewing Christian understanding and practice theologically and ethically in order that Roman Christians might perceive, within these ways, the nature of God's being and plan for all humanity without partiality (Rom 1:14) through Jesus' salvation activity demonstrated by his crucifixion, resurrection (e.g. Rom 6:34) and abiding presence with them (e.g. Rom 8:39). Into this complex two other features occur. First, Paul's missionary vocation and personal experience are described with the intention of inviting the readers to enter into his experience (e.g. Rom 7:13-20). Secondly, the current situation of the Roman church/churches (the problems of disunity as a result of meeting in households [?], Rom 16:11 and 17-20, also 14:1; 15:1-2) is discussed, not with the immediacy which occurs in 1 Cor for example, but in the sense of issues which Paul would like resolved, if possible in the present, but certainly when he arrives in Rome in person (see comment on 1:8-15). The text of Romans, therefore, fundamentally concerns how the Gospel (Rom 1:1; 1:3; 1:9; 15:19; 16:25) should be proclaimed, understood theologically, and lived ethically, not merely in Rome, although the particular contextualisation of the Gospel in the capital city of the Empire is of vital importance; but also, by implication, throughout the world.

SECTION 1 – STRUCTURE

A. OUTLINE

Romans is composed of three sections, the first of which contains two subsections, thus:

1:1-15	Opening greetings and stated intentions.
1:16-8:39	Theological

- 1:16-4:25 = the way to be 'in the right' before God.
- 5:1-8:39 = the way to progress in the Christian life.

9:1-11:36	The place of the Jewish people (Israel) within God's scheme of salvation in Christ.
12:1-15:29	Ethical: How Christians should live in terms of the Gospel.
15:30-16:27	Conclusion and closing greetings.

As with Galatians remember that the terms theological and ethical are for convenience of reference and should be seen as being inter-dependent.

B. LINES OF ARGUMENT

To determine these lines of argument is, in comparison to Paul's other letters, a most difficult exercise. Having experimented educationally with the text of Romans with students/participants, and in order to assist the reader, I have used a slightly different method of studying the text. Rather than offering a continuous verse-by-verse exegesis throughout, I have instead alternated between a close examination and a more reflective analysis of the central themes and keywords

131

that underlie the four lines of argument presented in the structural outline. This modified approach aims to assist the reader both to maintain a keen eye on the shifting lines of Paul's argument and to discern within those contours aspects of Paul's closely integrated, Theological, Christological and ethical thought.

Opening greetings and stated intentions, 1:1-15

In the opening greetings and stated intentions (1:1-15) the issue of Paul's Apostolic Mission is the major theme. This Mission, and the greetings which accompany it, should be read in relation to Romans 15:14-29. I have commented in detail on this passage in Section 2B. These opening verses (Rom 1:1-7) are an enlargement and refinement upon the opening greetings which Paul has written already (1 Thess 1:1; 2 Thess 1:1-2; 1 Cor 1:1-3 [the most elaborate so far]; 2 Cor 1:1-2; in this regard Gal stands apart, Gal 1:1-5). They form one sentence in which the concept of the Gospel (*euangelion*, Rom 1:1; 1:3) remains the focus as it unites the ministry of Paul to that of 'Jesus Christ our Lord' (Rom 1:4).

A Christological statement or confession of faith unites two aspects of Christ's saving work in terms of the Gospel. He was: 1. descended from David according to the flesh and 2. designated Son of God in power according to the spirit of holiness by resurrection from the dead. This designation is achieved as a result of the resurrection which, in turn, affirms Jesus as the Jewish Davidic Messiah. Thus, this continuity between descent and resurrection means that Jesus can be affirmed as 'Son of God' (Rom 1:4 based on Ps 2:7 and 2 Sam 7:14). In this context Paul affirms his apostleship (Rom 1:1; 1:5); his prophetic calling (set apart, Rom 1:1 also Gal 1:3-14 and Jer 1:4) but also his role as a 'slave (*doulos*) of Jesus Christ' (Rom 1:1). The Christological continuity is confirmed further by the assertion that the Christian Gospel is the fulfilment of what had been written in Jewish scriptures, in this case, especially the prophetic texts. The proclamation of the Gospel is a universal activity which includes both Jews and Gentiles, and is exercised as a result of God's grace (Rom 1:5 and 1:7b) and call (Rom 1:1). This universality is here focussed in Paul's relationship to the Roman Christians (Rom 1:7a; 1:15) who must perceive themselves as part of God's universal, sanctified community (called saints, 1:7; linked to the Risen Christ, spirit of holiness, 1:4). In Romans 1:7 and 1:15 the phrase 'in Rome' has been omitted by some later manuscripts. Such an omission may have been accidental or in order to provide the letter with a general, rather than local Roman, appeal. It seems certain that Paul wrote 'in Rome' but also perceived that its contents could be applied and interpreted universally by Christians.

The second part of the introduction (1:8-15) concerns Paul's stated intentions and should be read together with his rationale relating to his future missionary activity as set out in Romans 15:14-29. This activity is eschatological and represents the ingathering of God's people in Christ, both Jews and non Jews, in anticipation of the final age (cf. 1 Cor 15:20-28). This mission is also universalised. With Rome at its centre it encapsulates the whole of the perceived known world. Paul's return to Jerusalem is not merely to present a financial gift but is also symbolic in that it represents his engagement with the historical and theological origins of the Christian faith which are anchored in Jesus' activity for the salvation of all humanity (Rom 15:19). In using expressions like 'impart to you some spiritual gift' (Rom 1:12), 'harvest' (1:13) and 'obligation' (1:14) Paul may have intended to alert the Roman hearers/readers that he had some knowledge about the community divisions within the Roman churches. Thus, the letter had two particular pastoral functions which should be seen as complementary; first, to ask for support for the proposed Spanish mission and secondly, to offer a theological scheme by which they could rediscover their ethnic and social unity and equality in Christ.

Following these opening greetings it is necessary to ask: how is the rest of Romans to be read? To enable the reader to answer this question I summarise certain features regarding the way Romans functions as a literary text. The following four features can be noted:

1. For Paul, Romans is a 'projected text', it portrays what he hopes will happen in the future.

2. In this way Romans is a developing, not a final, text, as it represents Paul's 'developing' ideas, as can be seen when the letter is compared to his earlier letters.

3. Romans is a bi-focal text; it dwells upon: (a) community issues within the Roman church of which Paul had been informed, and (b) it presents a series of carefully argued theological and ethical maxims.

4. Romans is a theological text in that it speaks of God's activity: in the past (through Israel and the nations); in the present, and in the future. This activity is centred upon the claim that Jesus is God's Messiah and through him salvation is received. Paul demonstrates both: (a) how this salvation can be obtained, and by what means, and (b) how it can be sustained.

Theological, 1:16-8:39 – The way to be 'in the right' before God (1:16-4:25)

The themes of this section can be projected through the understanding of the basic vocabulary utilised:

— righteousness (*dikaiosune*); to be made righteous (*dikaioo*);
— faith (*pistis*); grace (*charis*); gift (*dorea*, lit. free gift);
— Law, in the sense of *Torah* (*nomos*);
— sin (*hamartia*); to sin (*harmartano*, lit. to miss the mark).

For the section Romans 3:21-26 note two words not used before by Paul: (a) expiation/atonement (*hilasterion*, note also, Heb 9:5), and (b) passover (*paresis*). On this basis, ask:

i.   how and why does Paul use this language;
ii. what were his sources; and
iii. compared with earlier letters (in particular, Galatians and 1 and 2 Corinthians) has Paul modified their meaning?

Consider first Paul's basic declaration in Romans 1:16-17

These verses form a basic statement of what the Gospel is in Paul's understanding and of which he is not ashamed; either, of its contents, or of proclaiming and living by its message. First, the Gospel concerns God's attributes and activity. His attributes of power and righteousness or justice (*dikaiosune*) are manifested by implication, through the ministry of Jesus Christ, the Gospel relating to whom (cf. Rom 1:9) Paul is proclaiming. In this context it should be understood that righteousness or justice (*dikaiosune*) had a range of meanings in both Jewish and Graeco-Roman literature given that justice, to act justly or ethically and to be regarded as righteous by an all-righteous God covers a vast range of concepts: political, social and religious. In Romans perhaps three areas should be noted: (i) righteousness as an attribute of God; (ii) righteousness as a general ethical and social quality and (iii) Paul's particular emphasis of 'being in the right' before God through the saving ministry of Jesus. This revelation of theology through Christology is based on Paul's interpretation of the Jewish scriptures (in regard to Rom 1:9 and 1:16 and 1:17, cf. for example, Ps 72:1) which, in turn, both confirms his ministry and provides the basis for the universalisation of the means of entry into God's offer of salvation which is gained through faith. This proposition is confirmed by references to Habakkuk 2:4.

It is worth noting how Paul interprets this text given that he differs both from the Hebrew original: 'The righteous (man) will live by his faithfulness (to God's *Torah*)' and the Greek (LXX) translation: 'The righteous (man) will live by my (God's) faithfulness'. For Paul, the text is to be understood as: The man who has faith in the ministry of Jesus Christ for salvation will be considered 'in the right' before God and he (the man) will live for ever with God.

On the basis of this understanding of Habakkuk 2:4 in Romans 1:17 two important questions emerge:

- *Why is it necessary to preach the Gospel?*
- *What forces have alienated humanity, both Jews and Gentiles, from God's salvation?*

Perspectives on how these questions might be answered are demonstrated in Romans 1:18-3:20. The next major theological statement, which enlarges upon Romans 1:16-17, however, is found at Romans 3:21-26. These verses provide the rationale as to why belief in God's salvation through Jesus Christ is necessary. It is because all humanity have sinned and fallen short of the divine glory which belonged to them originally (Rom 3:23). As we shall see behind this approach is the contrast between Adam, who forfeited the divine glory through disobedience to God's will and Christ who restored it through his obedience (cf. 1 Cor 15:21-22, later Rom 5:12-21). Mention of 'all humanity' would have doubtless raised the ethnic and religious tensions between Jewish and non-Jewish members of the church over the question as to whether, on the basis of scripture, Jewish members might not claim superiority of acceptance by God (Rom 3:1) against their Gentile counterparts.

Before that, in Romans 1:18-3:20 Paul indicates, first, to Gentiles (called either 'nations', Rom 1:13 or 'Greeks' and 'barbarians' Rom 1:14) and then to Jews, the reasons why 'all' (Rom 1:16 and 3:23) need to return to God's offer of salvation both theologically and ethically. These various threads are held together by the concept of revelation, what God has revealed (verb, *apokalupto*, compare the content of the revealing, Rom 1:17 and 1:18; later, 8:18) about himself and Christ in relation to humanity.

Romans 1:18-32 reveals the circumstances where God's wrath (Rom 1:18) will be exercised. Two particular areas are mentioned: (a) idolatry (Rom 1:19-25, concluding with the Semitic affirmation, *Amen*), and (b) unnatural sexual practices (Rom 1:26-27) and vices (Rom 1:28-31) which are ethically unacceptable within the orbit of monotheistic belief. Here, as elsewhere, theological affirmation and ethical practice run together. In this context Paul is likely to be using a variety of sources: the typical rhetoric against some Gentile practices used by Jewish teachers found, for example, in the Wisdom of Solomon (e.g. 13:1), the Jewish scriptures (Rom 1:23 uses Ps 106:20 where reference is made to the golden calf narrative, Ps 106:19) and the 'vice lists' found in ancient, usually Stoic literature. The outcome is that on receiving the Gospel of Jesus Christ non-Jewish believers must accept both monotheism and the ethical stances which accompany this interpretation of monotheism and reject those attitudes and practices which do not. The justification for this requirement is that these are the positions upheld by the Jewish scriptures which, by their very nature in the totality of God's plan of salvation, are binding on Christian believers for whom Christ is both 'the end, *telos*, of the law, *Torah*' (later, Rom 10:4) and, as God's Messiah, the fulfilment of scripture.

In Romans 2:1 Paul turns to his hypothetical opponent (a Jewish teacher?) and argues with him on the issue of judging of others, presumably regarding the Gentiles whose sins Paul has outlined in 1:18-32. The issue of judging others had become embedded in the developing Christian tradition probably having arisen from Jesus himself (e.g. Mt 7:1-5). Paul's argument is that God is the ultimate judge and any human judgements ought to be made in relationship to his judgement. Given that 'all' are sinners two particular questions arise in this context: who has the right to judge, and on what terms? Paul then uses three rhetorical questions (Rom 2:3-4) to demonstrate that before judgement is made about anyone else repentance on behalf of him who is making the judgement should be forthcoming. In this context God's eschatological judgement will be given to those who have violated the 'natural' divine law (Rom 2:2 alluding to Prov 24:12), a judgement which will be revealed on the day of wrath (Rom 2:5 cf. 1:18). Judgement will be made according to deeds done (Rom 2:6) which are set out dualistically (Rom 2:7-10). The same progression will be used (Rom 2:9) here as was used previously by Paul when he describes his scheme for preaching the Gospel (cf. Rom 1:16). These arguments conclude with the statement that God manifests 'no partiality' an expression which connects directly with the concept of humanity's total sinfulness.

In Romans 2:12-24 Paul confronts the concept of law (*Torah*, *nomos*). In Section 3 I shall attempt to describe how Paul has either refined, altered or reshaped his understanding of *Torah* from his discussion of the subject in Galatians. In the meanwhile, in the Romans context, Paul shows how the law has a dual function encapsulating all humanity. Jews will be judged by the biblical *Torah* on account of its fundamental importance as a response to God's covenant with his chosen people, Israel. Gentiles, who in response to the conscience within have followed the demands of *Torah* without being aware of the *Torah* have responded, nevertheless in their own way, to the demands of God. On these grounds, when the eschatological Day of the Lord comes the inner secrets, in addition to external deeds (Rom 2:6) of all humanity will be judged by 'Christ Jesus' (Rom 2:16 cf. the Christological confession of Rom 1:3-4).

In Romans 2:17-24 Paul places himself in his personal situation of being a Jew (continued in 9:1-5) and in doing so explains the facets of Judaism which are able to enlighten non-Jewish people (Rom 2:17-20). Within this exposition the critical question arises as to why the Jews have failed to perform this God-given task? In a series of rhetorical questions which follow Paul challenges his 'fellow Jews' to ask fundamental questions with regard to this vocation; have they fulfilled what God has asked of them with regard to adherence to the sacred *Torah*? Answer: No. On the contrary they have blasphemed God's name amongst the Gentiles, the evidence for which is provided by Isaiah 52:5 which is quoted in Romans 2:24. The discussion in Romans 2:25-29 now turns to the question of circumcision: the ritual means by which God's covenant is entered (Gen 17:9-14; note also Paul's earlier comments on the subject, Gal 5:6; 5:11 and 6:15) and with it the argument relating to the tension between the external and internal commitment to God. On this basis Paul is able to maintain that it is possible for non-Jews to keep the *Torah* without circumcision, while the circumcised Jews have failed to adhere to the internal obligations demanded by the *Torah*. In each case it is the disposition of the human heart which is significant (Rom 2:29).

In Romans 3 Paul begins by asking questions relating to the 'advantage' of being a Jew and of the value of the religious 'possessions' of Judaism: circumcision (means of ritual entry) and the scriptures. In this regard the objector (cf. the comment at 2:1) to Paul's argument is able to point to Israel's unfaithfulness, what difference does this fact make? Answer: it serves to highlight the faithfulness of God and to sharpen the difference between God's truthfulness and human falsehood. Israel's faithlessness in no way negates Paul's argument. In turn, does the 'advantage' of Judaism give Jews superiority over Gentiles? Again, the answer is no. This position is because all humanity finds itself under the 'power of sin' (Rom 3:9; cf. 2:12). This proposition contains an implicit reference to Adam's disobedience in relation to God (note Gen 3:17-19; for an explicit reference see Rom 5:14 and cf. 1 Cor 15:22 and 15:45) through whom it was believed that this 'power of sin' was communicated to all humanity, the consequences of which, and the resolution to which, will be described later in the letter (Rom 5:12-21).

But where is the evidence to be found for these arguments? Answer: in the Jewish Scriptures (Rom 3:10; cf. 3:2). In Romans 3:10-18 Paul cites a series of scriptural texts linked together by the phrase 'no one'. The purpose of these citations is to illustrate the claim (3:9) that all humanity, as a result of their disobedience to God's law and will, have become alienated from him. At a later stage the reader might wish to study these citations in detail with the following questions in mind:

(i)   what did the texts mean in their original setting;

(ii) how has Paul interpreted the Jewish scriptures (using mainly the Greek translation, the Septuagint = LXX) in his context and

(iii) to what extent was his interpretation of these texts 'original' (Christological?) and, in what measure was he following the 'usual' forms of Jewish interpretation of his time?

In the meanwhile, however, it should be noted that Paul uses a high level of scriptural interpretation to support his various arguments in Romans; on occasions, citing numerous passages together (e.g. here in Rom 3, and later 15:9-12). He begins each section with the traditional formulae for introducing scripture, 'as it has been written' (e.g. 1:17; 2:24; 3:4; 3:10; 9:13; 12:19; 15:9, some twenty times in all), indicating the solemn, sacred declarations from the biblical texts which follow: the purpose being to provide evidence for the arguments which Paul is offering. In Romans 3:10-18 Paul utilises: Psalm 14:1-3; 53:1-3 (3:10-12); Psalm 5:9; 140:3 (3:13); Psalm 10:7 (3:14); Isaiah 59:7-8 (3:15-17) and Psalm 36:1 (3:18). These references indicate the range of particular texts which Paul utilises: often quoting from the Psalms (the hymn book for Jewish worship) and from the prophecies of Isaiah (God's declarations relating to salvation). These citations in Romans 3:10-18 introduce Paul's defining statements found in 3:19-20: (i) this interpretation of 'no one' means that, in its alienation, the 'whole world' is under God's judgement, and (ii) humanity cannot become 'in the right' (*dikaioo*) before God through doing 'works of law' (cf. the language of Gal 2:6 and 3:11) because *Torah* produces the awareness of sin.

How then can (and has) this situation be resolved? Maybe using an existing theological structure Paul, in Romans 3:21-26, declares the answer and the remedy to this human alienation from God. Given both the importance and complexity of this passage I shall expound its argument in diagrammatic form:

3:21a   God's righteousness has been manifested to all humanity apart from the *Torah*. This proposition relates to Paul's view that God's nature can be discerned by all people when they contemplate the created order (1:20).

3:21b   Nevertheless the *Torah* and its prophetic inter-preters (found in scripture – thus the citations) bear witness to God's righteousness.

3:22   Given that there is no distinction between Jew and Gentile, how can this righteousness be now received by them? Answer: through faith in Jesus Christ.

3:23   Why is this faith necessary? Answer: all humanity have sinned (cf. 3:9) and fall short of God's original intention for human creation (Gen 1:26

	and 2:7): the possession of his divine presence, glory (*doxa*, cf. 1:23; note later, 8:18, and cf. 2 Cor 3:18).
3:24	How does this 'faith-possession' operate? Answer: God's righteousness is a freely given (and undeserved) gift to humanity through the freedom (*apolutrosis*, cf. 1 Cor 1:30- metaphor from the slave market/biblical image of the Exodus) offered in Christ Jesus.
3:25a	How did this method of demonstrating God's righteousness occur? Answer: God gave Jesus to humanity in the form of an atonement (*hilasterion*). This metaphor represents Paul's attempt to describe Jesus' sacrifice in terms of the Jewish Day of Atonement ritual (Lev 16:1-28) which occurred annually in the Jerusalem Temple. The irony behind this metaphor is that the Roman Christians were being directed, not to the Temple, but to the cross of Jesus in order that God's salvation could be understood correctly (cf. 1 Cor 1:17; 1:23 and 15:3).
3:25b	What does this situation illustrate? Answer: that God has passed over the former sins of humanity.
3:26	Also, (i) his righteousness is now revealed in Christ and that (ii) all humanity is offered the possibility of sharing in this righteousness through faith (cf. 3:22) in Jesus.

After these declarations Romans 3:27-31 ask: where does humanity stand now? A further series of rhetorical questions follow relating to righteousness, faith, law and God's universal appeal by means of which the Roman Christians are challenged to analyse their 'position' with regard to salvation. Paul concludes this challenge by two statements: (i) faith does not overthrow *Torah*, and (ii) 'we' (the believers in general?) uphold *Torah*. How these propositions ought to operate within the Christian community is revealed in the chapters of Romans which follow.

In Romans 4 Paul offers the example of Abraham as a believer who had faith in God without recourse to law (God had not yet revealed the *Torah*). This proposition is based upon Genesis 15:6: 'Abraham believed God, and it was reckoned to him as righteousness'. Paul has already utilised this text in his argument in Galatians 3:6. Here Genesis 15:6 is used to demonstrate that Gentiles can be included within the community of faith without first becoming Jews. In Galatians 3:8 Paul moves his argument forward by means of Abraham's role as presented by Genesis 12:3 and 18:8 and, with it, the ideas of blessing (Gal 3:9 and 3:14); promise (Gal 3:14-29) and, the opposite of these positive qualities, the notion of the curse (Gal 3:10 and 3:14). In Romans 4:3; 4:22 and 4:23 Paul returns to the interpretative possibilities inherent within Genesis 15:6 in particular with regard to 'believed' and 'reckoned'.

To describe further how God 'reckons righteousness' Paul quotes Psalm 32:1-2 to illustrate how, at a time after Abraham, David was able to pronounce God's blessing in order that sin can be removed apart from 'works' (of the law, Rom 4:6). Into this 'reckoning' is placed the ritual of circumcision (based on Gen 17:4-10) and God's promise that his fatherhood would include many nations (Rom 4:17-18; Gen 17:5 and 15:5). In returning to the issue of faith (Rom 4:20) Paul connects his readers again to the main theme: how to be 'in the right' before God. Through the interpretation of these Jewish texts it is not merely the case that some interesting insights about Abraham are given, rather the interpretation is 'for our sake also' (Rom 4:24). But how is this so? Answer: because Abraham and the texts about him should be interpreted Christologically (4:25). As a result the faith-inspired believers are able to be 'reckoned' as righteous before God through Jesus. In this way Paul returns his readers to the place where the letter began: the Christological statement of Romans 1:3-4.

Theological 1:16-8:39 – The way to progress in the Christian life (5:1-8:39)

In addition to the vocabulary indicated at the beginning of

the previous sub-section (1-16-4:25) new concepts are utilised in 5:1-8:39:

- peace (*eirene*); reconciliation (*katallage*) and to reconcile (*katallasso*);
- Spirit (*pneuma*); obedience (*hupakoe*) and to obey (*hupakouo*).

In this sub-section the following questions arise:

- *On what basis can believers in Jesus as the Christ understand their new 'status' before God?*
- *Given this new 'status' what should be their principles for ethical living?*

By using the past passive participle form of the verb 'to be in the right' (*dikaioo*, Rom 5:1, cf. 2:13; 3:24) Paul is able to link Romans 5:1-8:39 conceptually to the previous sub-section, 1:16–4:25. This observation, however, needs to be qualified in two ways. First, the use of the past tense does not here indicate finality but rather progress and development. Secondly, the passive form indicates God's action towards humanity. This action is centred in the ministry of Christ. It is the Christological theme, therefore, 'through our Lord Jesus Christ' (5:1), which unites the beginning of the new sub-section to the conclusion of the preceeding unit (4:25). In 4:25 Paul (maybe using an existing Christological couplet) describes the implications for believers of Jesus' death and resurrection. On this basis the 'faith-inspired' (cf. 3:26 and for Abraham, 4:16) believers obtain 'peace with God' (5:1). The use of the present tense ('we have', 5:1) indicates that believers now have been accepted by God into a renewed relationship with him. This concept of peace would have been recognised as coming from two sources. First, there is the biblical idea of *shalom* (Hebrew, peace) which God offers to his people, frequently through the agency of the Davidic king (Ps 72:7) and perhaps, in the first century AD, seen as a characteristic of the coming Messiah. Secondly, there was the Roman Imperial concept of the *Pax Romana* under which Paul and his hearers lived. With this reality the believers experienced peace on the basis of Roman power. For them 'peace with God' is said to bring different results. First, through the work of Christ access (note the 'Temple language' metaphor) to God is obtained and the hope of glory (*doxa*) given (5:2). Secondly, God's peace, paradoxically, is experienced through suffering (the implication is given of the identification with Christ's sufferings) which, in turn, leads to a chain of virtues and aspirations: endurance, character and hope (5:4-5). This hope (*elpis*, see later, 8:20 and 8:24) is based on the manifestation of God's love through the action of the Holy Spirit (5:5), a theme upon which Paul concentrates in chapter 8. Another link is produced by Paul's utilization of the concept of glory (*doxa*, 5:2 and 5:18, also 6:4 and cf. 2 Cor 3:18). This goal is reached by passing through eschatological tribulations (Rom 5:3). In this way, although believers are at peace with God (5:1), nevertheless they are still opposed by the forces of the world, both supernatural and political (8:21-23). This situation, however, will be concluded when Christ returns at his *parousia* (cf. 1 Cor 15:24-28) and the 'glorious liberty' (Rom 8:21) of God's rule in Christ will be established in totality.

In Romans 5:6-11 Paul describes both the process and the results of the manifestation of God's love in Christ. It was while humanity was in a helpless state of sin that the all righteous Christ died, the purpose of this death was in order that humanity might again be 'in the right' before God. In order to amplify this concept Paul utilises themes to which he has referred already in the letter: blood (Rom 5:9, cf. 3:25); salvation (cf. 1:16) and (the opposite state to righteousness) wrath (cf. 1:18), to which he has added the concept of reconciliation (5:10-11, cf. 2 Cor 5:18-20). In this way Paul is offering the Roman Christians a 'philosophy of time': God's action in the past through the historical events of Christ's death and resurrection, prepared for in the life of the Israelite nation; the present experience of 'peace with God' (5:1) and awaiting for the consummation of salvation in the future (5:10).

This Christological argument is advanced by means of 'therefore' to indicate that (i) a comparison between Adam and Christ can be made, and (ii) by perceiving the 'historical progression' from Adam to Moses the discussion of sin in relation to the giving of the *Torah* can be made (5:13). With regard to (i), although Adam is said to be a 'type' (Rom 5:14 or pattern, see 6:17 for a different sense of the word, also 1 Cor 10:6) for the Christ; it is indicated at the same time, however, that Christ's work is different to that of Adam (Rom 5:15) on account of the divinely-given free gift of God's grace which Christ offers. In this way the positive effects of the work of Christ far exceed any 'damage' done to humanity as a result of Adam's disobedience to God's command. The connection between them is that they are both representatives of all humanity yet, whereas Adam was disobedient, Christ was obedient to God's will and the effects of this obedience for humanity are: abundant grace and the free gift of God's righteousness (Rom 5:17, cf. 1:16-17; note also, 2 Cor 5:21). This free gift means that humanity is now offered the possibility of being 'in the right' before God.

In Romans 5:20-21 Paul returns to the implications of the 'historical progression' explained in 5:14 and, with it, to the discussion of the relationship between law, sin and grace. Accompanying this discussion is the Christological theme and the exposing of the dichotomy between (a) the sin and death brought by Adam, and (b) the righteousness and eternal life brought by Christ (5:21).

Does this situation mean, however, that sinful behaviour can be continued in the new life of grace (6:1-2)? To this question Paul gives the emphatic answer: no. In order to illustrate his answer Paul turns to Baptism (Rom 6:3; see also, Gal 3:27): the public, ritual and liturgical means by which God's new community is entered. Two important facts about Baptism are here presented. First, Baptism identifies the new believer with the saving activity of Christ (6:3-4; note also, 1 Cor 15:3-4). Secondly, living the baptismal life carries with it ethical obligations relating to righteousness (Rom 6:13) and the avoidance of sin (6:6). At their heart these ethical obligations are Christological and made possible on the basis of Christ's death, through which the sinful nature of humanity had been destroyed (6:6). In this regard the metaphor of slavery is used and, with it, a comparison between the 'old' and 'new' life. The 'old' life is characterised by sinful passion

(6:17) whereas the 'new' life is characterised by righteousness and holiness (6:19). The results of these different standards of living are now clear: the 'old' life would have lead to death (6:23) while, with the 'new' life there is the promise of eternity (6:23). From these observations arise the challenge to the believers to ask themselves: to which state of life are we enslaved?

Two further points ought to be made in this context. First, there is presented the tension between living under grace and not under *Torah*. Yet this new life of grace does not allow the licence to sin. With these propositions Paul walks a tightrope. What is the difference between Romans 6:14-15 and Romans 13:8-10? Do the believers need *Torah* for ethical living (note 3:31)? In a sense 'yes', because *Torah* provides an important basis for God's moral law but; in another sense 'no', because Christ has fulfilled the law (Rom 10:4; note also the expression, 'the law of Christ', Gal 6:2). It is with this ambiguity that Paul must wrestle as he presents his ethical norms based upon his theological and Christological arguments. Secondly, given that the discussion found in Romans 5:18-21 and 6:12-23 represents Paul's attempt to establish ethical principles, then the exposition of ethical norms found in 12:1-15:13 illustrate the practical application of these principles.

The tension observed in Romans 6:14-15 relating to sin, law and grace finds personal expression in chapter 7. This chapter illustrates Paul's own wrestling with the 'old' and the 'new' life (7:23). This wrestling is dissimilar to that facing the Gentile converts in the Roman church; as for Paul, it concerns his attitude to *Torah* in terms of adherence to its precepts in relationship to sin and his new life of grace. Where is his ethical framework now to be found? For Paul this question is never resolved satisfactorily. On one hand, with his Messianic belief in Jesus his need for *Torah* ends, it has become like 'widowhood' (7:3), the widow being free to marry again; thus, with Christ Paul has found a 'new partner'. On the other hand, the *Torah* has continuing value representing holiness, justice and goodness (7:12). Yet, by its very nature, *Torah* exposes sin: it demonstrates what is wrong with human behaviour (covetousness is cited as an example, 7:7; Ex 20:17;

Deut 5:21). But how can sinfulness be removed? (7:24): answer, through the saving activity of 'Jesus Christ our Lord' (7:25). Thus, the tensions and uncertainties within Paul's lines of argument on these subjects have to be seen against the background of Christ's activity and of Paul's sharing in that activity in terms of his mission and ministry. The use of the first person singular, however, in Romans 7:8; 8:18 and later in 9:1-18 demonstrate clearly that Paul is not afraid of entering personally into the narrative which he is creating. Perhaps this is his way of revealing his deep regard for the Christians of Rome (1:11-12)? This link between apostle and community illustrates the difficulty of interpreting the first person singular pronoun with precision. The contention which arises between various interpreters of 'I' centres on the extent to which Paul is being autobiographical or whether he is using 'I' as a way of describing what happens to humanity who are living under *Torah* (cf. 2:19-20). Given Paul's identification of his mission and ministry with the community he could be, very subtly, using both ideas.

In Romans 8 Paul summarises the new status of believers against the background of God's universal and cosmic activity (8:19-23). This activity is to be understood by reflecting on the work of the Spirit (*pneuma*). Paul's letters are filled with references to the Spirit; for example, in the giving of prophecy and other ministerial gifts (e.g. 1 Cor 12:9); as providing an ethical guide to living (e.g. Gal 5:16; Rom 8:4); as the means by which Jesus is professed as Lord (e.g, 1 Cor 12:3) and as the intercessor to the Father on behalf of the believers (e.g. Rom 8:27b). Primarily the Spirit is manifested as God's agent of re-creation and renewal (Ps 104:30; Rom 8:23b) who dwells within the hearts of the believers (Rom 8:11). Romans 8:1-2 are linked (cf. 7:21-25) by means of the ethical concepts raised: law, sin and death. In 8:4-8 a new way of expressing the tension between law, sin and grace is introduced: that between flesh (*sarx*), earthly living and Spirit (*pneuma*), heavenly living. Again, this discussion is set within a Christological framework, found in 8:2-3. In Romans 8:2 Paul uses the term law (*nomos*) ironically, exposing the tension between 'the law of the Spirit' and the 'law' which the work of the Spirit negates: that of sin and death. God has now acted apart from law/*Torah* which, because of its capacity to highlight fault, is not able to offer salvation (cf. 2 Cor 3:6). This divine action is revealed in a two-fold Christological structure (cf. 1:3-4 and 4:25):

(i) God sent his Son in the (sinful) human likeness and because of sin, and
(ii) as a result, sin is condemned.

This 'incarnational theology' can be seen in relation to Galatians 4:4, while 'atonement theology' which it contains can be seen in relation to 2 Corinthians 5:21. The concept behind the passage is that of the Day of Atonement ritual (Lev 16:1-28) which Paul has already utilised Christologically by the use of the word *hilasterion* found in 3:25a. The point, however, is clear: Christ identified completely with humanity in order that humanity might be enabled to return to God and to share the salvation which he offers. In Romans 8:4-8 this entry into God's salvation takes an ethical perspective: it is concerned with living in the Spirit not in the flesh. But the Roman Christians have entered the 'new life' and, as a result, the Spirit dwells in them (8:9). Given that the Spirit re-creates and renews the God-given life of humanity, his major work in this regard was the resurrection of Jesus (8:11) and, on the basis of this action, the believers are raised with him (cf. 1 Cor 15:20-28). This resurrection is bi-focal in concept: through faith and Baptism the believers can share in the present time in the righteousness of God (8:10) while, later, they will share in the totality of the resurrection when God's salvation will be finally consummated for them. This 'resurrection theology' also brings with it intimacy with God: sons sharing in his fatherhood. This intimacy is expressed through the ancient Aramaic word for father, *Abba* (8:15; Gal 4:6 and Mk 14:36) which links believers to Jesus' intimacy with the Father and which, in turn, became a liturgical feature in the Church's worship used to express the relationship which believers have with God. From this basis a chain of concepts emerge: inheritance, suffering and, through suffering, the prospect of glorification (8:17). In following this chain the believers are sharing in the pattern set by Christ himself (cf. 5:10-11 and 6:3-5).

The 'suffering theme' moves the argument forward to reveal the tension between the present and the future (8:18) and the 'status' of the believers within the totality of God's universal creative activity. The link between the two themes is provided by the idea that Adam's disobedience effects also the total fabric of the cosmic order. On this basis God offers through Christ the redemption of the cosmic order from decay in order that the totality of the cosmos, and humanity with it, can be said to be set free by God. Two further ideas are added into the narrative. First, that of adoption (note the comment at Gal 4:5): humanity has been taken back into God's care and secondly, that the notion of future salvation is to be seen in terms of hope.

But how else can believers be supported? Answer: through the intercessory work of the Spirit (8:26-27) who has been instrumental in providing resurrection (8:11) and who now helps believers in their vulnerability (8:26). In Romans 5:1 Paul has conceived of living the Christian life in terms of progress and development. This process is now demonstrated in 8:28-30. First, there is the injunction to conform (continually) to the image (*eikon*, note 1 Cor 15:49) of Christ and then, secondly, there is declaration of the believers' first-born 'status' (note later Christological use in Col 1:15 and 1:18). Thirdly, the progression of the believers' 'Christian pilgrimage' is revealed: chosen, called, found to be 'in the right' and the hope of glorification. On this basis the Roman Christians are both challenged and called to contemplate their status before God in Christ. In so doing (as with the Spirit, 8:26) they can be assured of God's protective care for them. To understand this care they must again turn to meditate upon the work of Christ (8:32). In their Roman context they would have understood well the notion of the conqueror. Now Paul tells them that they are conquerors (8:37) in Christ from whom they can never be separated even through the worst of human experiences. It was now necessary that the Roman believers reflect upon this tension between political conquerors and their role as conquerors and how they are to think and live as a consequence.

The place of the Jewish people within God's scheme of salvation in Christ, 9:1-11:36

This section raises for Paul one fundamental question:

- *What is the situation in God's plan of salvation for those Jews who (unlike himself) have rejected the claim that Jesus is God's Christ and who continued to look for a future (Davidic) Messiah?*

Related to this question is the issue as to whether Jesus can be equated with God's Messiah given the nature of his death by crucifixion. Inherent in this issue is the numerous views that various Jewish groups had about the geographical extent of Israel as a nation and how it should be governed (by the Romans?); the Jewish place within the Diaspora and the variety of attitudes taken to the non-Jewish nations. There is also the issue of the presence of Jews in Rome (in 57, see also Acts 28:17).

Paul's discussion is based on both his personal understanding and involvement in the issue and on a particular interpretation of scripture which perceives these scriptures as being fulfilled in and through Christ. In addition there is the issue of Christ's relationship to God and how literary and theological problems relating to how Romans 9:5 are to be understood. The following issues with which Paul is concerned in these chapters can be listed as follows. I note six points:

1. He is certain that Israel has been granted privileges by God (9:4).

2. He is grieved that some of his own people have not turned to Christ (9:2).

3. He maintains that not all Israelites belong to the 'true' Israel (9:6).

4. He is clear that Christ has fulfilled the Jewish *Torah* (10:4) and that a new basis for universal salvation has been found in him in which both Jews and Gentiles are included (9:24). Paul sees that in Christ's saving ministry the ancient prophecies have been fulfilled in that Christ is (i)

the saviour from Zion (Isa 59:20-2) and that (ii) through Christ's death sin has been removed (Jer 31:33).

5. He perceives that Gentile converts ought to willingly accept Jews into the fellowship of faith (11:13-14).

6. He maintains that God has not rejected Israel and that a remnant will be grafted into God's new community.

The overriding motivation behind these chapters concerns the activity of God. In one way the issues with which they are concerned are unresolved. For Paul, though, their resolution must be left to God for there is no way of knowing his mind (11:33-35 in which Isa 40:13-14; Job 35:7 and 41:11 are quoted). If it were so God would cease 'to be God'. God is known through revelation: in the natural order (1:20); through the Jewish *Torah* (7:12) but supremely and finally through Christ (9:1). Therefore it is fitting that the section should end with a hymn of praise to God (11:36) to which the hearers of the letter would reply with 'Amen'.

Having arrived at 11:36 it should now be possible for the reader to perceive the progression of Paul's lines of argument which began at 1:16-17. From the complexity of text two particular points emerge. First, Paul demonstrates the totality of God's promise both to Israel and 'the nations' and secondly, he declares that despite human disobedience God is able to have mercy upon *all* (11:32) people. This declaration represents both another aspect of the 'universality theme' and reveals again the tension between human sinfulness (received through Adam, 5:17a) and the magnitude of God's grace which is available through Christ (5:17b and 5:8-9).

Ethical, 12:1-15:29

This section raises two major questions:

- *How should the believers live within Roman society?*
- *How should the believers understand each other and live with each other as God's beloved holy ones (1:7)?*

The other issue concerns how this section ought to be understood both in terms of itself and in relation to the other sections of the letter. In order to address these issues five points need to be made:

1. The internal issues relating to the Roman church (e.g. 15:1-6) fan into Paul's discussion of universal mission found in 15:14-29. Also that the Roman Christians, although not physically present with him, are involved spiritually in Paul's mission. Thus, any discussion of 'local ethics' is to be seen against a much broader background.

2. In the section 12:1-15:13, Paul presents a coherent series of ethical injunctions which inter-relate with each other. These injunctions should not be seen as a series of random ideas.

3. Earlier in the letter Paul has discussed the theological principles of sin, law, grace, death and eternal life. The ethical injunctions outlined in 12:1-15:13 should be regarded as representing the practical application of these principles. In this way principles and application; theology and ethics ought to be seen together as offering a unified response to God.

4. The sources which form the basis for Paul's ethical discussion are two-fold. First, there is the priority of biblical ethics illustrated by the numerous references to scriptural precepts (e.g. Rom 13:9 using Ex 20:13-17 and Deut 5:17-18). Secondly, it seems that Paul is also aware of some of the general ethical maxims found in Graeco-Roman thought, in particular those based on Stoic ethics. Of these maxims it can be supposed that some of the Roman church members would have had knowledge of them.

5. Some of Paul's injunctions were, or came to be, a feature of general Christian teaching. This observation might go some way to explain why some of the injunctions are paralleled in the recorded sayings of Jesus (e.g. Rom 13:8, note Mt 22:39-40).

Paul begins by perceiving ethical living in terms of temple sacrifice (12:1). Ethical living is, therefore, to be seen in terms of an offering to God and of linking ethics with worship. In this living believers are to be 'in the world' but not of it and to be mentally transformed by right ethical thinking. This position is the basis on which church life is to be governed: by humility (12:3) and by the recognition of the diversity of ministries within the body of Christ (12:4-8; 1 Cor 12:12 and 12:27). In Romans 12:9 Paul introduces the concept of love both in its verb (13:8-9, *agapao*) and noun (12:9; 13:10; 14:15, *agape*, note also its use in 5:5; 5:8; 8:35 and 8:39) forms which illustrate how love becomes the controlling factor in guiding ethical behaviour which is seen also in the context of God's love for the believers (note 5:5). Love should always be present within the believing community as the injunction to demonstrate brotherly affection (12:10) testifies. All the injunctions which follow (12:11-21), concerning living within the believing community, develop from this love concept.

With Romans 13:1-7 Paul deals with the issue of living under the Roman Imperial social and political order. The injunctions contained here have been open to numerous interpretations and differences of opinion. Other than the comments I have made on the matter in this chapter I should add that 13:1-7 ought to be considered in its context: the historical context of AD 57 and its literary context within Romans. This latter context has two aspects. First, the notion that love both fulfils the *Torah* but does not negate its precepts (13:8-10) and that, secondly, within Romans a powerful eschatological perspective (retained from 1 Thess) is to be found in that God would soon come to the world in judgement. This perspective retains traditional eschatological metaphors: awakening from sleep (13:11; 1 Thess 5:6); the arrival of the daylight and the expelling of darkness (13:12; 1 Thess 5; 8) and the command to perceive eschatology in terms of the exercise of virtue rather than as providing an excuse for licentious behaviour (13:13; 1 Thess 4:12; Gal 5:19-21). The discussion concludes with a two-fold statement: (i) that the believers are to remember their baptismal obligations (being clothed in Christ, cf. 6:3-11 and Gal 3:27), and (ii) on that basis to live 'in the Spirit' rather than 'in the flesh' (13:14; cf. 8:1-9).

Romans 14 contains a long discussion relating to food; which types of food is it proper for believers to eat? Paul works his way through this discussion: (i) by indicating the important issues which are the consideration of righteousness, peace, joy and the Holy Spirit in the context of ethical living (14:17) and (ii) by suggesting that the strong ought to support the weak (15:1). Through these injunctions a glimpse is received of the social and pastoral difficulties faced by believers (especially Gentile believers) who encounter the religious and political pressures of living in a Graeco-Roman urban environment. Paul is sympathetic to these pressures as evidenced by his advice to the Corinthian Christians in 1 Corinthians 8. In Romans 15:6 Paul summarises the ethical discussion and the implications of that discussion which are: first, for the Roman church to strive for unity ('one voice') in the numerous ways which have been suggested and secondly, to return to the 'fountain head' of the faith, the glorification of God in Jesus which recalls a state of life which the believers are given the hope of achieving (8:24-25).

Given the difficulties with regard to the conclusion of Romans I set out here the possibilities in diagrammatic form.

Possibilities as to the shape of the conclusion of Romans

These possibilities relate to the various manuscript traditions and to the placing of the doxology, Romans 16:25-27.

1. 1:1-16:23 + 16:25-27
2. 1:1-14:23 + 16:25-27 + 15:1-16:24
3. 1:1-14:23 + 16:25-27 + 15:1-16:23 + 16:25-27
4. 1:1-16:24
5. 1:1-15:33 + 16:25-27 + 16:1-23 (found in one of the oldest collections of Pauline letters, papyrus = P^{46})
6. 1:1-14:23 + 16:24 + 16:25-27.

Readers who wish to pursue this study further will need to:

(a) Research the manuscript traditions relating to Romans and

(b) Ask why the copyists made changes and the reasons why
they believed that changes were necessary.

SECTION 2 – THE CONTEXT

A. THE ENVIRONMENT

The discussion relating to the environment in which the
Roman Christians received the Letter to the Romans,
AD 57, operates on three levels. First there is the issue of
the topographical features of the city of Rome at the time.
On this issue a vital distinction ought to made between the
'shape' of the city in 57, in 60 when Paul arrived in Rome,
and in 64 at the time of the 'great fire' (consult Amanda
Claridge's book, *Rome*, Oxford Archaeological Guides, Oxford,
Oxford University Press, 1998, pp 15-16). Architectural
interconnections between temples and civic buildings (e.g. The
Forum, containing a large temple dedicated to Julius Caesar)
afford a glimpse into the intertwined aspects of political and
religious power in the imperial capital, and highlight tensions
in the degrees to which Christian believers chose to share in
the civic, social and political life of the city.

Rome was (and had been since the accession of Augustus)
a developing city. New buildings were being erected constantly
reflecting the vital conjunction between city of Rome,
Empire and Emperor, all designed to manifest both Roman
traditions and Roman power. In the case of Emperor Nero
in particular, conjunctions between his political policy, his
'cultural philosophy', promoting Hellenism, and his building
projects hint at future conflicts with theistic religions, given
their perspective on theology and ethics, but which remained
at the level of projection in c. AD 57.

This issue leads to the second level of environmental
investigation which concerns the areas of the city where the
earliest Christians resided and where their house-churches were
to be found. Considerable research has been undertaken over
these issues with one conclusion being that Christians lived in
some of the poorest and densely populated areas of the city;

155

for example, Trastevere and along the Appian way outside the Porta Capena. It is also likely that Christians settled between Puteoli (Acts 28:13) and Rome (Acts 28:16) and this route represented one of the important trade highways into Rome from the south (left hand part of Map 5).

These issues lead to the third level namely the 'character' of the church in Rome. I have discussed already the implications of the Edict of Claudius and the possible return of some Jewish Christians in 54 (on the accession of Nero) but two other possible areas of community conflict are implied from the above discussion. The first relates to how the Roman church was organised corporately. Did the presence of numerous house-churches lead to a lack of theological and pastoral coordination such that disharmony was created (e.g. 12:14-21)? Was there continuing disagreements between Jews, Jewish and Gentile Christians (the argument in 9-11)? Secondly, does the primary location of Christians in socially deprived areas also sow the seeds for social and educational disharmony amongst the majority and minority social groups? Also the question emerges as to how such a sophisticated text as Romans was received, appreciated and acted upon by all the Christian believers in Rome. On this basis it could have been the case that some Christians lived in more affluent parts of the city; again illustrating, as with the Jew/Gentile composition of the church, that there was some diversity also in its social and educational composition.

A note concerning the study of the Roman Forum

The readers who wish to research the development of the Forum might consult:
> http://dlib.etc.ucla.edu/projects/Forum

Timemap:
> http://dlib.etc.ucla.edu/projects/Forum/timemap

B. ROMANS WITHIN PAUL'S MISSIONARY ACTIVITY

The key to understanding the letter to the Romans within the context of Paul's missionary activity is to be found in Romans

15:6-32 and, for Rome, Romans 1:8-15. In Section 3, and in order to illustrate the theological innovations which Paul demonstrates in Romans, I shall argue that, central within these innovations, is his concept of 'universal' mission and ministry found in Romans 15:18-20 and 15:23-29, which marks a development from what he has argued before. In this section I shall be highlighting the three localities on which this concept is based: Jerusalem (15:19; 25-26); Rome (15:22-23; 1:7; 1:11-13) and Spain (15:24 and 15:28). This development is based upon Paul's own realisation that there is 'no longer any room for work in these regions' (15:23a; in particular, the Roman provinces in Macedonia, Achaia and Asia) and therefore, in AD 57, he must seek new pastures for his missionary ministry.

Locality 1 – Jerusalem (15:19; 15:25; 15:26; 15:31; also 1 Cor 16:1-4; 2 Cor 8:1-9:15)

The reason Paul offers to the Romans for his return to Jerusalem is in order to deliver the collection gift offered to the church there by the Christians of Macedonia and Achaia (Rom 15:26). Is this presentation of the information a sufficiently good reason as to why he cannot immediately visit Rome? I suspect that there is a deeper motive: that of involving the Roman Christians in his entire project, Jerusalem, Illyricum, themselves, Spain. Interestingly Paul does not ask them for a contribution – this gift has come from the churches which he has founded (15:26; also 15:20-21) rather his purpose is to highlight the status of Jerusalem in his theological and evangelistic understanding.

With regard to this understanding Paul betrays a certain ambivalence of approach and at least three layers of perception. First, Jerusalem is the location where both the prophets and Jesus were persecuted and martyred by their own countrymen, the Jews (1 Thess 2:14-15). In Galatians Paul considers Jerusalem as a 'city of slavery' (Gal 4:25), whereas the heavenly Jerusalem (the city of Christian believers) our 'mother' is the 'city of freedom' (Gal 4:26). Secondly, Paul has expressed a desire to be at least semi-independent (note Gal 1:17 and

1:18) of the Jerusalem Christian 'ecclesiological structure' (Gal 2:1 and 2:7-10). This structure was (is?) represented by the Jerusalem apostles (note inference in 2 Cor 11:5 and 12:11) and James, the Lord's brother, the leader of the Jerusalem church. Paul believed that Jerusalem was not the central location of the Gentile mission (note Acts 13:1-3, for the place of Antioch in Syria in this regard). Thirdly, and perhaps more profoundly, Jerusalem represents the origin and centre of the fulfilment of God's purpose for salvation (Rom 11:26-27 where Isa 59:20-21 is quoted). This purpose is focussed in the historical origin of Christianity determined as a result of Jesus' death, resurrection and his appearances to the initial believers (1 Cor 15:3-7). The Roman Christians, therefore, must never lose sight of either (a) the material plight of their Jerusalem brothers and sisters (15:27), or (b) of Jerusalem as the historical and theological location of the origin of the Christian movement (implied in 15:19). It can be assumed that (by 57) Paul expected every church to think in this way and when he reached Spain he would remind the Spanish believers of this perception and obligation. He may have even intended to return again to Jerusalem with the 'sacrificial offering' of the Spanish mission. In this regard Paul is able to utilise and interpret the Jerusalem Temple liturgical language and practice of 'priestly service', 'offering' and 'acceptability' before God (Mal 3:4) in his ministerial understanding which is here focussed on the evangelisation of the Gentiles (Mal 1:11; note also, Isa 60:5-7). From childhood Saul/Paul would have understood Jerusalem as being the centre of his religious world to which, in the eschatological age, all nations would return. Now in his late 40s his earlier perception is being reinterpreted. In this context Jerusalem is seen as the source of his Christian, Messianic faith from which the glorious Gospel of Jesus' saving power has originated and to which the redeemed believers would return. Biblical interpretation forms the basis for this reinterpretation: the way in which the Jewish scriptures can be expounded in the Christian era (e.g. Rom 15:9-12 and 15:21).

Locality 2 – Rome (1:7; 1:15; 15:22; 15:28; 16:1-16)

Fundamental to the understanding of the Letter to the Romans is (i) its context, AD 57, and (ii) that it represents what Paul is projecting for his continuing and future mission and ministry. In this latter category, however, it should not be presumed that he was ignorant of the political or the ecclesiological position in Rome. Within the Christian communities there were clearly social, ethnic and religious divisions which Paul attempts to resolve (e.g. 14:17-19; 15:1-2). On whose authority and on what ecclesiological basis could he attempt a resolution? His claims in these areas are expounded in Rom 15:15-21. They are based on the God given grace (15:15b) which Paul has received. In this case he is more 'measured' than he has been in Galatians 1:6-17 (note especially, 1:15-16). The Galatian churches, however, were his own foundation (e.g. Gal 3:15) whereas the Roman church was founded by others (Rom 15:20) and, in 57, Paul had no part in the leadership structure although Prisca and Aquila would have provided a possible means of communication between Paul and the Roman church (16:3-4; 1 Cor 16:19). Thus, for him, the ministerial authority remains the same while the context in which the ministry operates is different. On this basis, therefore, it might be asked: what was Paul's purpose in the composition of Romans – to summarise his theological position, to prepare for this apostolic mission to the city and in Spain, to resolve pastoral crises in which he was not directly involved or to challenge opponents (note the use of rhetorical diatribe; e.g. Rom 2:1-4)? These questions highlight areas of unresolved debate. Most likely Paul's reasons for writing were numerous. It could have been that various areas of theological, ethical and pastoral issues are being raised in preparation for his projected visit. This letter, essay, preparation discussion paper, however Romans is to be classified, if studied correctly, would maximise the 'spiritual gift' and 'mutual encouragement' (1:11-12) which can be shared when Paul eventually arrived in the city. In the meantime the Roman Christians ought to resolve their internal differences in order that the church might be evangelically effective in the city and also that it might be prepared spiritually to act as the base from which Paul's projected Spanish mission might be undertaken (15:28).

In this process Paul's own understanding of the 'place' of Rome in his thinking had to be enlarged. As a Roman citizen he would have perceived Rome as the centre of his political understanding (implied in 13:1-7). In this view Paul was agreeing with the Roman conventions of the time; the geographer, Strabo (c.AD 20), for example, writes about the grandeur of Rome. As a Christian minister (15:16) Rome has developed in his mind as the centre of his newly-discovered missionary vision.

Locality 3 – Spain (15:24; 15:28)

Other than being somewhat vague the question arises as to why Paul should choose Spain as an area for Christian evangelisation. Two observations can be made in this regard. First, Spain was a Latin speaking region. Paul's discourse, however, seems to have been almost entirely Greek perhaps with some Hebrew. He may have gained some experience of Latin from his missionary work in Illyricum. On this basis we might speculate that Paul's horizons: intellectual, linguistic and experiential, were being broadened. Secondly, Spain was not an area where Jews had settled in any great number. The possibility of using the synagogue as the basis for his ministry would be remote. The Spanish mission, therefore, would have been almost entirely Gentile (note 15:9). In this regard Paul wished to seek virgin territory for his mission (note 15:20-21). This view would have most likely ruled out North Africa; for example, Alexandria or Cyrene, as (by 57) Christianity had spread already to these regions (note Acts 2:10). It is probable that, writing later c. 96, Clement provides the clue to the 'Spanish issue' when he observes that Paul 'taught righteousness to all the world, and when he had reached the limits of the West...' (1 Clem 5:7). For Paul (and for others of his time) Spain would have marked 'the limits of the West'. Thus a vast missionary panorama is presented, the possibility of 'all the world' being under 'the obedience of faith' (1:5) in Christ, from Jerusalem to Illyricum (15:19), considered as the northern most part of his missionary activity, including Macedonia and Achaia (15:26), Rome, and finally to Spain (15:28) – all enjoying 'the fullness of the blessing of Christ' (15:29).

SECTION 3 – THEOLOGICAL, PASTORAL AND HERMENEUTICAL ISSUES

It is my intention in this section to explore the 'new features' which the letter to the Romans offers. On occasions these 'new features' emerge from themes that Paul has utilised already (e.g. Adam, 1 Cor 15:22; Rom 5:14; Law, Gal 2:16, works of Law; Rom 2:12-13), at other times new concepts are employed (e.g. Rom 15:29). Sometimes these 'new features' are conditioned by the particular context of Romans: that Paul was not a founder member of the Roman church (15:20); that the letter represents Paul's intentions with regard to his future ministry in which the church is to play a central role (15:28-29) and the need for inter-community harmony within the house churches (12:14-21). Thus Romans, as I have argued, should be understood as being vitally important in our perception of Paul's missionary strategy, 56-57: leaving one area of missionary endeavour (15:26) and seeking others. Given that Paul had not visited the Roman church, merely been informed about its life (by Prisca and Aquila) the tone of the letter varies from its nearest antecedent: Galatians. In Romans 'measured' argument more often, certainly not always, prevails. Another related feature is how Romans has been 'received' as a text: interestingly often in times of spiritual and theological crisis; for example, St Augustine, St Thomas Aquinas, Martin Luther and John Wesley. We 'receive' Romans, not merely be enquiring why Paul originally wrote the letter, but also by being aware of the rich tradition of its theological interpretation, both Evangelical and Catholic.

Given the large scale of these approaches my modest intention is to present these 'new features' in the context of a hermeneutical dialogue with our contemporary setting. I offer the following list with no particular order of importance merely as ideas to be discussed with a view to uncovering still more features of the letter's rich complexity both in terms of biblical commentary and subsequent interpretation.

Mission

The way in which Paul presents his 'new features' relating to mission in Romans has been one of our principal concerns. The concepts revealed in 15:6-29 demonstrate an enlarged universal and eschatological understanding of mission from that which Paul has related before. Christian Mission is now perceived on a grand scale covering a large area around the northern Mediterranean, originating in Jerusalem, arriving in the capital of the Roman Empire, moving to the 'limits of the West' – Spain. This perception would now become a feature of Christianity (note Mt 28:19 and Acts 1:8). To understand this concept geography is necessary (compare with the extent of the Roman Empire) but insuffcient without theology. The mission is Christ centred (15:29). It is a declaration of the totality of the Gospel (10:14-17) of which Paul is a slave and apostle (1:1). This ministry occurs during 'the middle of time': the period between Christ's death and resurrection (6:4-5) and the coming judgement (13:11-14). The mission concerns entry into the 'new community of faith' by Baptism (6:3-11) which is the liturgical means of identifying the new believer with the saving activity of Christ: unity with his death and resurrection. The resurrection remains a source of hope: it is given but not finalised. This finalisation will occur at a future date known only to God (6:5). Entry into this community also brings with it ethical obligations (6:6) relating to sin, righteousness (6:18) and right conduct (13:8-10).

Through the investigation of these 'new features' (which build upon some of Paul's earlier themes) contemporary challenges with regard to missionary strategy are revealed. These challenges relate both to the concept and practice of universality and the 'ministry of welcome' (15:7): the ability to perceive of the Church's mission as a vast inter-connected organism between peoples and nations in which all are equal before God (2:11). Our mission should also be ethical in that people have the 'right' to justice which is to live under God's Law (13:8). Fundamentally, Christian mission is Christological: the projection of the 'fullness' (15:29) of Christ's total ministry in terms of incarnation (8:3b); crucifixion (5:15-17), resurrection and glorification (8:34). In all these aspects of Christ's work believers are able to share and, in turn, to demonstrate them in their missionary activity.

Judaism and the Law (*Torah*)

In Romans Paul confronts his former life in Judaism (cf. Gal 1:14) in a way in which he has not done before. The starting point for this confrontation is chapter 7 with its powerful first person singular statements relating to Paul's personal experience. This chapter is not easy to interpret but it is clear that Paul is engaging (in AD 57) with his past life, perhaps in preparation for his visit to Jerusalem (15:25 and 15:31)? The confrontation concerns the notions of sin and law (*nomos*) with the question as to whether the law (in terms of *Torah*) is itself sin (7:7). Paul is clear that this is not the case, rather the law (and its precepts) is holy, just and good (7:12). His conception of law, therefore, is more positive than that presented in Galatians (note 2:16). In Romans the law becomes the basis for an over-arching moral framework for living under God ethically, a position which forms the foundation of Paul's injunctions in 12:1-15:6. In this regard the knowledge of law highlights sin and assists us, as we all must, to live under law. As we shall see in the next section Paul retains the view that the *Torah*, or its precepts, cannot make us righteous before God, the restoration of a primal glory and the abolishing of sin is only possible through faith in Jesus Christ (3:22). Paul declares that 'Christ is the end (*telos*, could also be translated 'goal') of the Law (*Torah*)' (10:4) which could mark either its fulfilment or its annulment. This ambiguity reflects the tension here between seeing *Torah* as a 'thing-in-itself' or as text to be interpreted. In this context, I would argue, that it is not that the *Torah* which ceases to have value in the Christian era, rather it is the way in which *Torah* is used: fine as an ethical guide (thus, 'goal') not as the means of gaining God's salvation in Christ (thus, 'end'). For Paul's ethical training *Torah* is a major building block on which it is based and within his writings there are numerous quotations and allusions to the *Torah* text. In the end, however, it is the saving activity of Christ (cf. 10:4) which puts the *Torah* into a Christian perspective.

The confrontation by Paul with his Jewishness begins in 3:1 with the question as to the advantage of being a Jew, the answer being that they have been entrusted with God's oracles (3:2), the precepts of the *Torah* which God mediated to Israel through Moses. The question of 'advantage' is explored with great profundity in chapters 9 to 11. By 11:33 it is clear that Paul still remains uncertain as to how Jews and Gentiles can be incorporated together within God's plan, in particular if some Jews have not believed that Jesus is God's Messiah. In the end Paul cannot know God's mind on the matter (11:34 quotes Isa 40:34-35). Paul is wrestling with the issue both personally (9:1-5) and corporately in terms of membership of God's new community. This wrestling should be a distinctive hallmark of Church as demonstrated within the document produced by the Pontifical Biblical Commission of the Roman Catholic Church, *The Jewish people and their Sacred Scriptures in the Christian Bible*, 2002, where reference is made to Paul's example in Romans 9-11 which shows that: '…an attitude of respect, esteem and love for the Jewish people is the only Christian attitude in a situation which is mysteriously part of the beneficent and positive plan of God. Dialogue is possible, since Jews and Christians share a rich common patrimony that unites them' (p. 199). It is only in this spirit, I should argue, that both the continuity and discontinuity between Judaism and Christianity can be researched and appreciated, a position made possible because of the personal and corporate tensions which Paul confronts in Romans.

Acceptance by God in Christ

The issue as to how humanity can be accepted by God in Christ is the single most important theme in Romans (note 1:16-17). On the basis of this thesis two other points emerge:

1. For Paul the issue of acceptance interlocks with the other topics with which the letter is concerned: community life (12:9-13); 'progress' in faith (5:1); the proclamation of the Gospel (10:17) and how Judaism and the *Torah* should be interpreted within this acceptance claim (2:17-24).

2. From our contemporary perspective the investigation of these issues is truly 'good news' as the door is opened for us to reflect profoundly on the nature and purpose of theology, humanity and ethics.

The statement as to how this 'acceptance theme' operates is found in 1:16-17 and with it five 'new features' emerge. First, acceptance is linked to the preaching and power of God's Gospel in Christ (e.g. 1:16; 15:19). Secondly, the application of this Gospel is offered to humanity on the broadest possible terms: to all who have faith (1:16). Thirdly, the theme is linked to Paul's (new?) systematic understanding of mission, 'to the Jew first and also to the Greek': rooted in Judaism and then taken to all nations (the Gentiles). The division of labour between the Pauline mission to the Gentiles and that of the 'pillar apostles': James, Cephas and John to the Jews (Gal 2:9-10), in Romans 1:16 disappears (also a feature of Luke's presentation of Paul's mission; e.g. Acts 13:14 and 13:46). Fourthly, saving righteousness/justice (*dikaiosune*) is an attribute of God (alongside other attributes such as love, 5:5; and wrath, 1:18). Fifthly, this acceptance process is confirmed by biblical interpretation (Hab 2:4 quoted in 1:17 with a changed meaning different both from the Greek text and the Hebrew original).

From this initial statement other issues must be confronted before 'full acceptance' can occur. First, the roots of human sinfulness, originating in Adam, with different manifestations for Jews and Gentiles, must be abolished. Sinfulness produces alienation from God, the opposite state of life to acceptance. For Paul sin is removed through the means of Christ's sacrifice. In this regard Romans 5:6-21 outlines the 'theology of the cross' which reveals how Christ's death has ensured forgiveness and reconciliation with God: our acceptance is confirmed by identification with Christ's sufferings (5:1-5). Secondly, there is the question of the continuing place of the *Torah* in God's plan. I have considered this issue above and suggested that there is ambiguity here. For while the Jewish scriptures (the law and the prophets) bear witness to Christ and he fulfils their precepts (10:4) yet, at the same time, God's manifestation in Christ is independent of them (3:22). This ambiguity, rather than demonstrating weakness, is a source of strength as it forces us to encounter what is 'old' and 'new' in the presentation of the Gospel: the wrestling with tradition and innovation at the same time. Given its profundity, metaphors are utilised to express this 'acceptance Christology' (3:24-25): the law court showing God's justice; the slave market (redemption) his freedom and the temple sacrifice (expiation) his offering of his Son (8:3; also for Paul's ministry, 15:16). These metaphors are also chosen to demonstrate God's action in Christ towards believers. What attributes of acceptance are now available to us? The answer is: grace, gift, forgiveness, the promise of eternal life with God and the regaining of divine glory (*doxa*, 3:23; 8:18-25). Evidence of this process can be detected in Judaism through the faith of Abraham (4:3 quoting Gen 15:6). Yet Abraham (coupled with his willing sacrifice of his only son, Isaac, Gen 22:1-19) provides a pathway into Christian experience illustrated by the fact that Paul's reflection upon Abraham's faith concludes with a Christological summary. 'Jesus our Lord' (4:24) is one who: (i) died for our sins but was, (ii) raised by God in order that we might share in his righteousness (*dikaiosune*, 4:25; cf. 1:17 and 3:25).

Yet for Paul in Romans this 'acceptance theology' operates on the basis of a subtle blend between the 'I' and the 'we'. As you study the letter this interaction becomes clear (e.g. 'I', 1:16 and 7:1; 'we', 3:31 and 5:1). It is true that we receive God's acceptance individually on account of our faith but the whole issue of receiving God's righteousness is also corporate. We might illustrate this argument by reference to Paul's discussion of Baptism (6:3-4). Baptism, although it demands an individual profession of faith in Christ's saving activity and that, individually, new believers are 'drowned' in Christ's death in order to rise with him, from the water, into the future risen, glorified life; nevertheless, the operation of Baptism is corporate: acceptance into the company of believers who by their faith and living (6:11) demonstrate God's righteousness and Christ's saving power. Two other points need to be noted in this context. First, 'acceptance theology' is dynamic not static. The statement in 5:1: 'having been made righteous therefore by faith' should not be seen as a conclusion to the 'justification argument' but rather as a continuation of it. In our 'progress' in Christian reflection and experience we should be aware that God's acceptance of us through justification demands our continuing attention in the same way that Baptism should be considered as a 'once-for-all' sacrament (in parallel to Christ's death) but the implications of our baptismal calling and 'progress' in baptismal understanding remain as a source of constant reflection and challenge for the living of the Christian life (12:3-8). Secondly, as we have seen in Section 2, Paul is anxious about the 'state' of the Roman Christian community (e.g. 14:1-4). On this basis we should utilise this 'acceptance theology' for the up-building of the Church: the harmony of its communal life (15:7) which, in turn, will aid its effectiveness for mission (15:28-29). In this way the thematic links; for example, between 1:1-17 and 15:5 and 15:30, illustrate that Romans ought to be seen as an integrated text, not a text marked by divisions; for example, at 5:1; 9:1 or 12:1. These references are markers for the progression of the argument, which is focussed throughout on the implications of God's acceptance of believers in Christ and in the implications for faith and living of that acceptance.

Yet Romans also portrays this 'acceptance theology' as being painted against the broadest possible framework. We have considered already Paul's 'universalist' concept of mission (15:22-29) which encompasses Jerusalem and the 'limits of the West'; in 8:18-24, however, the proclamation of the Christian faith is seen within the total cosmological order of the created universe. The creation shares in the tension between the present and the future glory, a glory which will include the release of the entire universe from its slavery to decay. Thus, believers ought to perceive their faith, mission and living as against the totality of God's plan both for all humanity (1:16) and for all creation (8:22). In case the contemplation of this 'acceptance theology' with its multiple implications appears too great for our comprehension we have always the prayerful help of the Spirit. It is the Spirit, God's agent within creation, who also enters into the individual human heart and works within the believing community. In this way the creative, corporate and individual aspects of our acceptance by God in Christ are united.

In case such an expression of theology should appear to be too abstract Paul brings into his discussion the theme of the reality of suffering (5:3-4; 8:18), which finds its focus in the sufferings of Christ (6:3) with whom the believers are identified. Later, in AD 64, the Roman Christians, including Peter and Paul, are to experience terrible sufferings on the orders of the Emperor Nero. In AD 57, however, it can be supposed that Paul imagined that the proclamation and living of the Gospel in Rome (and elsewhere) could be subsumed within the Roman political order. In this thought there was always to be tension. The *Pax Romana* was based on military power and upon imperial administration as demonstrated by the policies of the first Emperor Augustus being described in terms of good news/Gospel and of his power as bringing salvation. Paul's conception of 'Gospel' was based on the saving activity of God in Jesus Christ and of the construction of eschatological (13:11-12), non-violent, law-abiding missionary communities of believers.

In Romans 13:1-7 Paul demonstrates, perhaps naively, how the Roman leadership is to be viewed (13:1-3), with optimism. Nero's tutor, the Stoic Seneca (also optimistic) had written (AD 55-56) to the Emperor on the subject of clemency (*De Clementia*) because this concept would act as a 'mirror' by which his good conscience might be inspected. The logic of both Seneca and Paul is to encourage support for the Emperor. In Romans 13:7 Paul lists the actions that Christians should take in terms of being good citizens (13:7). As a result of Nero's subsequent actions (for which he was criticised by the later Roman historians, Tacitus and Suetonius) the way of living the Gospel (not merely Christians but Seneca and the Stoics also suffered as a result of Nero's later policies and actions) under tyrannical and despotic regimes is demonstrated. My point here is that acceptance by God in Christ is costly, often in ways that are not clear at the time but are revealed later. Under such circumstances our acceptance by God is ever constant and the living of the Gospel is, paradoxically, ever renewing and always 'good news'.

CHAPTER 5

FROM PRISON

Paul's four short letters to the churches of Philippi, Colossae and Ephesus and to his friend and fellow worker in the ministry, Philemon, have been grouped together as 'the letters from prison' as in each case Paul is writing from captivity.

Philippians   1:7; 1:13; 1:17
Philemon   1; 10; 13; 23
Colossians   4:3; 4:18
Ephesians   3:1; 4:1; 6:20.

The first issue is where and when should these imprisonments be located, remembering that they need not be in the same location or at the same time for each letter. Given that Paul says that he has been frequently in prison (2 Cor 11:23) three suggestions have been made:

1. Paul is writing from an Ephesian prison (a possible hint from 1 Cor 15:32 and Acts 19:38; here merely the possibility of a court appearance). Although there is no specific evidence that he was in prison in Ephesus, especially given the proximity to the other cities mentioned, this location has been advanced particularly in connection with Philippians. The possible dates here are 54-56.

2. Paul is writing from his Caesarean prison (Acts 23:35; 24:27) where, according to Luke, he was held for two years, between c. 58-60.

3. Paul is writing from his Roman prison (Acts 28:16; 28:30) where, according to Luke, he was under house arrest, awaiting trial before the Emperor to whom Paul, as a Roman citizen, had appealed. The possible dates here are 60-62.

As we shall see when we come to consider 2 Timothy the final years of Paul's life between imprisonment and martyrdom are difficult to reconstruct historically. In addition, although in these prison letters Paul speaks of the possibility of death in the near future, at the time he seems to be also contemplating his release and the possibility of exercising further apostolic and pastoral ministry (compare Philem 1 with 22 and Phil 2:17 with 2:24).

Two other related issues need to be addressed by way of introduction; first the question of authorship. There is no foolproof way of dealing with this issue (note the various arguments relating to vocabulary, literary style and theological content) as it centres on whether we are dealing with Paul and his intellectual development, or with the Pauline tradition which emanated from him. If we consider the letters in the reverse order, Ephesians is the most likely candidate to be thought of as post-Pauline, written by a disciple acting in Paul's name and within the orbit of Pauline authority, outlining for the Pauline churches (for Ephesus, see Acts 18:19-20:1; 20:17-38; 1 Tim 1:3; 2 Tim 1:18 and 4:12; Rev 1:11 and 2:1-7) what Paul had achieved and why his thought was of continuing importance. It does not (as do other Pauline letters) deal with specific circumstances with the exception of a reference to Tychicus and his ministerial relationship with Paul (Eph 6:21-22). In addition there are textual difficulties in relation to Ephesians 1:1. At this point the question must be asked as to the original text of this verse. This issue arises because the destination of letter to the believers being 'at Ephesus' is omitted from some of the earliest manuscripts or from the original copies of them. On this showing Ephesians 1:1 reads as:

'Paul an apostle of Christ Jesus through the will of God to the saints being...
[at Ephesus] ... and faithful in Christ Jesus.'

If this is the case then the Greek sentence is made grammatically difficult by the juxtaposition of 'being' (*ousin*) and 'and' (*kai*). A number of suggestions have been made to account for, and to resolve, this issue. Did the author intend to leave a space between 'being' and 'and' (represented by dots above) in order that the precise location could be added? If this is the case then the letter would have been a circular one written to a number of churches perhaps with Ephesus as the principal destination. Maybe the location of 'and' in Ephesians 1:1 means that the letter was written to two churches (Lincoln, *CCStP*, 134)? It might have even been the case that the letter was 'from Ephesus' composed in order to give theological and ethical guidance to other local churches. On two grounds, therefore, authorship (Eph 1:1 and 3:1) and destination (Eph 1:1? and the role of Tychicus, Eph 6:21; Acts 20:4; Col 4:7; Titus 3:12 and especially, 2 Tim 4:12) makes the placing of the Ephesian letter uncertain.

A further complication is the literary relationship between Ephesians and Colossians. The parallels between them have been presented diagrammatically by Raymond Brown (*INT*, 628). Does this evidence mean that Colossians should be also considered as post-Pauline? Unlike Ephesians, Colossians refers to specific circumstances (Col 1:7 and 4:7-17) yet, on the other hand, both in terms of grammatical construction and theological content the case for post-Pauline authorship might be made. In turn there are close links between Colossians and Paul's personal letter to Philemon; what does this observation say about the authorship of Philemon?

In the case of Philippians Pauline authorship has never been seriously doubted. This observation highlights the problems of seeing these letters from prison as a corpus. Given the complexities outlined above, how should they be studied together? In addition to historical and literary issues (the structure and vocabulary of the letters) there is also the question of theological interpretation. These questions relate primarily to Christology and Ecclesiology. Are the views expressed about Christ and the Church in Ephesians and Colossians in tune with what Paul would have said or do they represent developments based upon his ideas? The problem related to expressing the question in this way is subjectivity and with it the issue of how the material in the text may be interpreted without the overuse of prior contemporary presupposition. It is impossible to give dogmatic answers to these questions. I raise them, however, merely to draw attention to the issues themselves. As with the issues surrounding the unity of Paul's Corinthian correspondence I suggest that the best way of handling the material, whilst avoiding prejudicial answers to questions of authorship and date is to:

1. Study the arguments presented in the Prison Letters;

2. To highlight problems relating to interpretation and any possible solutions by which they can be solved;

3. To outline your own evaluation of the texts.

Secondly, there is the question of literary structure and type. Not only is Ephesians a clearly structured letter dividing neatly into two sections, (i) 1:3-3:21; (ii) 4:1-6:20, but it is composed grammatically of long sentences with numerous clauses.

Ephesians has the feel of a general theological and ethical essay encased within a letter framework. Although the conclusion has a 'Pauline ring' (Eph 6:21-24; cf. Phil 4:14-23; 1 Cor 16:10-24) the opening greeting (Eph 1:1-2), as has been mentioned, poses literary and contextual difficulties. Colossians has more of the structure of a typical Pauline letter (note Col 1:1-2; 4:7-18) and the body of it is internally coherent. Philippians, however, is more variegated. The apparent breaks in its structural argument have lead some exegetes to argue that (like 2 Cor) the present Philippians is a combination of perhaps three letters:

– Philippians 4:10-20 – acknowledgement letter.

– Philippians 1:1-3a; 4:4-7; 4:21-23 – justification of Epaphroditus' position and call for unity letter.

– Philippians 3:1b-4:3; 4:8-9 – arguments against opponents letter.

Both this fragmentation of the letter and the Ephesian prison context have been challenged. On the grounds that Philippians 4:10-20 reflects the vocabulary used in 1:3-11 therefore the overall integrity of Philippians ought to be accepted (Hooker, *CCStP*, 108). Equally the conjectures made about Paul's imprisonment are uncertain but, given that Paul was apparently imprisoned on a capital charge (1:19-26; 2:16-17) and that references are made in the letter to the Roman military and political organisation (1:13; 4:22), the Roman imprisonment context and the date of writing in the early 60's remains the most likely solution (Hooker, *CCStP*, 106).

Philemon remains a personal letter in the sense that it was written to leading members of a particular church. These personal letters were not unknown in the ancient world. The Latin writer Pliny the Younger, for example, wrote to his friend Sabrinianus (in c.110) requesting him to receive a slave back into his household (Book 9, Letter 21). Clearly Sabrinianus accepted Pliny's request as another letter expresses gratitude that the matter had been resolved satisfactorily (Book 9, Letter 24, the texts of these letters can be found in the Loeb Class. Lib., ed., no. 59). In Philemon's case, however, it is the Christian implications of the action which are paramount.

Thus these letters from prison have a common context yet their forms, structures and contents vary. Given their brevity and the number of interesting issues which they raise historically, theologically and ethically they are worthy of patient study.

TO THE PHILIPPIANS

SECTION 1 – STRUCTURE

A. OUTLINE

1:1-11   Opening greetings, thanksgiving and prayer

1:12-3:1a   Information on Paul's situation, how the Philippians should live the Christian life

3:1b -4:1   Warning against false teachers

4:2-9   Paul's call for unity, rejoicing and declaration of God's peace

4:10-20   Paul's apostolic ministry and gratitude for the Philippians' gift,

4:21-23   Concluding greetings and blessing.

B. LINES OF ARGUMENT

Opening greetings, thanksgiving and prayer, 1:1-11

The Letter to the Philippians opens in a way similar to other Pauline letters yet here Timothy seems to be associated with Paul's correspondence rather than being a 'co-author' for the remainder of the letter Paul writes in the first person singular with a particularly personal form (note 3:5-11). Paul and Timothy are described as 'slaves (*douloi*) of Jesus Christ', maybe the particular context of imprisonment, of giving up all for Christ, is being emphasised rather than their apostolic status. As elsewhere the Christian congregation are described as saints and their leaders as bishops (*episkopoi*, overseers) and deacons (*diakonoi*). While the latter term seems to have been established in relationship to Paul's earlier ministry (1 Cor 3:5; 2 Cor 6:4) which in turn is based on Christ's 'serving-servant' ministry (e.g. Mk 10:45); *episkopoi* is a new term which in Christian ministerial understanding and practice is to become increasingly important in describing Christian leadership (1 Tim 3:1-7; Titus1:7; Acts 20:28; I Eph 1:2). Its origin stems from the role of guardianship or oversight in relation to a political, social or religious community (1:1). This term was adapted within Christianity to indicate the oversight leadership of a number of house churches or regional churches. The traditional acclamation of grace and peace from 'God our Father and the Lord Jesus Christ' is then included (1:2).

Paul's thanksgiving for the Philippian Christians is based on his 'joy' (1:4) for them, which is introduced here and which will become an important feature of the letter, as also is unity, which is here expressed in terms of partnership or communion (*koinonia*, 1:5) in presenting and living the Gospel. The eschatological nature of Christian experience is also raised and the framework in which Christian ministry and living should be understood ('the day', 1:6; see 'The Day of the Lord' theme, 1 Thess 5:2). Paul's declaration of his particular relationship with the Philippians follows with the hope that they will grow in love, knowledge and discernment (1:9-10). The familiar Pauline righteousness – justice language is here added to the argument; in Philippians, righteousness is seen as a fruit, (1:11; cf. Gal 5:22, 'fruits of the Spirit') a characteristic which is to be demonstrated theologically and ethically as a result of their relationship with God through Christ.

Information on Paul's situation and living the Christian life, 1:12-3:1a

Paul begins by communicating the present situation of his imprisonment (1:13). This imprisonment has had the effect of: (1) strengthening the Christian believers (1:14); (2) Paul proclaiming the Gospel without fear (1:14b, the possibility of death focussing his thoughts and speech) and (3) his bearing in prison being an example to the praetorian guard (1:13, the whole praetorium). This guard was responsible for the personal safety of the Emperor. Paul's idea here may also have been linked to the greetings to the Philippian church from 'the saints' especially those belonging to 'Caesar's household' (4:22). The view being communicated is that somehow the Christian example was being reflected within the heart of the Imperial establishment. Yet here in Philippians 1, Paul seems to feel the need to justify (1:16) this activity in terms of the difference between the motives of Christian preachers concerned with 'envy and rivalry' and those (like Paul himself) who minister out of good will and love. The former group are said to preach Christ 'out of partisanship' (1:17) with the intention of even troubling Paul during his imprisonment (1:17). The rhetorical question, 'what then?' (1:18) leads forward to the idea that whatever the motives of the Christian preachers are deemed to be, nevertheless, Christ is still proclaimed and in view of this proclamation Paul can only 'rejoice' (1:18).

The theme of rejoicing is extended to the next section (1:19-26) in which Paul reflects upon his imprisonment and its implications for the future. Whether in death or in freedom through his experience Christ will be honoured (1:20). This honouring is based upon the implications for the salvation of humanity through his death and resurrection (cf. 1 Cor 15:3-4; forward to, Phil 2:8-9). On balance Paul hopes for freedom (1:24) in order that his ministry amongst the Philippian

Christians (and elsewhere) may be continued and renewed (1:24; also 2:24).

This renewal stands in the heart of the letter in that the Philippians are exhorted to live ethically according to 'the Gospel of Christ' (1:27). This call for ethical living is juxtaposed with the call to withstand opponents. As elsewhere in Paul it is difficult to pinpoint who the opponents were and what was the manner of their teaching and how it differed from that of Paul. In Philippians opposition to Paul seems to have been operating at two locations: that of his imprisonment (1:17, probably Rome) and within the Philippian church (1:28). In the latter case it could have been that Paul's call for Christian ethical living had meant that some of the city's religious and civic customs had been curtailed (Acts 16:21) and with them the accompanying financial rewards (Acts 16:16). In this situation the duality between the opponents who will face destruction and the true believers who will obtain salvation is maintained (1:28). The common link between Paul and the Philippians is the suffering of Christ which remains the 'model' to imitate in their respective situations (1:29-30).

This theme is continued in chapter two which represents a further Christological reflection upon the Philippians' theological and ethical living. The themes of communion (*koinonia*, 2:1) in the Spirit, love, sympathy, humility, mutual sharing and unselfishness (2:1-4) are set within the framework of Christ's ministry (2:5). This ministry is outlined in a well-structured rhymic liturgical section (2:6-11, beginning with 'who', *hos*, referring to Christ). I shall discuss this passage later in Section 3; in the meanwhile, it needs to be noted that the meaning of the passage is gathered from its context: the need for the Philippian Christians to imitate Christ within their understanding of God's plan of salvation available to all humanity. It is interesting that, for this purpose, Paul is utilising a liturgical structure which would have been familiar to his readers and opening them to the rich 'theology of imitation'. This imitation involved more than copying Christ's obedience to God. It concerned also the eschatological transformation through the activity of the Spirit (2:1) and being conformed to the image of Christ as the last Adam thus placing the believers within the orbit of the new creation (cf. 1 Cor 15:20-28; 2 Cor 5:17-21 and Rom 5:15-17).

This theme of imitation is highlighted in Philippians 2:12-13 in which the Philippians are exhorted not only to reflect upon God's offer of salvation in Christ but also to live in a manner worthy of the Gospel. How this ethical living is to be done is outlined in 2:14-16 where this way of living is to be seen in terms of the eschatological return of Christ ('the day' 2:16; cf. 'the day of the Lord' theme in 1 Thess 5:2). This theme is related by Paul both to his own ministry in relation to the Philippians (Phil 2:16b) and to his present imprisonment. As we shall see later in relation to 2 Timothy, there is an ambivalence between Paul's imprisonment leading either to imminent martyrdom (2:17; religious sacrificial language is used, see also 2 Tim 4:6) or to freedom in order that his ministry might be continued. The section concludes with the need for mutual rejoicing (2:17b-18).

In Philippians 2:19-30 Paul leaves the 'imprisonment theme' to concentrate upon the missionary and ministerial organisation of the Philippian church in relation to Timothy (2:19-24) and Epaphroditus (2:25-29). Timothy has been entrusted already with the difficult task of mediating between Paul and the Corinthians (1 Cor 4:17). His task in this instance was to remind the church of Paul's way of portraying Christ in his pastoral and evangelistic ministry. The precise nature of Timothy's task in relation to the Philippians appear to be similar: (a) to provide Paul with information about the spiritual progress of the church (2:19) with regard to the maxims which he has outlined already (2:1-5) and (b) to confront Paul's opponents (3:2-3) with the true way of living the Gospel (2:21). Timothy is praised by Paul in filial terms (2:22), a relationship which I shall summarise when the Pastoral letters are discussed. Whilst Timothy had a wider ministry among the churches, Epaphroditus (also 4:18) appears only in Philippians and in the context of being a local minister and envoy (apostle) of that church. In terms of this ministry he was sent to minister to Paul in his imprisonment where Epaphroditus became his co-worker and co-soldier in terms of the Gospel (2:25). Paul uses the letter to explain why he is sending Epaphroditus back to Philippi. His return is not caused by any personal difficulties which have arisen between them, on the contrary, they have shared in each others ministry, rather it was on account of Epaphroditus' serious illness (2:26-28). The Philippians are requested to receive him 'with all joy' (2:29). In this situation it should be noted that ministerial terms have differing levels of application and meaning (for 'apostle' compare, 1 Cor 1:1 with Phil 2:25; for 'minister', compare Phil 2:25 with Rom 15:16).

This section is concluded with 3:1a which summarises the preceding section 1:3-2:30 that in every circumstance believers are to 'rejoice in the Lord'.

Warning against false teachers, 3:1b-4:1

The warning against false teachers is prepared for in 3:1b with the statement that it is Paul's intention to protect the Philippian believers by keeping them 'safe'. There follows a three fold warning for them to be watchful for the dogs; the evil workmen; those of the 'mutilation party'. It is to be assumed that the three categories embrace the same group: Judaizing Christians. The reference to 'dogs' picks up ironically the offensive language used by some Jews to describe their non-Jewish neighbours (Mt 15:26) and inverted by Paul, evil workmen speaks for itself and rather than speaking here about circumcision speaks (this time offensive to Jews) of mutilation. There also might be an allusion, which could be recognised by Gentiles, to Cynic-style itinerant preachers who were pejoratively referred to as 'dogs' (Greek, *kunes).

Thus, this opening warning is formed in both rhetorical and ironical terms. The difficulty is to know to whom Paul is referring given that his problems in Philippi were connected with the non-Jewish civic authorities (Acts 16:19-40) and the presence of Jews in Philippi was either small or non-existent (see the discussion about the existence of a synagogue in Philippi in Section 2). It might be concluded, therefore, that between Paul's initial evangelistic ministry and the composition of Philippians Jewish-Christian teachers arrived in the city from outside.

Paul's answer to these false teachers is to make claims both for the Christian community (3:3) and for himself (3:4-6). Given the irony over word-play between mutilation and circumcision Paul declares that the community are the 'true circumcision' (3:2), the fulfilment of God's promises to Israel (Gal 6:16). This fulfilment is manifested by: (i) spiritual worship; (ii) glorifying in Christ Jesus (cf. 2:10) and (iii) having no need for circumcision given that, by implication, entry into this renewed community is through Baptism (Gal 3:27-28; Acts 16:33).

Paul's personal claims are listed in 3:5-6 where he recites his Jewish credentials (note also, Gal 1:13-14 and 1 Cor 15:9). Although he can claim to have a better Jewish pedigree (perhaps in the sense of being more observant of the *Torah*) than the false teachers, (Phil 3:4) nevertheless in comparison with his knowledge and faith in 'Christ Jesus my Lord' (3:8; note the Christological position, cf. 2:6-11) this pedigree is rubbish (lit. dung, 3:8). In this context two further Pauline themes are introduced: first, the tension between law (in the sense of *Torah*) and circumcision, and faith (*pistis*) and righteousness (*dikaiosune*). This theme is familiar (in different ways) from Galatians and Romans. In Philippians 3:9 they are personalised. Paul makes them his own both in terms of his understanding of Christianity and as the basis for his own ministry. The second theme relates to his identification with Christ's death and resurrection. This theme is familiar from the Corinthian correspondence. In Philippians 3:10-11 Paul again personalises the theme. On this occasion he hopes to share 'in the resurrection from the dead' (cf. 1 Cor 15:12; 2 Cor 5:1-5), maybe an observation sharpened as a result of his imprisonment and the possibility of death (cf. Phil 1:19-26).

Paul's 'interim' position in relation to salvation is stated in 3:12. Although he once accepted the call (note use in 3:14) of Christ Jesus (cf. 3:7) Paul knows that, as a result of his failure to conform fully to the image of Christ, his salvation has not yet been totally consummated. He has not yet obtained God's ultimate perfection. Rather (as in 1 Cor 9:24-27) he describes his Christian pilgrimage in terms of an athletic metaphor of a race to be won and a prize (3:14) to be obtained. These perceptions, however, are extended by Paul to include the Philippian community. They are: (i) to rely on God's revelation in this regard (3:15) and (ii) to imitate the apostolic example which they have been given (3:17; cf. 1 Thess 1:6; 1 Cor 4:16 and 11:1).

The context of this injunction is provided by those who have not imitated the apostolic example and who, as a result, are 'enemies of the cross of Christ' (Phil 3:18). Paul is here using very stern language or, to extend the athletic metaphor, regards these enemies as running on the wrong track. It is unlikely that this group are the same as the Jewish teachers mentioned in 3:2. More likely the group referred to in 3:18 held a hedonistic philosophy similar to that mentioned in 1 Corinthians 15:32. Yet the effect of this Epicurean philosophy upon discipleship is the same. In 1 Corinthians 15:33 Paul says that 'bad company ruins good morals' while, to paraphrase Philippians 3:19, he maintains that 'bad philosophy ruins good theology'. Over-indulgence is an affront to the humility and obedience represented by Christ at the crucifixion (cf. 2:7), while mere earthly reflection is an affront to the theology of resurrection and eternal life. This observation allows Paul to turn the argument of the hedonistic teachers to enhance his own position. First, using political metaphors, he declares that the true home (*politeuma*, citizenship) for Christians is heavenly and that it is from heaven that Jesus Christ as Lord and Saviour will come as Judge (3:20). Thus, it is implied that the ultimate destiny for Christians is not within the Roman Empire nor is their ultimate leader the Emperor; rather the Christian 'homeland' is heaven and their Saviour is Jesus, to whom all cosmic worship is due (2:10). Secondly, the over-indulgence of the body in 3:19 is noted in order to illustrate that the lowly, humiliated body (note 1:20) of the Christians will be transformed into the glorious (cf. 3:19; but note 2:11) body of Christ.

As with the preceding part (3:1a), this section concludes with the two-part summary structure of 4:1. First, there is the imperative injunction for the Philippians to stand firm (note also 1:27). This standing firm could refer to persecution from the civic authorities, the various groups of false teachers and, positively, to adherence to the Christian faith as outlined in the letter. Secondly, Paul uses a number of epithets to describe his relationship to the Philippian Christians: love; joy and crown (cf. 1 Thess 2:19-20) all of which signify a situation of deep affection in terms of preaching and living the Gospel.

Paul's call for unity and general injunctions, 4:2-9

The picture of the church described in 4:1 is not without alloy. Paul asks an unnamed companion (4:3) to assist in the resolution of a quarrel between two female members of the Philippian church: Euodia and Syntyche (4:2). In giving this request a further glimpse (cf. 1:1) is provided into the life of the church as it illustrates a corporate ministry between men and women in a context in which Clement (a Roman name) and other co-workers (4:2) are recognised. Their ministry is also given a heavenly dimension given that their names are written 'in the book of life' (4:3), a conventional expression which recognises their eternal destiny (note Rev 3:5). Into this appeal Paul adds a series of general injunctions and statements. These relate to rejoicing (4:4; a common theme in Philippians, note the various uses in 1:18; 1:19; 2:28; 3:1 and 4:10); forbearance, anxiety, and the offering of prayer and thanksgiving to God (4:6; cf. 1:3-5). Their setting is eschatological (4:5b; 'The Lord is at hand', cf. 1 Cor 16:22 for *Maranatha*) and embraced by a liturgical form which offers God's peace and his protective power in keeping the believers linked to the 'mind' of Christ Jesus (4:7; cf. 2:5). In 4:8-9 this offer of God's peace is repeated, together with the injunction for them to imitate Paul (4:9) and to pursue the path of virtue (4:8).

The Philippians gift, 4:10-20

Philippians 4:10-20 provides a series of loosely connected injunctions which continue the theme of rejoicing but in the context of the issue of financial support for Paul during his imprisonment and ministry. Some of the same issues underlie this section as they do in 1 Corinthians 9:1-23 but in another context. The Philippians apparently have contributed already to Paul's work and for this contribution they are thanked. Paul emphasises, however, that he did not seek the gift (4:17) and he affirms that in his apostolic ministry, especially in the context of suffering, imprisonment and the possibility of imminent death, he knows how to face hardship (4:12). Epaphroditus is mentioned as the bringer of the 'gifts' (4:18) emphasising his role as the ministerial envoy who links Paul in his imprisonment to the Philippian community (cf. 2:25-30). These gifts are represented as a sacrificial offering (note the metaphor of religious sacrifice which refers either to Jerusalem Temple sacrifices or those offered in Graeco-Roman temples; in different contexts note the use of this metaphor in Rom 12:1 and 15:16) which God accepts. This section of the letter concludes with the doxology (4:19-20).

Concluding greetings and blessing, 4:21-23

The letter concludes with the traditional greeting which is to be offered to every believer and by all those Christians who are in some way or another sharing in Paul's imprisonment. The reminder of the Imperial setting is given (4:22) which has the effect of bringing the letter full-circle (cf. 1:12-14). It concludes with the grace (4:23).

SECTION 2 – CONTEXT

A. THE ENVIRONMENT

Like Thessalonica, the city of Philippi was situated on the Via Egnatia which assisted in the ease of communication between the port of Neapolis on the coastline of the Aegean Sea and the Adriatic. In 360 BC Greek colonists from the island of Thasos settled on the site of what later became known as Philippi. Threatened by local tribes, in 356 the Thasians requested the military and political assistance of Philip II of Macedonia (father of Alexander the Great) who conquered the territory, fortifying the city and renaming it Philippi in his own honour. He constructed new city walls, populated it with his own Macedonian mercenaries and exploited its local resources.

These resources were two fold: agricultural and mining, chiefly silver and gold. This commerce greatly increased the city's economic potential.

The city gained further prominence by being the location of the battle of Philippi in 42 BC between the armies of Octavian (later the Emperor Augustus), Mark Antony and Brutus and Cassius which occurred as a result of the civil war emanating from the assassination of Julius Caesar in Rome in 44 BC. The supremacy of Octavian (defeating Brutus and Cassius at Philippi and later Mark Antony at Actium in 31 BC) ensured that Philippi became a Roman colonial city, being populated by Roman army veterans. The citizens were granted, by the Emperor Augustus, political, legal and property rights, with the city's civic administration being based on that found at Rome. For Luke, Philippi was both 'the leading city of Macedonia and a Roman colony' (Acts 16:12; site details, *BSGT,* 103-110). This fact explains why the inhabitants were composed both of native Greeks and a newer Roman population mainly of Italian origin. This observation also explains why the believers mentioned by Paul in his letter have either Greek names (Epaphroditus 2:25, 4:18; Euodia and Syntyche 4:2) or, in one case, a Latin one (Clement 4:3).

What is more uncertain is the place of Judaism within Philippi at the time of Paul's arrival. According to Luke, Paul and his apostolic company ('we', Acts 16:12) shared in Jewish, Sabbath day worship, mainly with the women who gathered by the river for prayer (Acts 16:13). Although this evidence would seem to imply that the Jewish presence was minimal given that Philippi seemed to be without a synagogue (Hooker, *CCStP*, 105) this need not necessarily have been the case. A grave marble inscription (from the third century AD) has been discovered, however, which makes reference to the city's synagogue (*BSGT,* 102) which would indicate that, at a later date, the Jewish population expanded and the building of a synagogue became necessary. It would appear, therefore, that the majority of converts from Paul's initial evangelistic campaign were Gentiles and that (as I have indicated with reference to Phil 3:1b-7) his Jewish, or Jewish Christian, opponents mentioned came from outside Philippi, either from

Thessalonica (1 Thess 2:14-16), Galatia (Gal 3:1) or Judaea (Gal 2:12-13).

B. PHILIPPI WITHIN PAUL'S MISSIONARY ACTIVITY

The context for the apostolic mission to Philippi is placed by Luke within Paul's second missionary journey (see Map 3). Paul and his apostolic company arrive in Macedonia as a result of the divine call to evangelise in this province given at Troas (Acts 16:9-10). After arriving at the port of Neapolis (Acts 16:11) they travel the ten miles to Philippi (Acts 16:12). Luke highlights three incidents within the Philippian mission:

First, the conversion of the 'God-fearer', Lydia, a native of Thyatira in Asia Minor (note at a later date, the establishment of the Christian community in that city, Rev 1:11; 2:18-28). She was engaged in the purple cloth dyeing trade (purple clothes were considered to be a luxury item and worn by the Roman elite) who responded, with her household, to the Christian Gospel and, in recognition of their conversion, were baptised (Acts 16:14-15). It can be supposed that Lydia and her family were reasonably wealthy, and that their house was of sufficient size, for Lydia to be able to offer hospitality to the apostolic company. It is likely that the Philippian church community developed from Lydia's household and that their financial position ensured that they were able to support Paul continually in his apostolic activities (Phil 4:14-20, both at Thessalonica and later in prison).

Secondly, Paul is instrumental in the healing of a slave girl. In this activity Luke: (i) sees Paul following the earlier exorcism ministry of Jesus (Acts 16:18-19; e.g. Lk 9:37-43); (ii) compares the ineffectiveness of local exorcisms with the new divine power offered in the name of Jesus (Acts 16:16-18) and (iii) uses the incident for members of the local community to bring charges against Paul and Silas and, as a result, to indicate the relationship between the Christian Gospel and the Roman legal and political system. This intention lies at the heart of Luke's presentation of Christianity and its perceived role within Roman civic society.

Thirdly, Luke presents a long narrative (Acts 16:19-40)

relating to the illegal treatment of Paul and Silas at the hands of the Philippian magistrates and their subsequent apology and request for them to leave the city (Acts 16:39). At the heart of this discussion the status of Paul and Silas as Roman citizens (Acts 16:37-38) is raised, a theme which is of importance for Luke with regard to the troubles of Paul in Jerusalem (Acts 22:22-29) and his subsequent appeal to Caesar. Luke is anxious to (i) provide for his readers details of the Roman legal system (Acts 16:19-24 and 35-39) and (ii) to imply that this system is basically just (Acts 16:35).

Luke records a further visit to Philippi during Paul's third missionary journey (see Map 4). On this occasion the apostolic company divided, with some of them (including Timothy) going on ahead by land to Troas (Acts 20:4-5) while 'we' (Paul and the narrator of Acts) remained at Philippi for the 'days of Unleavened Bread' (Acts 20:6, including the Passover). By this comment Luke presents the reader with a puzzle. Why should Paul be concerned about the Jewish festival of Unleavened Bread in a Christian community which was largely Gentile? Equally, how can the circumstances which Paul has outlined in his letter to the Philippians be related to Luke's narration in Acts? Whatever answers can be given to these questions it is clear that the church in Philippi flourished, as demonstrated by Polycarp's letter to the church written in the mid second century.

TO PHILEMON

SECTION 1 – STRUCTURE

1-7   Opening greetings and thanksgiving

8-20   Body of the letter
- Appeal to Philemon to welcome back his slave Onesimus into his household.
- Report of Onesimus' service to Paul while in prison.

21-25   Concluding request, greetings and blessing.

186

B. LINES OF ARGUMENT

Opening greetings, 1-3

Paul writes as a prisoner (also 10 and 13). Timothy, as elsewhere, (Phil 1:1; Col 1:1 also 2 Cor 1:1; for both Timothy and Silvanus note 1 Thess 1:1 and 2 Thess 1:1) is the co-author. Although often seen as a personal letter from Paul to Philemon, the remainder of the text being in the first person singular and, according to the mores of the time, Philemon, as Onesimus' master, has sole authority in the execution of Paul's request; nevertheless, there is a Christian corporality about the letter. Not only is Timothy part of the authorship and others of Paul's company join in sending greetings (23-24) but the letter clearly involves the leadership and members of Philemon's house church. Philemon is described as Paul's 'beloved fellow worker' (*sunergos*, a familiar Pauline theme for sharing the ministry, e.g. Phil 2:25; 4:3; Philem 24). Philemon shares the ministry with Apphia (maybe his wife?), with Archippus (also Col 4:17; either a soldier in the actual or metaphorical sense), and with their church membership. The nature of Philemon's response to Paul will have serious implications both for the theological and social life of the church. The greeting of grace and peace from God and Jesus follows the usual pattern found in other Pauline letters.

Paul's thanksgiving for Philemon's support, 4-7

As is usual in Greek letters of this type Paul lists the reason why he is able to show gratitude to Philemon. The difference here is that the thanksgiving is Christological and ministerial. Paul's thanksgiving and prayerful support for Philemon are based on his 'love' and 'faith' which he has demonstrated 'towards the Lord Jesus' (5) and, by implication, to all believers. Philemon's faith is also orientated in mission, promoting the knowledge which is experienced in Christ (6). In addition to being a fellow worker (1) Paul considers Philemon to be a 'brother' (7; 20) which cements a close ministerial relationship in the work of the Gospel and in the upbuilding (lit. refreshing) of the Church. It is clear that Paul is communicating with a person whom he knew well.

The body of the letter, 8-20

The question raised is: on what grounds is Paul able to speak to Philemon on the future of Onesimus? Within this question there is a tension. On one hand Paul considers that he has the authority to command (8); on the other, it is out of love that he makes his appeal (9). There is a tension also over Paul's present status. He claims to be an elder (*presbutes*, 9, perhaps used here in the sense of an old man? *RSV* trans. ambassador, see 2 Cor 5:20); in actuality he is a prisoner. Thus any appeal to Philemon must take into account Paul's position. In a sense this position heightens the ministerial bond which Paul and Philemon have forged.

The appeal concerns Onesimus (10, Col 4:9). As the body of the letter unfolds more of the circumstances relating to Onesimus' separation from Philemon becomes clear. What is not certain is, if Onesimus was escaping from Philemon's service, how was it that he reached Paul in prison? The answer to this question is difficult to answer; what is known is that Onesimus has become an effective servant to Paul who has taken on the role of 'father' (10). It could have been that Paul was instrumental in Onesimus' conversion to Christianity. He is now Paul's child (11).

Onesimus' effectiveness becomes the subject of a wordplay on his name (*oninemi*, 20) between effectiveness (*euchrestos*) to Paul's benefit, but previously being ineffective (*achrestos*) in Philemon's service (11). Yet probably for both legal and pastoral reasons Onesimus must be returned to his lawful master (12) although Paul would have preferred that he remained in his service (13). Paul's appeal is based on Onesimus' future permanent residence in Philemon's (church) household (15).

Between leaving and returning, however, Onesimus' status has changed. Socially he remains a slave (*doulos*), ecclesiologically he is a believer (a beloved brother, 16) sharing in the Christian religious status as Philemon and the other members of the church. The tension between these two aspects of 'status' is Paul's request that Onesimus be received by Philemon for work ('in the flesh') but also as a believer ('in the Lord', 16).

An aspect of the circumstances by which Onesimus left (escaped?) originally are then revealed: he owed or had stolen Philemon's money which Paul now offers to repay (18). The letter, being written in Paul's own handwriting from prison, emphasises the seriousness with which he understands this particular personal/pastoral problem (cf. Gal 6:11). On this basis Paul believes that Philemon should submit to his apostolic authority by granting his request (19, cf. 8). Yet this authority is based on their common service of Christ and the Gospel and represents the true foundation on which any request can be made and answered (20, cf. 9).

Concluding request, greetings and blessing, 21-25

Is Paul's concluding request to Philemon to allow Onesimus his freedom (cf. 1 Cor 7:21-24)? Does the tension between social slavery – freedom and Christological slavery – freedom lie behind this statement? (21). Perhaps surprisingly Paul now changes the subject. He is hopeful of his release and requests a guest-room to be prepared for him (22).

A list of personal greetings follows from:

- Epaphras (23- also a prisoner; Col 1:7-8; 4:12-13)
- Mark (24, Col 4:10)
- Aristarchus (24, Col 4:10)
- Demas and Luke (24, Col 4:14) described, like Philemon (1), as Paul's fellow workers (*sunergoi*). I shall add further details relating to the activity of these Church members when 2 Timothy 4:9-14 is discussed. The letter concludes with the Grace.

SECTION 2 – PHILEMON WITHIN PAUL'S MISSIONARY ACTIVITY

As the list of names which Paul has recorded in Philemon 23-24 has parallels with those mentioned in Colossians

4:10-17 and that Archippus, Epaphras and Onesimus came from Colossae, it is not unreasonable to suppose that Philemon's house church was located in Colossae or in a nearby location in the Lycus valley. This linking of the two letters has produced difficulties. If Philemon was written at the same time as Colossians what does this assumption say about the date of composition in relation to the fact that some interpreters argue that Colossians is a 'post-Pauline' letter? Equally if the Ephesian prison context is accepted (1) that assumption would mean that Philemon was written c.54-56. This Ephesian hypothesis, it is claimed, has the value of close proximity: Ephesus and Colossae being 120 miles apart thus making Paul's desire to visit Philemon shortly (Philem 22) more feasible. Most of these ideas, however, are speculative as is also the view that the Philemon – Onesimus saga had a 'happy ending' and that, as a freed slave, Onesimus became at a later date in early second century, Bishop of Ephesus.

TO THE COLOSSIANS

SECTION 1 – STRUCTURE

A. OUTLINE

1:1-2	Opening greeting
1:3–2:6	How to understand Church, Christ and the apostolic ministry
2:8-3:4	False teaching and the Colossian response,
3:5-4:6	Living the way of the Gospel, Ethically,
4:7-18	Closing pastoral information and greetings,

B. LINES OF ARGUMENT

Opening greeting, 1:1-2

The opening greeting found in the letter to the Colossians is similar to that found in Paul's earlier letters. Like 2 Corinthians 1:1 Paul describes himself as an 'apostle' whose call to this ministry is based upon God's call and is issued in accordance with his will. Timothy, described as 'the brother', is again associated with the composition of the letter. Although addressed to the Christian community in Colossae it is clear that the contents of the letter are to be linked to the neighbouring churches of Laodicea (2:1; 4:13; 4:16) and Hierapolis (4:13). God's blessings of grace and peace are offered.

How to understand Church, Christ and the apostolic ministry, 1:3-2:6

With 1:3 the literary style found in earlier letters alters with the development of longer sentences, 1:3-1:8 being one continuous sentence. This technique gives the idea of a 'flowing' rather than a 'step-by-step' argued narrative. Thus, thanksgiving to God for the churches' faith and love leads to the assurance of the hope of the heavenly inheritance (later, 3:1-4) which, in turn, is the result of the churches' fidelity, known throughout 'all the world' (1:6). Into this framework is placed the ministry of Epaphras (later, 4:12; also Philem 23) whose ministry Paul describes both in terms of the metaphor of slavery (fellow-slave, Col 1:7; note also Phil 1:1) and that of service (*diakonos*, Col 1:7, qualified by the adjective, faithful). Like Tychicus (cf. Col 4:7), Epaphras had been commissioned by Paul to undertake evangelistic ministry in the Lycus valley, most likely from Ephesus. In Epaphras' case, however, he was imprisoned with Paul (Col 4:12-13; Philem 23) and therefore the on-going strengthening of the churches had to be undertaken by Tychicus and others.

The next long sentence runs from 1:9-20. Within it is included Paul's prayer for the believers together with a rhymic structure which includes thanksgiving for the work of God (1:12-13) and a statement relating to the activity of the 'Son' (1:14-20) in connection with creation and salvation. The 'flow' of the literary structure ensures that the various aspects of the theology represented are to be 'read' as being part of a unified framework. The initial prayer (1:9-11) is concerned with the profundity of the Christian experience and the full knowledge and the totality of the spirit-filled wisdom (*sophia*) of God which is offered. The tension and ambiguity of these concepts of knowledge and wisdom found, for example, in 1 Corinthians (e.g. 1 Cor 8:1-8:11, for knowledge; 1 Cor 2:12-13, for wisdom) is not found here in Colossians. Instead the hearers are directed to the biblical wisdom tradition where the recognition of God's loving activity is the true source for the recognition of divine wisdom. As with that tradition so in Colossians the hearers are exhorted to live ethically by walking in the Lord's path (Col 1:10) and being open to the reception of spiritual growth given as a result of the divine empowering (1:11) which manifests itself in the believers through their endurance, long suffering, joy and the offering of thanksgiving to God (1:11). The 'flow' of the narrative is provided by the use of the participle form 'giving thanks' (1:12) which leads forward to the theological statement concerning God's activity. This activity is allied to the narrative by means of *hos*, 'who', followed by a description of that activity (1:13; cf. Phil 2:6 in relation to Christ; who, *hos*, being in the form of God...). God's activity concerns salvation: the journey from darkness (1:13) into light (1:12). The language of kingdom or reign (first used in Paul at 1 Thess 2:12 where it refers to God's kingdom; note also, Col 4:11 used here in terms of the ministry) is used to describe this transfer into the dominion of the 'beloved Son' (note the use of 'Sonship Christology'; see, for example, Gal 4:4 and Ps 2:7). The extent to which this transfer involved conflict with civic society is difficult to evaluate. What is certain, however, is that Christian belief involved adherence to a new set of theological (e.g. 2:2-4) and ethical (3:5-11) values. The implications of this Christology for the believers are then noted. For them 'redemption' (*apolutrosis*; cf. 1 Cor 1:30; Rom 3:24 and 8:23) and forgiveness of sins (1:14, the forgiveness idea found only here and in Eph 1:7 in the Pauline literature) are offered through the activity of Christ.

This Christological activity is, in turn, described by the formulation of a second *hos* (who) clause (1:15) which unites this description into the totality of the narrative. The description contains inter-related statements which affirm who the Son is, what he has achieved in terms of salvation for humanity and how this salvation operates.

The first theme relates to creation and image (1:15-17). This theme unites incarnation and creation within God's plan. Incarnationally the Son bears the image (1:15; *eikon*, note the diverse applications of this notion, 1 Cor 11:7; 15:49; Rom 8:29 and Col 3:10) of the invisible God. The background to this idea is found in Genesis 1:26-27 with humanity being created in the image (*eikon*) of God. In Colossians 1:15 it is implied that the 'beloved Son' (1:13) remained in the image of God in terms of his total obedience, whereas humanity at large had disobeyed God, sharing in Adam's sinfulness (Gen 3:17-19; note also, Rom 5:15-17). Prior to the incarnation, however, the Son shared in the totality of the Father's work of creation (1:16). Yet this created work and the continual renewal of creation remains part of the Son's ministry within the Godhead, now based upon the Son's glorification which ensures that, for all eternity, the Son is able to cohere creation together in a single unity (1:17). The background to this idea is the figure of wisdom as portrayed in biblical wisdom literature (e.g. Wis 7:26). In the Christian era, however, this wisdom tradition had to be recast. First, the ancient biblical figure of wisdom was feminine. In Christian theology, and in order to describe Jesus' ministry Christologically, the attributes of this earlier wisdom figure were transferred to, and reinterpreted in accordance with, the masculine person of the Son. Secondly, the creation of wisdom was seen as one of the first of God's activities (Prov 8:22). In Christian thought, however, the Father and Son remained eternally united, a view found in the liturgical structures of both Philippians and Colossians: Christ Jesus always being 'in the form of God' (Phil 2:6) and the Son sharing with God in the work of creation (Col 1:16). The value of the biblical wisdom tradition is that it unites Christology and ethics: the categories of wisdom inform perceptions of Christ's ministry, while the truly wise in the ways of God will always 'walk' according to his will (e.g. Col 3:5-17).

The second theme relates to church and reconciliation (1:18-20). Given that the themes in Colossians 1:15-20 overlap, their binding force is provided by the concept of the first-born (*prototokos*) Son. This concept is an ancient biblical one (e.g. Gen 17:15-21; 22:1-19; 25:25-26; texts which provide much interpretative potential) which gives the first-born son both primacy in rank and dignity and offers the familial and legal basis for inheritance and continuity. Christologically, for the Son, this first-born status is related (i) to creation and (ii) to resurrection. He is:

    (i)   the first-born of all creation (1:15) and
    (ii) the first-born from the dead (1:18).

Thus the resurrection can be seen as the 'new creation' into which believers might now enter as 'first-born' because they can be conformed to the 'image' (*eikon*) of the Son (Rom 8:29). In Colossians, this relationship between the Son and the believers, provides the Son with the status of the headship (*kephale*, 1:18) over the believers who are conceived of as the assembly (*ekklesia*) and the body (*soma*) of God's faithful in Christ, a community which is entered liturgically through Baptism (2:12). These civic metaphors for the Christian community of the new Israel of God (Gal 6:16) would have been familiar given Paul's earlier use of them (e.g. 1 Cor 12:27-28). What is new, however, in Colossians (1:18; 2:10; 2:19) and Ephesians (Eph 1:22; 4:15; also note 1 Pet 2:7) is the application of Christ's headship over, and above, this community of believers which is conceived of, in the first instance, in universal rather than in local terms.

Recourse to the Wisdom Christology found within the theme of 1:15-17 is maintained by the use of beginning or origin language (*arche*, 1:18) which is applied in order to provide a further statement relating to the Son's primary status within the Godhead. This status is amplified by the utilisation of 'fullness' language (*pleroma*, 1:19; 2:9; also note Eph 1:23; 4:13). The use of 'fullness' in relation to Christ seems to be a feature of Colossians and Ephesians whereas Paul's earlier use (Rom 15:29) is concerned with his missionary activity in which the fullness of Christ's blessing is to be found. The origin of the Christological use of 'fullness' is difficult to determine. As a basket could be overflowing with the collected fragments of bread (e.g. Mt 14:20; 15:37) so, using the idea metaphorically, Christ is filled completely with the being of God (Col 1:19; see a later use in Jn 1:16). The implications for salvation of this 'fullness' are two fold. First, the saving work of the Son has brought reconciliation to the entire universe. This language extends, in one direction – that of cosmic salvation, the reconciliation statements found in 2 Corinthians 5:16-21 which concentrate on God as the initiator of reconciliation and of the Pauline ministry in terms of this reconciliation. Secondly, the idea is presented that the crucifixion has the effect of bringing the whole universe back into the orbit of peace with God (Col 1:20).

Two further points need to be made in relation to this section. First, as with Philippians 2:6-11, I have avoided the use of 'hymn' to describe their structure, given that hymns are viewed in a particular way in contemporary Church worship (see any hymn book). Rather, I have spoken of liturgical, rhymic structures. These structures were developing in various ways within the churches (e.g. Col 3:16), sometimes in short statements (e.g. 1 Cor 16:22) or in longer forms based on the Jewish psalms (e.g. Lk 1:46-55). In each case these structures should be interpreted within the particular contexts in which they are now found in the New Testament. Secondly, when Colossians 1:15 (or 13?)-20 is compared with Philippians 2:6-11 it is clear that, within the various churches – in this case Philippi and Colossae, the one act of the saving work of Jesus Christ was interpreted in various directions with recourse, for example, to either Adam (in Phil 2) or wisdom (in Col 1). What is clear is the interpretative Christological possibilities relating to the texts were numerous and, as a result, the theological creativity emerging from them was both exciting and inspirational.

As with the situation in Philippi, the Colossians liturgical structure is embedded within its context. The Colossians are reminded of their former, pre-Christian life and of the new ethical requirements which Christian belief demands (Col 1:21-22, cf. 1:13). Emphasis is placed upon continuing pilgrimage within the faith, a context in which Paul identifies himself (1:23). This identification provides the opportunity for Paul to expand, first in general terms, upon his ministerial vocation. This vocation, as before (cf. 1 Cor 4:8-13), is linked to Christ's sufferings (1:24) and thus identifies Paul's ministry with that of the crucified Christ (cf. 1:20). In Colossians, however, the ministry (both of Christ and of Paul) is perceived in terms of providing for the stability of the ecclesial community (1:24; for the body metaphor cf. 1:18). This stability, however, should not distract from Paul's evangelistic calling to bring Christ to 'the nations' (1:27; cf. Gal 1:16). The message, which was known to God from the beginning in terms of mystery (*musterion*, probably best understood as 'sacrament': outward activity which demonstrates the inner working of God), has now been revealed in the person of Christ (1:27). Paul's task is to act as a servant (*diakonos*, 1:25) to him and his message, acting as a steward (1:25; note household language) of God in terms of preaching, teaching and wisdom (1:28; cf. 1:9) for the purpose of offering spiritual maturity in Christ (1:28).

In Colossians 2:1-5 Paul relates these general observations to the specific circumstances in Colossae and Laodicea. In this context, unlike his situation in Galatia and Corinth, Paul is not thinking of 'personal contact ministry' (2:1 and 2:5; this work has been undertaken by Epaphras, 1:7; and Tychicus, 4:7) but of offering a 'spiritual message' from prison which relates to the Christian pilgrimage in terms of the mystery of God's action in Christ (2:3-4). Coupled with Paul's intention in this regard is to offer encouragement to the Colossians to remain steadfast (2:5) in faith and to ensure that the churches are in good order (2:5, both military metaphors). Colossians 2:6-7 form a summary of the argument and the themes presented in the letter so far: walking in the way of Christ theologically and ethically; being rooted, built up and confirmed in faith and, supremely, offering thanksgiving to God for his mercies (cf. 1:12).

False teaching and the Colossian response, 2:8-3:4

This section is prepared by Paul's statement that no one should beguile the believers 'with persuasive speech' (2:4). It would appear that Paul is providing a warning against the persuasive rhetoric presented by those who offer intellectual arguments (philosophy, 2:8) against the portrait of Christianity given by Paul and his fellow ministers. This observation, however, raises considerable difficulties. First, there is the issue relating to the nature of this 'empty deceit'. Clearly one aspect of it is connected with Judaism given the references to 'circumcision' (2:11 and 2:13) and the 'sabbath' (2:16). The reference to philosophy (2:8), however, indicates that Jewish thought and practice is being interpreted against a wider Greek intellectual framework. The reference to the 'worship of angels' (2:18, note Stuckenbruck, CCStP, 120, for the translation of the verse) is not clear. Is reference being made to an aspect of Jewish theology where angels are considered to be intermediary messengers between God and humanity or is Paul complaining about the identification of the worship of the Risen Christ (3:1-4) with that of the cosmic deities found within the cultic practices related to the various mystery religions prominent in Graeco-Roman cities? It is also likely that an ascetic element was also involved, given the references to food (2:16) and the mortification of the body (2:20-23). If there is uncertainty as to the nature of the 'empty deceit' (2:8) so also is the identity of those (2:18, 'let no one disqualify you...') who advanced this teaching and religious practice equally doubtful. The most that can be said is that this form of Christianity represents a synthesis between aspects of Judaism, contemporary philosophical insights ('elemental spirits', 2:20), ascetic practices and the worship of Jesus as Christ.

Secondly, throughout 2:8-3:4, Paul reminds the Colossians of how Christian theology and practice ought to be understood. Entry into 'the Body' (2:9; cf. 1:18) is through Baptism not circumcision (2:12; note Gal 3:27-28 and 5:2; 6:12). Salvation, with forgiveness and the restoration of a right relationship with God, comes through Christ's death (Col 2:14; cf. 1:20), as a result of which, the cosmic powers have been 'disarmed' (2:15; with military metaphors and the question in 2:20 relating to 'elemental spirits'). The section concludes with statements relating to Christ's glorification (3:1; allusion to Ps 110:1) and to his future return (3:4). Into this picture of his cosmic triumph and authority (cf. 2:15 and note 1:16) the Colossian believers are placed. They are: (i) to model themselves on this heavenly perspective (3:1) and (ii) to share in the effects of Christ's death (3:2 and baptismal implications in 2:12) in order that, through their thoughts and actions, the totality of God's saving action through the work of Christ might be known (cf. 1:13-14 and 2:6-7).

Thirdly, although the situation in Colossae has resonance with that in Galatia (e.g. compare Col 2:11-12 and 3:11 with Gal 3:27-28; 5:2 and 6:11-16), nevertheless the contexts are different. In Galatia Paul has deep personal involvement: his apostolic authority has been challenged (e.g. Gal 1:1-2; 1:10). His dispute with the Judaizers concerned the fundamental issues of law (in the sense of *Torah*), justification, grace, faith and entry into the new covenant relationship with God in Christ (e.g. Gal 3:10-14). Paul's arguments abound with quotations from scripture. In Colossae, however, his involvement is, it seems, at a distance (e.g. Col 2:1), his scriptural allusions are less obvious and the nature of the so called false teaching is much less precise. Another difficulty relates to the dating of Colossians. If the letter is to be considered to have been written by a disciple of Paul (Horgan, *NJBC*, 877) in c. AD 75-80 (after Colossae partly recovered from the earthquake of 60) then the question emerges as to the forms of Jewish synthetic religion which existed in Asia Minor after the destruction of the Temple in 70 and their possible effect upon the Pauline interpretation of theology. In dealing with the intellectual and pastoral problems in Colossae we are left with a certain vagueness and considerable uncertainty. If with the Judaizing theology in Galatia Paul was confronted by solid opposition then it would appear that with the synthetic theology in Colossae Paul, or the Pauline writer, the confrontation was with religious systems which were far less substantial.

Living the way of the Gospel, ethically, 3:5-4:6

In presenting the way that Christians should live ethically Paul returns to his method of listing vices and virtues (e.g. Gal 5:19-21, vices; 5:22-23, virtues). In Colossians the vices listed in 3:5 and 3:8 should be compared with the virtues found in 3:12. These lists were conventional in Greek ethical thinking but here (as also with the household codes, 3:18-4:1) this conventional morality has been placed in both a theological and Christological framework. Believers are to shun vices because the practice of them will incur the wrath of God (3:6). Vices belong to the old life (3:9; cf. 1:13-14) while, in the new Christian life, the image of the Creator (3:10; Gen 1:26) is renewed across ethnic, religious and social boundaries (3:11). In this process the totality of Christ's Lordship and universal, cosmic action is again stressed (3:11; cf. 1:15-20).

It is within the Christological framework, therefore, that the virtues are to be understood and demonstrated (3:12). In this context two metaphors are used, both linked with Baptism (3:12). First, there is the idea of clothing. The effects of the baptismal life are that the believers are clothed in Christ's garments manifested by faith and the practice of the virtues. Secondly, the believers have been called and chosen by God (noun, *eklektos*, 3:12). Both in its noun and verb form this concept is a frequent one in the Pauline literature. Originally connected to God's choice of Israel as his chosen people the concept is now transferred to embrace all (cf. 3:11) Christian believers. The particular characteristics of this Christian body (cf. 1:18) are now listed: forbearance, forgiveness, love and harmony (3:14). An insight into Christian worship is now offered (3:16) in which many of the features enunciated already in the letter are summarised: the community as the body (3:15; cf. 2:19 and 1:18) which lives in unity and the all-embracing power of Christ within and above the community through the offering of his peace (3:15), his word and wisdom (3:16; cf. 2:2-4). The 'name of the Lord Jesus' is to be evoked (3:17; note also Phil 2:10) with the effect of offering thanksgiving to God (3:17; a continual theme in the letter beginning at 1:3). In Colossians, Christology is both all-embracing and multi-faceted, in which both traditional and new emphases are to be found; for example, Christ as bearing God's fullness in bodily form (2:9) and Christ as God's Son (1:13) and as the bringer of his wisdom (2:3; also 1:9; 1:28; 2:23; 3:16; 4:5). Yet it must be stressed that this Christology is not 'mere theory'.

It is imperative that Christ's gifts are manifested both in the worship and theological perceptions which the churches have about themselves and in the ethical positions which ought to be seen in the lives of the believers.

Colossians 3:18-4:1 contain household codes of behaviour in terms of the reciprocal relationships between wives – husbands; children – parents; slaves – masters. The ethical issues relating to these codes will be discussed in Section 3. In the meanwhile it should be noted that: (i) in literary terms they have not been integrated into the argument of the letter given that the text could be read straight from 3:17 to 4:2 without them, as the sections 3:12-17 and 4:2-6 concern injunctions relating to Christian conduct and can be read together. Colossians 3:18-4:1 represent a conventional ethical code which has been Christianised. (ii) This text is proposed by the expression in 3:17, 'and whatever you (the believers) do, in word and deed…', thus worship (3:16) – 'in word' is united to 'deed' which includes appropriate behaviour within the Christian household which should act as an example to wider society (cf. 1:10).

Colossians 4:2 returns to the themes of 3:12-17: worship and prayer (3:16) and thanksgiving (3:17) into which Paul includes his particular circumstances (4:3-4; cf. 1:23). His present imprisonment is recalled (implied in 1:24) as is prayer for the apostles ('us', twice in 4:3; they are praying for them, 1:9) which the churches are requested to offer. The object of their prayer is evangelistic: the continued declaration of the mystery (cf. 1:27-28) of Christ. Colossians 4:5-6 returns to general imperative injunctions for believers in relation to outsiders (4:5; Christians as an example) which includes their manner of speech which should (using the metaphor of salt) always be communicated with grace (4:6; note another use of *charis*).

Closing pastoral information and greetings, 4:7-18

Pastoral information about individuals, groups and situations given at the conclusion of Pauline letters (cf. Rom 16:1-16; 1 Cor 16:15-20; Philem 23 and 24) are important as they offer insights into the scope of the Pauline mission, the Pauline representatives involved in it and the 'networking' between Paul, the Pauline tradition, represented by his subsequent followers and the churches. These closing greetings should be seen also in conjunction with the opening greetings of each letter which frequently reveal co-authorship. This study should help to mitigate against the impression that Paul was an inspired individualist. While, on occasions, he does attempt to justify his personal claims (e.g. note the use of the first person singular in Gal 1 and 2), often against opposition (e.g. Gal 3:1; Phil 3:2), nevertheless considerable emphasis is placed on the corporate nature of his missionary activity.

The pastoral greetings found in Colossians (4:7-17) should be compared with those found previously in Philemon (23 and 24). In the Colossian greeting emphasis is placed on the ministries of Tychicus (4:7-8, also Acts 20:4; Eph 6:21 and later, 2 Tim 4:12 and Titus 3:12), Epaphras (4:12-13; cf. 1:7; also, Philem 23) and Onesimus (4:9; cf. Philem 10), although in his case no personal details are given other than hints about his particular circumstances (Philem 8-21).

The other points of interest related to greetings sent to the churches are: (i) Mark (Col 4:10; Philem 24); is the reader to assume that he has been reconciled to Paul (cf. Acts 15:37-39)? (ii) Like Saul-Paul (Acts 13:9) both the Jewish and Graeco-Roman names are given for Jesus-Justus, whose Jewish origin is emphasised (Col 4:11). Why he (and Mark) are described as 'men of the circumcision' (4:11) is less clear. Does this expression describe their background or their particular 'Judaeo-Christian' stance within theology? (iii) Aristarchus (Philem 24; also Acts 19:29; 20:4; 27:2); Luke (Philem 24; later, 2 Tim 4:11) and Demas (Philem 24; later, 2 Tim 4:10) also seem to have been associated with Paul's imprisonment as well as sharing in his ministry.

However the phrase 'men of the circumcision' is to be interpreted and, taken together with the other Graeco-Roman names, it is clear that those involved in the Pauline mission came from a variety of social, ethnic and religious backgrounds. In addition there is the issue of gender. The church in Laodicea, to whom Paul sends greetings, seems to have met in the house of Nympha (4:15). It is uncertain as to whether Nympha should be considered as either male or female (details, Murphy-O'Connor, *OBC*, 1198). If female, then it would infer that the Laodicean church was led by a woman which raises, in turn, Paul's attitude (and that of the Pauline tradition) to issues of gender within the ministerial life of the churches (e.g. note also, 1 Cor 14:33b –36; Rom 16:1-2; Phil 4:2-3 and later, 1 Tim 2:11-12). Again, as in other areas of Pauline practice, there appears to be some variability, and perhaps ambiguity, of approach, not merely to wives in relationship to their husbands, but also to their 'role' in church life and, by implication, even within their civic communities.

The letter concludes with: (i) the injunction of a shared ministry and a shared reading of the letter between the churches (Col 4:13 and 4:16), and (ii) with the encouragement (perhaps admonition?) to Archippus to fulfil the ministry that he has received from 'the Lord' (4:17). Paul says that he has written this greeting with his own hand (4:18). Although he uses secretaries (Rom 16:22) it is clear that his purpose here, and elsewhere (2 Thess 3:17; Gal 6:11; 1 Cor 16:21 and Philem 19) is to authenticate, and to give authority to, the contents of the letter. The question raised for contemporary readers is what does this statement say about the debate over the authorship of the letter: Paul or a later disciple?

The final statements request (i) prayer for Paul in his imprisonment (see Section 3) and, (ii) as is usual, the offer of the Grace (4:18).

SECTION 2 – CONTEXT

A. THE ENVIRONMENT

Little of ancient Colossae remains. The site of the city was discovered by W.J. Hamilton in 1835 but still awaits major archaeological excavation. Colossae is situated near the Lycus river and in the fifth and fourth centuries BC was regarded as one of the leading cities of the area (details, *BSGT,* 172-174). This prominence was due both to its flourishing wool industry, Colossae being important for the purple coloured wool which was produced locally (rivalling Laodicea's black wool), and to its geographical location on the trade route which linked the river Euphrates to the Aegean Sea. In the Greek and Roman periods, however, Colossae's status was eclipsed by superior development of the neighbouring cities of Laodicea and Hierapolis due to them being favoured by the Seleucid rulers. In AD 60 a major earthquake struck the area. Although the cities of Laodicea (*BSGT,* 235-240) and Hierapolis (*BSGT,* 210-217, now a world heritage site) were rebuilt, Colossae never recovered fully from the destruction and in the ninth century was abandoned finally. Josephus records that in 213 BC Antiochus III settled 2,000 Jewish families from Mesopotamia into the Lycus valley region with the purpose of increasing trade and commerce (details, Murphy-O'Connor, *OBC,* 1191). This migration ensured that a reasonable Jewish presence could be found in the area.

B. COLOSSAE WITHIN PAUL'S MISSIONARY ACTIVITY

Paul had not visited Colossae when he wrote the letter. The evangelisation of the area had been undertaken by Epaphras, who was a native of the city (Col 4:12-13) and who acted on Paul's authority. This evangelisation may have been envisaged by Paul as an extension of his Ephesian ministry into Asia (Acts 19:26). This missionary activity also concerned the cities of Laodicea (2:1; 4:13; 4:15; 4:16) and Hierapolis (4:13). As a result, these three churches ought to be seen as being engaged in an apostolic and ministerial partnership represented by the shared reading of the one letter. As noted when the letter to Philemon was discussed, the slave Onesimus also came from Colossae (Col 4:9) and it is likely that Philemon's house church was situated in the same area. As Paul requested that Philemon prepare a guest room for him on his release from prison (Philem 22) it is likely that Paul intended to visit the Lycus valley churches on that occasion. Eventually the Colossian church declined in line with the general disintegration of the city following the earthquake while the churches of Laodicea (Rev 1:11; 3:14-22) and Hierapolis (Papias, c. 60-130 was bishop there in the second century) remained strong.

TO THE EPHESIANS

SECTION 1 – STRUCTURE

A. OUTLINE

1:1-2	Opening address and greeting
1:3-3:21	Theological exposition – God's plan revealed and accomplished in Christ
4:1-6:20	Ethical exposition: Living through Christ in society
6:21-24	Concluding information and blessing

B. LINES OF ARGUMENT

Opening address and greeting, 1:1-2

I have considered already the textual difficulties relating to the phrase 'in Ephesus' and to the issues which these difficulties raise for the destination of the letter and its authorship. In other ways Ephesians 1:1-2 follows a structure similar to the opening addresses found in other Pauline letters. In Ephesians Paul's single authorship is stressed together with his apostolic role in accordance with God's will together with the status of his readers who are declared to be saints (also 1 Cor 1:1 and Rom 1:1) reflecting the sanctity of God and being faithful (also Col 1:2) in God's service (Eph 1:1). The offering of grace and peace follow: divine gifts which emanate from God, addressed traditionally as 'our Father' (note Mt 6:9), and Jesus who is given his Christological titles as 'Lord' (see 1 Cor 12:30) and 'Christ' (Eph 1:2; also note 1 Thess 1:1).

Theological exposition, 1:3-3:21

As is clear from the structure outline of the text Ephesians falls into two clear parts: Theological exposition, 1:3-3:21, and Ethical exposition, 4:1-6:20.

Naturally these parts inter-relate and are not mutually exclusive, yet it is the author's intention to demonstrate clearly that, with regard to Christian faith, its ethics derive from its theology and that the basis for understanding this arrangement is Christology. This position explains why the body of the letter begins with (what is now) an eleven verse single sentence blessing in praise of God's action in terms of what Christ has achieved and what, in turn, the believers can achieve through the ministry of the Holy Spirit. The literary method of the single sentence reveals theologically the 'flow' of the narrative of salvation and the inter-connectedness of the different parts of it. The over-arching framework is provided by the theological concept of declaring God as 'Blessed' (*eulogetos*; see use in Rom 1:25, in the NT used only in relation to God; note Mk 14:61) who, in turn, has blessed us (the believers) with the totality of Christ's heavenly blessings and salvation. The form of 'Blessing God' liturgical structures was already familiar within Judaism; in Ephesians, however, this Jewish form is transformed by the author's Christological understanding. Using the term 'liturgical' here highlights the point that the three liturgical passages in the Prison Letters: (i) Philippians 2:6-11; (ii) Colossians 1:13/15-20 and (iii) Ephesians 1:3-14, take different forms.

In my judgement 'The Blessing' of Ephesians 1:3-14 is best explained in terms of an 'antiphonic dialogue' between (i) what God offers in Christ in terms of blessing and (ii) the blessings which the believers are able to receive as a result of this offer. This 'dialogue' is represented by the following diagram (implicit divine blessings placed in brackets):

Antiphonic Dialogue (through Christ): Ephesians 1:3-14

Ephesians	God, Father	Lord Jesus Christ	Saints/Faithful
	(I) Divine gifts	Mediated in/through Christ	(II) Human receipt and response
1:3a	**Blessed**	(blessed) in Christ	**Blessed** **Blessed be God!**
1:3b-4	(Holy) residing in *Heavenly places*	(chosen) in Christ	Holy and blameless In presence of God Chosen before foundation of the *world*
1:5-6	Divine will/purpose (Grace)	(in love) through Christ (bestowed) in his Beloved	Destined in love to be sons of God Praise his glorious **Grace!**
1:7-8	**Grace**	in him, through his blood	Redemption Forgiveness **Grace**
1:9-10	Made known Mystery of Divine Will Things in *heaven*	(set forth) in Christ (united) in Christ	Wisdom Insight Things on *earth*
1:11-12	Divine Purpose (Glory)	(destined and appointed) in Christ	Hope in Christ Live for the praise of God's **Glory**
1:13-14	(Glory) (residing in Heavenly places)	(sealed) in Christ	The word of truth/Gospel Holy Spirit Heavenly inheritance Praise God's Glory

One way of understanding 1:3-14 is by analysing the way in which the two prepositions 'in' and 'through' are used.

'In' is found in:

1:3 'in the heavenly places...in Christ'; 1:4. 'in him'; 1:5. 'in love';

1:6 'in the Beloved'; 1:7 'in whom';

1:9 'in him'; 1:10. 'in the Christ'; 1:10. 'in him'.

1:11 'in whom and...'; 1:12. 'in the Christ'; 1:13. 'in whom and...' (twice).

'Through' is found in:

1:5 'through Jesus Christ';

1:7 'through his blood'.

The language of 'in' describes both the mystical union between Christ and the believers which God has initiated and also locates the source of this union *in* the heavenly realms (1:3). Being *in* Christ means that freedom (redemption, 1:7; also 1:14; cf. Rom 3:24) can be obtained. 1:11-14 adds the extra elements (by including 'and') that can be obtained through this 'in' status: first, election (1:11) and secondly, sealing by the Holy Spirit (1:13). The thought form of 2 Corinthians 1:22 is used to illustrate that believers receive a guarantee (1:14) of the promised inheritance through the activity of the Spirit.

The language of 'through' describes the process by which the totality of this activity occurs. It is through the saving activity of Christ, his crucifixion (1:7) and glorification (1:3), that redemption becomes a possibility which is accompanied by the manifold blessings which are offered including the wisdom and understanding to perceive the mystery of the totality of God's plan and will (1:8-9). This over-arching vision, however, is focussed in Christology. The author's model is the rhetorical one of summing up or recapitulating an argument at the end of a speech. This sense of the concept is used in Rom 13:9 where Paul summarises the *Torah* commandments which describe the modes of conduct which God declared ought to be found amongst the Israelites (Ex 20:13-17). By 'summarising' these commandments with the phrase 'You shall love your neighbour as yourself' (note also, Mt 19:19) Paul demonstrates the maxim by which the Roman Christians are to behave towards each other. In Ephesians this 'summarising' concept has been transformed. It is Christ who now 'heads up', 'summarises' or 'recapitulates', not the argument of a speech, but the entire universe (1:10). He is portrayed in cosmic terms as fulfilling God's eternal plan (1:4) for the inclusion of all humanity into God's redemptive promised inheritance (1:14).

If Ephesians 1:3-14 states the overall theological framework in which Christian experience is to be placed then 1:15-23 (again, as 1:3-14, a single sentence) should be interpreted as including the ministerial activity of Paul into this framework and of being its natural outcome (note the use of 'therefore', which begins the section at 1:15). Paul's ministry is expressed initially in the form of a prayer (1:16) which develops into a theological statement centred upon Christ's saving work. The basis for this prayer is twofold: (i) the faith which the readers have shown 'in the Lord Jesus' and (ii) the love which they have demonstrated to other believers (cf. 1:1, note the use of these virtues in 1 Cor 13:13). This conduct is the cause of Paul's thanksgiving and prayers for them (1:16) in which intercession is made to God that they be open to receive more of his wisdom (1:17; cf. 1:8-9) and the revelation of his knowledge (see Col 1:10). This wisdom and knowledge occur on the basis of the readers' heavenly enlightenment. In this area there is a tension between what the believers received (1:8-9; perhaps through Baptism, note 4:5) and what they are still capable of receiving (1:17); thus preserving the 'Pauline tension' between 'the now' and the 'not yet' (e.g. note Rom 6:5). Here, in Ephesians 1:16-19, many of the same concepts are used which have occurred already in 1:3-14; for example, glory (1:18; cf. 1:6 and 1:14) and inheritance (1:18; cf. 1:14), states of life into which the believers have been called (1:18). The purpose of reflecting upon the lives of the believers is in order to demonstrate the magnitude of God's activity towards them. This activity is centred in the work of Christ, illustrated by the series of Christological affirmations which follow. These affirmations (1:20-23), included in the context by the use of the relative pronoun 'which' (1:20), relate to: (i) Christ's resurrection and glorification; (ii) his universal Lordship (note Phil 2:9-11; based on Ps 110:1); (iii) the naming of Christ in worship (note Phil 2:10) is the means by which earth is joined to heaven; (iv) the entire universal order has been subjected to Christ (based on Ps 8:6, also Col 2:10); (v) the purpose of Christ's headship (note Col 1:18) is for the sake of the entire believing community, the Church (here conceived of in universal terms) and (vi) two other features about the Church are added; first it is conceived as Christ's body (1:23; note the 'body language' in the remainder of the letter: 2:16; 3:6; 4:4; 4:12; 4:16 [twice] 5:23; 5:29; 5:30; also, 1 Cor 12:12-13 and Col 1:18). Secondly, as if to explain further the notion of the Church as Christ's body, the concept of his fullness is used which radiates from the body filling the whole universe.

What has been said about the mystical union between Christ and the community of believers (into which Paul's ministry is incorporated) places great responsibility upon both the thinking and the activity of the Christian adherents. In the two sections of chapter 2 (2:1-10 and 2:11-20) the author attempts to analyse both the status and the ministry of Christians in terms of God's call and activity and to describe the union of all humanity (both Jews and Gentiles) in this renewed community of faith.

Ephesians 2:1-3 highlights the features of their pre-Christian existence in terms of their sinfulness (2:1); following the path of Satan, one of the demonic forces which existed immediately above the earth (2:2) and their unethical living (2:3). For the author this existence is part of the 'natural' (2:3) state of humanity which makes them 'children of wrath'. As a result of this understanding of human nature the emphasis upon the saving activity of God is all the greater. His activity is narrated in terms of riches, mercy, love, new life, grace and salvation (2:4-5). Into this narrative, once again (cf. 1:20-23), the work of Christ is placed. A series of Christological affirmations follow (2:5-6) which begin with the declaration of God's action which ensures that the believers share with Christ corporately in the divine life which is received through his ministry of salvation. The corporate nature of this Christology is continued with the expressing of the believers sharing with Christ in his resurrection and glorification (2:6; cf. 1:20-21). This affirmation develops into the continuation of this saving experience for future generations thus giving the Church future continuity (2:7). The Pauline 'theology of salvation' is reiterated by the use of the traditional concepts of grace, faith and gift (2:8). Also, the negative, 'no salvation by works' (2:9) is affirmed. Although the thought of Galatians 2:16 may be behind this affirmation, in Ephesians, the 'works' probably refers to the believers' former Gentile life (cf. 2:1-3 and 2:8, 'not of your doing') rather than the 'works of the law'. Nevertheless the Pauline notion of self-confidence or boasting (2:9; cf. Rom 2:17 and 2:23 [for Jews] and the general use, Rom 3:27) in relation to 'salvation by works' is retained with the implication that salvation can be received only on the basis of faith, grace and gift (cf. 2:8). In Ephesians 2:10 a series of new ideas is introduced: first, the believers are God's workmanship (see also Rom 1:20 for general use of this creation concept), created by him in Christ. Secondly, taking up the 'works theme' of 2:9, this creation is for the purpose of the believers' living ethically in the way of God. Thirdly, in line with God's creative activity, this state of life was prepared previously by him (note 1:4).

Ephesians 2:11-20 uncovers further the origin and nature of the community into which the believers have been called. What for them was difficult to achieve through Judaism is now made possible through the body (2:16), the Church. In this context the author restates the elements which previously prevented Gentiles from entering God's covenant (2:12): not being circumcised – the physical sign of entry into the covenant (Gal 6:12-13; Gen 17:10) – and, on this basis, being alienated from God's chosen nation, Israel. The net result for non-Jews was hopelessness and permanent separation from God.

Following the structure of 2:1-10; 2:11-12 presents a picture of despair while 2:13 (cf. 2:4) emphatically demonstrates the Christological position. There follows a list of what God has achieved through Christ: strangers (2:12) are now included within the covenant; Jews and Gentiles are now unified; salvation through 'the old law' is abandoned, a new ethical code of 'walking with God' is now in its place; access to the Father is through the work of Spirit (2:18) and all believers (both Jews and Gentiles) are equal members within the family of God (2:19). This new situation results from Christ's saving death by crucifixion (2:13 and 2:16; also note Phil 2:8). The embodiment of this new situation, however, is ecclesiological which can be interpreted only Christologically. Thus, this new situation is explained by the metaphor of a building structure. Apostles and prophets form the ministerial foundation of it but they, in turn, have been called by Christ. The building metaphor is continued when Christ is described as its cornerstone (2:20) without which stone the building would collapse. Three other ideas are included within this metaphoric approach. First, the building 'develops': its structure is dynamic rather than static. Secondly, the building is conceived of in terms of temple. Either this is a reference to one of the numerous temples founded in a Graeco-Roman city or, in my judgement more likely, a reminiscence of the Jerusalem Temple (note Isa 6:13) where God's presence was thought to dwell (see 1 Kings 8:27-30, for the 'tension' between heaven and earth). Within the Church, therefore, God's presence is encountered as it was previously in the Temple. Thirdly, the believers are themselves the temple (2:21; cf. 1 Cor 3:16-17) because the Spirit dwells in them. Believers are corporately God's temple because the Spirit dwells within the community and, as such, they are afforded access proleptically to the heavenly temple as a result of being 'in Christ' (Eph 1:3 and 2:6).

Three further points need to be made in this context. First, the building metaphor is one of several by which the author describes the Church and Christians, the others being; for example, the bride (5:23-33) and the body (beginning at 1:23). These metaphors must be seen collectively as representing the Church, its believers, and their relationship to Christ. Secondly, the author has an overwhelming desire to present the unity, the oneness (note 2:16; 3:6; 4:4) of the Church, perhaps presenting an ideal to which all ought to aim. Thirdly, although based on biblical images, a sense of 'newness' pervades his understanding: the Church being a 'new person' designed to accommodate a 'new humanity'.

In Ephesians 3 (note that 3:1-12 is a single sentence) Paul again (cf. 1:15-16) places his personal ministry within the broader framework of the redemptive action of God in Christ. Having mentioned the ministry of 'the apostles and prophets' in terms of their foundational role within the Church (2:20) he casts his own role (now as a prisoner, 3:1) and ministerial identity in similar terms (3:5; for prophecy and prophets note 1 Cor 12:10 and 14:5).

The first item relates to Paul's ministerial 'status' (3:1-6). Using the conditional (if, 3:2) Paul restates that the gift of ministry offered to him occurred as a result of the grace given through God's revelation (note Gal 1:16). Did his readers doubt this fact, or were they ignorant of it (cf. the conditional, 3:2)? Whatever is the case it is not clear as to the precise reason as to why the basis of Paul's ministry apparently needs to be justified (3:4). The purpose of his ministry is to communicate how the Gentiles (you, the readers, 3:1) have become joint-heirs, in a corporate body and sharing in the same Christological promise as, by implication, the Jews.

The second item relates to the form of Paul's ministry (3:7-13; note his role as minister/servant, *diakonos*, 3:7). The connecting link between revelation and ministry is the Gospel (3:6 and 3:7) which Paul has been commissioned to proclaim. This Gospel, as enunciated here, concerns: (i) the bringing of 'the unsearchable riches of Christ' (3:8, cf. 2:7) to the Gentiles; (ii) the revealing of God's hidden plan through his creative activity (3:9, cf. 1:10); (iii) through the Church, God's cosmic wisdom and activity is made known (3:10, cf. 1:23) and (iv) the total focus of this activity is realised in the person and ministry of 'Christ Jesus our Lord' (3:11). This focus is seen in terms of 'access' to the Father thus reviving the Temple metaphor of 1:21. Two further points about Paul's ministry should be noted. First, he declares himself to be 'the very least of all the saints' (3:8). This statement represents a variant on Paul's earlier declaration that he is 'the least of the apostles' (1 Cor 15:9). Being the 'least' is explained on the grounds that Paul had persecuted the 'Christian group' within Judaism (also Gal 1:13). In Ephesians this background is assumed but, like Galatians and 1 Corinthians, Paul's subsequent ministry is explained by him in terms of 'grace' (3:8). Secondly, the suffering which Paul is enduring in prison is for the sake of the believers. It illustrates his exhortation that they are not to lose heart (3:13) which restates the Pauline theme in 2 Corinthians 4:16 where, the directive not to lose heart, is allied both to the identification with Jesus' suffering (2 Cor 4:10-11) and with the hope of eternal glory (4:17).

The injunction not to lose heart becomes the entry point into Paul's prayer of worship to the Father (Eph 3:14). This personal stance then develops into a series of theological statements about God's activity in which Paul includes intercessory prayers for his readers. The declaration is that every familial institution (3:15; cf. the household image of 2:19) is included within God's cosmic orbit and, on this basis, the inner self can be strengthened through the work of the Spirit and the indwelling of Christ. In this context the 'love theme' is introduced which should be the hallmark of the believers (1:15; 3:17; 4:2; 4:15; 4:16; 5:2; 6:23) as it is dependent upon the love offered by God (1:4; 6:23) and which is an attribute of Christ (3:19; 5:2; note here the juxtaposition of 'love', 3:17 [believers]; 3:19 [Christ]). This 'inner reflection', however, must be seen alongside the panoramic cosmic vision which Christian belief represents (3:18). To aid the understanding of this vision familiar themes are utilised: knowledge (3:19; cf. 1:17, later at 4:13; also, Col 1:9-10; 2:2 and 3:10) and fullness (3:19; cf. 1:10 and 1:23; also, Col 1:19 and 2:9). All the time, however, this visionary scheme is theological and Christological, it concerns God's action in Christ. On this basis the first part of the letter concludes with the Doxology (3:20-21). Its theme is the overwhelming, eternal abundant work of God within the Church, the purpose of which, by implication, is the salvation of all humanity through Christ as mediated through the apostolic and prophetic proclamation of the Gospel (e.g. 3:8). The Semitic affirmation 'Amen' (note also; e.g. Gal 1:5 and 6:18; 1 Cor 16:24; 2 Cor 1:20; Amen can form a conclusion or express an important affirmation part-way through a letter) concludes the section. This doxology illustrates how Pauline letters were received in a liturgical context and played a part in the Church's teaching ministry within the framework of its worship (Eph 4:19; Col 3:16). This worship would have been perceived as part of the cosmological vision in which God offered Christ's fullness (Eph 1:23). The believers, in their turn, would be able to share in the heavenly vision of, and in the mystical union with, the exalted Christ (1:17) which the prayer found in 3:14-21 summarises. Such visionary experience is featured also in both Jewish and Graeco-Roman revelatory and mystical literature which, in turn, would have imparted divine knowledge (1:17; 4:13; note also, Col 1:9-10; 2:2 and 3:10).

Ethical exposition, 4:1-6:20

The section of ethical exposition is linked to the previous section by means of a personal reminder as to Paul's state as a 'prisoner for the Lord' (4:1; cf. 3:1) which here is used as the basis for Paul's ethical injunctions to the readers. They are 'to walk' (also 4:17; 5:2; 5:8 and 5:15) in the way of the Lord. This metaphor is a fundamental tenet of Jewish ethics. It is used here to demonstrate how believers ought to live ethically and, in turn, this 'walking' metaphor is adapted to include Baptism which includes the necessity of living in terms of the baptismal faith existence (note 4:4-5). In answer to the issue as to what 'walking in the Lord' means, Paul lists a series of virtues (4:2) in the context of the maintenance of unity. This unity is provided by the Spirit (4:3 and 4:4). In a passage similar to that found previously in 1 Corinthians 12:12-13 the focus of this unity is provided by reference to Baptism, faith and theology; ultimately unity can be seen as a characteristic of God's nature which radiates throughout the universe (4:6). The Christological focus ('one Lord', 4:5) is introduced in terms of grace (4:7) which is measured by the various ministerial gifts (later in 4:11) which are offered to believers by Christ (4:7).

First, however, the author presents a Christological pattern related to Christ's glorification and triumph here seen in terms of ascension (4:9; note also Acts 1:9), justified on the biblical basis of Psalm 68:18. This reference was interpreted in Judaism either as the victorious Davidic King returning to Jerusalem or Moses ascending Mount Sinai to receive the *Torah*. In either case there is a statement about God's saving power being manifested to his people Israel. Yet talk of ascension presupposes descent. But what does descent 'into the lower part of the earth' (4:9) mean in this context? Could it have a similar meaning to the phrase used in 1 Peter 3:19 that after his crucifixion and burial Christ 'preached to the Spirits in prison', in Hades beneath the earth? Or is the reference incarnational, expressing in different language the thought of Philippians 2:6-7 that Christ 'emptied himself taking the form of a slave?' Whatever the case, the Christological progression operates in the same way: Christ's descent, ascent, the giving of grace and the gift of ministry.

Secondly, and the basis of Christology, a list of the different ministries is presented (4:11) with an emphasis upon the issue of unity. As before this ministerial list is based on that found in 1 Corinthians 12:28. The single sentence which forms Ephesians 4:8-16 interlocks both the (i) purpose, (ii) function and (iii) timescale of these ministries.

4:12 Purpose

1. To equip the believers for their ministerial work;
2. To build up the body (a concept which unites the two parts of Ephesians) of the faithful in Christ.

4:13 Timescale

1. Until unity of faith;
2. Knowledge of Christ's Sonship;
3. Maturity is reached, perfected manhood which equals the perfected person of Christ.

4:14 Function

To avoid false teaching and teachers.

4:15-16 Purpose again, for the believers

1. To develop into Christ's headship (Col 2:19) and

2. The continued integration of Christ's body (cf. 1 Cor 12:14-26) accompanied by the themes of 'up building' and love.

In Ephesians 4 the timescale presented emphasises the movement towards maturity and perfection while much of the earlier eschatological language is omitted.

Ephesians 4:17 returns to ethical exposition which is continued until 6:9. In the first section, 4:17-24 (again a single sentence) Paul counsels his readers to consider the contrast between the 'old' and the 'new' way both of thinking about ethics and living ethically. This clear division is represented by 4:20 with its forceful statement, 'But you have not so learned Christ'.

The 'old life' is characterised by a failure to walk (used twice in 4:17) in the ways of God. The notion of 'the Gentiles' returns to the meaning given in 2:11 and illustrates Jewish obligations to 'the nations' who do not follow God's precepts (4:18). These obligations include mental vanity which, in turn, is demonstrated by intellectual darkness (cf. 1:18) and alienation (cf. 2:19) from God's life. These states of life are seen by the practice of vice, lewdness, uncleanness and greed (4:19) see also Galatians 5:19-21; 1 Corinthians 5:10-11; 6:9-10; Romans 1:29-31 and Colossians 3:5; 3:8. Such vice lists, however, are not specially Jewish; they are also found in Graeco-Roman ethical discourses, particularly Stoic sources (details, Harvey, *CNT*, 620-1). It could be that the theological background to the division between the 'old' and the 'new' life is to be found in the Adam/Christ contrast found in earlier letters (cf. 1 Cor 15:22 and Rom 5:12-17).

The 'new life' is Christocentric and illustrated by the metaphor of clothing (for baptismal implications, Col 2:12 and 3:12). The 'old life' is to be abandoned, like old clothes (4:22) and the new, Christological clothes to be worn instead (4:24). The former language of mental activity is transferred to the 'new life', seen in the process of spiritual renewal and identification with the life of God concerning righteousness and holiness.

Building upon these general ethical maxims, Ephesians 4:25-32 contains a series of injunctions designed to address specific areas of behaviour. Given that the passage contains sentences of shorter length than those used before it is possible that the author is using existing Christian, perhaps Pauline, ethical tradition. This tradition can be tabulated as follows:

Ephesians

4:25 the need for truthful speech (2 Cor 6:7) with regard to apostolic ministry;

4:26 injunction against anger (Gal 5:20; 2 Cor 12:20; Col 3:8);

4:28a injunction against stealing (Ex 20:15-16; Deut 5:16-20);

4:28b the need for honest work (1 Thess 4:11);

4:29 injunction regarding graceful speech rather than evil talk (Col 3:8).

These specific maxims are placed within a theological framework provided by reference to God's creative and renewing Holy Spirit, which unethical behaviour 'grieves' (4:30) and to whom is given the role of 'sealing' (2 Cor 1:22; Eph 1:13) the believers for the promised eschatological day of redemption. This assurance provides the basis for a return to the types of behaviour by which the 'old' and the 'new' life are characterised: on one hand bitterness, anger, wrath, blasphemy and the evil vices of the 'old' life; but on the other, for the believers (you, 4:32) the virtues of tender heartedness and forgiveness. The presence of this virtue of forgiveness is again theologically based on God's forgiveness which the believers have received through Christ (4:32, Col 3:13; Mt 6:14-15).

Ephesians 5:1-2 form a 'bridge' section between 4:32 and the next series of ethical injunctions which begin at 5:3. First, there is the imperative that believers should be 'imitators' of God. Paul's earlier 'imitation language' has been used in connection with the apostolic ministry: the Corinthian Christians are to imitate him as he in turn imitates Christ (e.g. 1 Cor 11:1). In Ephesians 5:1 all the believers are commanded to 'imitate' God; first, because the ethical patterns presented are theological ethics and secondly, on the grounds of this proposition the believers are to 'walk' in love. The basis of this injunction is Christological dependent on the self-giving offering of Christ (cf. Gal 1:4) which is seen in terms of a temple sacrificial offering. Once again temple imagery recurs.

The list of vices to be avoided is continued in 5:3-18a, among them immorality, impurity and covetousness (5:3). Thanksgiving (*eucharistia*; cf. 1 Thess 3:9; 1 Cor 14:16; 2 Cor 4:15; 9:11, Phil 4:6; Col 2:7; 4:2) is to replace idle talk (Eph 5:4). Immoral persons will not enter the 'kingdom of Christ and of God' (5:5); cf. 1 Corinthians 6:9-10. This maxim leads to the injunctions that these immoral persons are to be avoided and with it a sharp contrast is made between disobedience (unbelievers) and obedience (believers) and ethics in terms of light and darkness (5:7-14). This dichotomy between light and darkness was a characteristic of the Jewish theology of the 'Two ways' found also in the Qumran community rule and which became a feature of Christian ethics. The contrast between the 'old' and the 'new' of the believers is repeated (5:8; cf. 4:17-24). The behaviour which belongs to darkness will be exposed by God (5:13) and the whole series of injunctions is confirmed by reference to a fragment of an early liturgical structure (5:14, with a possible antecedent in Isa 60:1). This structure is twofold: (i) there is a progression from death to life and from sleep to being awake. This progression might refer to the movement from the 'old' to the 'new' life, a 'faith journey' symbolised by Baptism which, in turn, would equate to 'burial' and then 'resurrection'. (ii) This progression is Christological being provided by Christ who himself offers 'light'.

This liturgical structure provides the foundation for another ethical injunction in terms of 'walking' (5:15a) in which the Jewish wisdom tradition is utilised to demonstrate the dichotomy between wisdom and foolishness (5:15b; 5:17 also note Ps 1:1-6). The eschatological nature of the context (Col 4:5) in which this wisdom/foolishness exists is emphasised (5:17) as is the liturgical context in which its drama is re-enacted (5:19). The thanksgiving theme is renewed (from 5:4) but on this occasion in honour of God and the Father and in the name of 'Our Lord Jesus Christ'. Given the contrast between drunkenness and the spirit-filled proclamation (5:18; note Acts 2:15-20) of Christian worship, drunkenness is condemned (note also Rom 13:13) while the power of Spirit inspired worship is praised as being a vital expression of Christian character. With this observation worship and ethics are combined; both are placed within the power of God's saving activity (cf. 3:14-19).

Ephesians 5:21-6:9 deals with household relationships. I shall be giving detailed consideration to these behavioural codes in Section 3. In the meanwhile it needs to be noted that the author is utilising an existing code (note Col 3:18-4:1) which he has overlaid with its own interpretive structure relating to Christology and ecclesiology (5:32).

Ephesians 6:10-20 offers an interpretation of the Christian life using the metaphor of Roman military armour, each section of which is given theological meaning. This metaphor, however, is given a cosmological interpretation. The warfare is concerned with the cosmic battle in which the believers are involved, 'the spiritual hosts of wickedness' (6:12). A threefold repetition of the injunction 'to stand against them' (6:11; 6:13; 6:14) is demanded. One of the interesting features of this passage is that Christians were content to utilise the imagery of Roman Imperialism and its military power in connection with the exposition of the nature of Christ's 'empire'. Was the appropriation of this metaphor designed to conflict with the Roman military or to assimilate it into Christian thinking?

Reference to the cosmological activity of Christ takes the letter 'full circle', given that the author has said already that Christ inherits the totality of cosmic space (3:18-19) and that it is from the 'heavenly places' that the believers receive Christ's spiritual blessing (1:3). The metaphor of the 'armour' and the 'battle' develops into a series of injunctions to the readers that they should pray in the Spirit (6:18a; cf. 5:18) and make intercession for the universal Church (all the saints; 6:18b; cf. 2:18-19).

Into this scenario Paul's personal circumstances are placed. The readers are to intercede for (i) his life in prison where he remains an apostolic 'ambassador' (6:20) and (ii) that he may continue to proclaim boldly 'the mystery of the Gospel' (6:19; cf. 3:3).

Concluding information and blessing, 6:21-24

The information relating to Tychicus found in 6:21-22 is similar to that related already in Colossians 4:7-8. The purpose of this news is to identify Tychicus with the Pauline mission and for him to act as Paul's ambassador. He is probably to be identified as the bearer of the letter.

The letter concludes with the offer of peace and love from God and Jesus (Eph 6:23) and with the Grace (6:24). In this case the Grace declaration contains two related ideas: (i) it is imparted to 'all the ones loving', that is who share in the love and imitation of God and Jesus and (ii) who love the Lord Jesus Christ in incorruptibility (*en aphtharsia*). The translations which render this expression as 'undying love' miss the powerful resonance produced by seeing the phrase in terms of immortality. To understand this concept we must return to Paul's resurrection discourse in 1 Corinthians (note 1 Cor 15:42; 15:50; 15:53-54) and to the first century BC Jewish wisdom tradition which linked humanity to God's incorruptibility (Wis 2:23 and 6:19). The recipients of the letter are invited to love Christ with the same intensity and with the same eternal perspective in mind. The reference is also Christological given that, throughout the letter, and by implication, the picture of Christ presented is one of incorruptibility.

SECTION 2 – CONTEXT

Given the difficulties relating to the Pauline authorship of Ephesians and lack of precise pastoral details within the letter relating to Ephesus (cf. the question of Eph 1:1) I have decided to deal with contextual issues in the reverse order from what I have done elsewhere. I shall consider first what can be gleaned from Paul and from Luke about the place of Ephesus within Paul's missionary activity and secondly, how our knowledge of ancient Ephesian civic life can assist our perceptions of Paul's (and successive) ministry in that city.

A. EPHESUS WITHIN PAUL'S MISSIONARY ACTIVITY

The fullest account of Paul's Ephesian ministry is given by Luke. Given that Acts 18:19-20:17 (together with the Miletus sermon which follows, 20:18-35 and its aftermath, 20:36-38) is a complex section which sees Paul, not merely in Ephesus, but also engaging in ministry in Macedonia and Achaia, 19:21, it is possible here to offer only a brief summary of significanct aspects of Paul's Ephesian missionary activity as recounted by Luke.

Four prominent features of Paul's Ephesian ministry according to Luke

1. Acts 19:1b-7. The issue of 'Christian' Baptism over against John's Baptism is raised, with regard to the receiving of the Spirit (cf. 1 Cor 14:1-5).

2. Acts 19:8-10. After a three-month ministry in the syngogue disputes occurred. Ministry in the hall of Tyrannus for two years. Ephesus becomes the centre for church activities in Asia (note ministry to Colossae, Laodicea and Hierapolis, Col 4:13).

3. Acts 19:11-20. Paul's ministry of exorcism is portrayed as superior to that of the Jews; Paul is following the example of Jesus (e.g. Lk 8:26-33).

4. Acts 19:23-40. Luke offers a substantial account of the Ephesian riot which occurred in connected with the erosion of the Artemis (Diana) cult revenue caused as a result of Paul's ministry.

Luke's account of Paul's Ephesian ministry offers a retrospective interpretation of its significance (c. 80-85 AD), influenced, in part, by the prominence of Ephesus as a major Christian centre in the latter decades of the first century AD (cf. 1 Tim 1:3, 2 Tim 1:18, 4:12; Rev 1:11, 2:1-7; Johannine literature; Ignatius' letter to Ephesians). Nonetheless, Paul's own references to his ministry in Ephesus suggest opposition (1 Cor 15:32 and 16:8-9; see also the general reference to affliction in

Asia, 2 Cor 1:8). This opposition no doubt came from both Jews and also the native, Graeco-Roman population. Paul's metaphoric reference to 'fighting with beasts' (1 Cor 15:32) in the context of his discourse on resurrection could also have been linked to his conflicts with the city's various religious cults, in particular the civic cult of Artemis. Accordingly, it might be concluded that Luke's portrait of Paul's Ephesian ministry (c. 53-56), reflecting internal and external tensions in the city, is substantially correct. Paul's Ephesian ministry, therefore, provides important insights into the relation of Christianity both to the civic religion which was confronted and to Judaism from which Christianity was emerging (e.g. compare Eph 2:11-22 with Acts 18:24 and 19:8-9).

B. THE ENVIRONMENT

The Ephesian environment offers an important urban context against which the reception or rejection of Paul's message can be appreciated. (For the remains of ancient Ephesus see *BSGT,* 183-207).

The particular features of Ephesus in this regard are: first, its antiquity. The city was apparently founded c. 1100-1000 BC by Ionian Greek colonists led by the Athenian prince, Androclus. These colonists assimilated the worship of the local mother goddess Cybele to that of the Greek goddess, Artemis, known as the virgin hunter with multiple breasts (illustration and information, *BSGT,* 205-6) whom the Romans identified as Diana (*BSGT,* 178).

Secondly, Ephesus developed as a city of considerable historical, political, religious and commercial importance. This importance was enhanced by the presence of a sizable port and by good land communications both north and south and by highways to the east. One of these highways, called 'the common way', was the ancient Persian royal highway which linked Ephesus to the river Euphrates and beyond. Ephesus came under direct Roman rule in 133 BC and, especially in the early Imperial period under Augustus from c. AD 29, the city flourished, evidenced by the increase in prosperity and in its civic importance. By the time Paul arrived in the city

c. AD 52, it acted as the capital of the Roman province of Asia and contained an estimated population of between 225,000 and 250,000 inhabitants. Thus, in status, it was reckoned as the third or fourth city of importance in the Roman Empire behind Rome, Alexandria and perhaps Antioch in Syria.

Thirdly, from the religious perspective, the city housed numerous religious cults which, combined with the other social factors mentioned above, gave Ephesus considerable additional prestige as a centre for religious pilgrimage and for the gathering of sacrificial (including financial) offerings. Three cultic areas need to be mentioned:

I.   Primary among these cults was that of Artemis (Diana), linked to the city's foundation as above, and evidenced by the presence of the Temple of Artemis, or the Artemision, one of the architectural glories of the city (details, *BSGT,* 202). Archaeological research upon this building, together with other parts of the city, was begun by John T. Wood between 1863-74, and continued by the Austrian Archaeological Institute.

While the silversmiths (led by Demetrius, Acts 19:24) objected to Paul's Christian evangelising mission in Ephesus, their grievances were not merely financial. The implied attack on Artemis (Acts 19:28-29) struck at the heart of the city's identity. Artemis was worshipped on account of her primacy over supernatural forces and, as such, was acclaimed as 'saviour', 'heavenly goddess' and 'queen of the universe'. In these roles she offered the city protection, prosperity and 'fertility'.

II. Ephesus was also the regional centre for the Imperial cult. This cult, together with its related temple buildings, was begun by Augustus and developed through the various Julio-Claudian and Flavian Emperors. This cult ensured that the political connection between Ephesus and Rome was maintained. On at least four occasions (the first was probably during Nero's reign as evidenced by the title being found on a coin from the period) Ephesus was given the honorific title of *neokoros* (temple warden) for protecting and advancing the Imperial cult (details, *BSGT,*

179). In return, the city would enjoy the privileges and blessings (also linked with Artemis) which accompanied the honour. Thus, all references to the 'Cosmic Christ' in the literature associated with Ephesus should be seen against this background.

III. In addition there was a multiplicity of other cults linked, for example, to Isis, Dionysius and, in particular, to Hestia Boulaia, goddess of the hearth. This cult was centred upon her temple, the Prytaneion, where the sacred fire in her honour was kept burning constantly (*BSGT,* 187). The Prytaneion also served as the city hall which again illustrates the intrinsic connection between the religious cults and the political organisation and well being of the city.

Fourthly, there is the question of the nature and influence of the Jewish presence in Ephesus. In this context it should be noted that: (i) Paul was recognised by the assembly as a Jew (Acts 19:34); (ii) preached in the synagogue (Acts 19:8), and (iii) it can be presumed that some of his early converts were Jews. Yet no remains of any synagogues have been discovered. Jewish presence is indicated by several inscriptions which identify tombs belonging to Jews and which state that the Jewish community has undertaken care of them. Other evidence relating the presence of Jews in Ephesus is provided by the Jewish historian, Josephus. It is likely that some Jews settled in the city in the third century BC while in the mid first century BC Josephus notes that the Roman authorities allowed Jews exemption from military service and the freedom to practise their religion. There appears to have been hostility to them from the native population from 49 BC to AD 2. After that date relations between Jews and non-Jews were generally harmonious. In Paul's time it can be estimated that roughly 5-10% of the city's population were Jews, c. 25,000.

Two further points need to be made. First, whereas in AD 52 Judaism seems to be able to be accommodated within Ephesian culture, the arrival and development of *Pauline Christianity* (according to Luke) challenged it. Maybe the

Christological emphasis of Paul's message was responsible? As a result, and from different directions, opposition to the Christian Gospel came both from sections of the native population and from Jews. Secondly, this discussion on the context and environment of Paul's Ephesian mission (and its aftermath) provides a rich tapestry against which his activity and literature related to it might be appreciated.

SECTION 3 – THEOLOGICAL, PASTORAL AND HERMENEUTICAL ISSUES

The hermeneutical importance of Paul's letters from prison is that they have set the pattern within Christianity for correspondence from prison especially from those who have been imprisoned unjustly and who have been persecuted under tyrannical and violent regimes. Probably the most well known form of literature in this regard is Dietrich Bonhoeffer's *Letters and Papers from Prison*, yet numerous other examples can be cited. Another fine example is that of Archbishop Francois-Xavier Nguyen Van Thuan who was imprisoned for thirteen years in Vietnam.

From this literature, and in connection with Paul's prison letters, I intend to highlight two features: Christology and Ethics. Those unjustly imprisoned often express their identification with, and dependency upon, Christ. In Paul's prison letters this feature takes the form of the inclusions of liturgical, rhymic structures which express aspects of Christology and were used most likely in the worship (Col 4:16; Eph 6:18b -20) of the churches. In turn identification with Christ teaches Christians how they ought to live. For prisoners like Paul, the pattern set by Christ teaches them how suffering might be endured (e.g. Phil 1:19-26); for Christians who belong to the various churches, Paul exhorts them to allow Christ to model their conduct ethically (e.g. Phil 2:1-5; 12-13; Philem 20; Col 2:6-7; Eph 4:1-3). In this regard I offer the example of Philippians 2:6-11.

CHRISTOLOGY

1. The Liturgical structure in Philippians 2:6-11

I outline this structure as follows (although there are many ways of presenting the structure):

Phil 2:5 Christ Jesus

I. 2:6 who (*hos*) being in the form (*morphe*) of God, did not grasp equality with God

2:7 **but** emptied himself, taking the form of a slave becoming in the likeness of men and being found fashioned as a man.

II. 2:8 He humbled himself becoming obedient to death, the death of a cross

III. 2:9 **Wherefore** also God highly exalted him and gave him the name above every name in order that in the name of Jesus every knee shall bend in heaven and on earth and under the earth and every tongue might acknowledge that Jesus Christ is Lord to (the) glory of God (the) Father.

2. A hermeneutical reflection upon Philippians 2:6-11

It is impossible here to deal with the numerous literary and theological issues related to this text. Instead it is my intention, in the context of prison literature and exhortations from prison, to uncover one aspect of hermeneutical reflection by attempting to illustrate the theological and ethical issues concerned with living in conformity with the pattern of Christ which, I should argue, is the most satisfying and challenging 'good news for today' that we can offer in terms, in particular, of our 'prison context'.

Part I of the structure is concerned with Christ's incarnation. It proclaims that he shares the form of God and is thus identified with his divine nature. The liturgical form which Paul has inherited uses the metaphor of 'grasping' in this regard. Like all metaphors it must be interpreted with care. What I believe is *not* meant is that Christ attempted to steal (or grasp) that which was not really his, rather 'equality with God' was rightly his but, for the sake of humanity and for its salvation (and in obedience with God's will) he emptied himself of this right deciding rather not to lay claim to it. The incarnational form which Christ took was that which is lowest in the human political and social order: being a slave and being bound by the institution of slavery. Paul has already used this metaphor with regard to his apostolic ministry by declaring that he is a slave of Christ (e.g. Phil 1:1), thus illustrating how his ministry aims to be in conformity with that of Christ. The incarnational form means also that Christ entered in the totality of the human condition. Anthropologically this condition is two-fold: humanity sharing the glory of God as a result of being the 'crown' of his creation but, as a result of human disobedience towards God, humanity is scarred by sin. Behind this perception lies the story of the first man, Adam. He was conceived in the divine likeness (Gen 1:26), bearing the divine image but, as a result of disobedience (Gen 3:22-24), became the agent of sin in which all humanity now partakes. Christ's incarnational role has been to reverse Adam's disobedience but his obedience which, in turn, affirms Christ's supremacy over Adam (1 Cor 15:45; Rom 5:15-17), offers divine light in the midst of human darkness. Paul has dealt earlier with this incarnational theme and its implications for humanity (Gal 4:4; 2 Cor 5:21; Rom 8:3) now, in Philippians 2, by utilising an established liturgical structure he illustrates how conformity with Christ means (i) understanding Christ's incarnational pattern and the reasons why this action was necessary and (ii) the reasons why Christians should conform to it. This incarnational pattern also provides the clue as to how the Church should exercise its ministry in the world: identification with humanity in every respect while attempting to bring both to political and social structures and to individuals the light of the Gospel of Christ amidst the darkness.

Part II of the structure summarises the supreme act of Christ's obedient self-offering to the Father (see also Gal 2:20;

3:13; 2 Cor 8:9): 'a death of a cross'. As we have seen Paul, in his letters, dwells frequently on 'the theology of the Cross': the explanation and interpretation of God's action and saving power through the crucifixion of Jesus (e.g. Gal 3:10-14; 1 Cor 2:1-5; Rom 3:21-26). In Philippians 2:8 the crucifixion of Jesus is mentioned without elaboration except that the Philippians are to demonstrate the same humility which he showed (cf. 2:3). This fact is not surprising given the 'summary form' of this liturgical structure. When, in 1 Corinthians 15:3, Paul takes another 'summary form' of the basic confessional facts of Christianity the crucifixion is explained in terms of: (i) the fulfilment of scripture and (ii) on account of human sin. Yet Philippians 2:8 like 1 Corinthians 15:3 makes a historical point upon which theological and ethical reflection might be based: the hearer is returned to the historical event of the crucifixion of Jesus which took place outside the city of Jerusalem c. AD 30. In Philippians 2:8 there is another implication: the identification of those unjustly imprisoned and punished with Christ who was likewise punished unjustly (see 1 Pet 2:18-25). By sharing in the extreme terror of crucifixion Christ identifies himself with the depths of human terror, injustice and despair. Yet there is another layer of meaning which probably occurs here in Paul's writings for the first time: the possible and actual tension between the Christians and the Roman state (Phil 1:13; 19-26; 4:22): the conflict between two ways of interpreting and living the Gospel. Paul is apparently facing this conflict in Rome and wishes to make the Philippian Christians aware of the issue even though they are not experiencing this form of suffering themselves. In this context Paul uses 'political' language by exhorting the Philippians to 'only conduct yourselves as citizens (verb, *politeuomai*, used only here and in Acts 23:1) in a way which is worthy of the Gospel of Christ' (Phil 1:27). It is in this injunction that the irony between Christian discipleship and political obedience lies (see also, Rom 13:1-7). As will become apparent later in Paul's life the conflict between Christ and Caesar emerges in stark terms as a result of the persecution of Christians by Nero. The Roman Christians wished to live as good citizens but, as a result of Nero's policy, they made the ultimate sacrifice. Through martyrdom and unjust suffering they identified themselves with the sacrificial offering of Christ.

These events lie in the future. In the meanwhile Paul is preparing his readers for what might happen by offering through a 'theology of suffering' based on Christ's crucifixion which, in its turn, represented the supreme act of obedience to God's will. These circumstances, however, have symbolic meaning for all righteous sufferers: Christ, through his particular form of suffering death, identifies with all those righteous sufferers who endure similar forms of human terror. This interpretation provides another important aspect to Paul's multi-layered and multi-sided 'theology of the cross'.

Part III of the structure demonstrates the implications (Phil 2:9, wherefore also) of this 'theology of suffering': the 'theology of glory'. The humiliated Christ is now 'highly exalted' (2:9) in terms of exaltation with God, given an exalted name and granted universal Lordship and Messiahship (Phil 2:11). Attributes of God (see Isa 45:23) are now attributed to Christ. The purpose of this exaltation is in order that all humanity are able to worship Jesus (his historical roots are affirmed) as Lord and Christ (2:11). The political perspective is implied through the cosmic totality of this worship: Christ's power is far greater than that of any earthly ruler, including Caesar. The implications of this theology and Christology for Christian believers are two form; first, the exhortation to obedience. Christians, in their theological and ethical conduct, are called to obey God (Phil 2:12). This obedience should be modelled on that of Christ (Phil 2:8; note also Rom 1:5, 'the obedience of faith'). Secondly, there is the promise that Christ will change (note future tense) the believers' 'body of humiliation' to be like the glorious risen and exalted body of Christ (Phil 3:21). This promise is based on Christ's willingness to humble himself even to death (Phil 2:8). As a result of persecution and possible martyrdom Paul, and all Christian believers, can be assured of sharing in Christ's eternal heavenly glory. In this context Paul again uses 'political' language. Not on this occasion of earthly political order (cf.

Phil 1:27) but of a heavenly citizenship (Phil 3:20, *politeuma*, used only here in the NT).

Allegiance to the totality of the pattern of Christ set by the three sections of Philippians 2:6-11, therefore, offers the promise of a 'colony' which is eternal and above and beyond that of existing, earthly, political structures. This promise, however, does not remove Christians from giving political loyalty to the state rather, it affirms that, like Christ (Phil 2:7), the Church must be 'incarnate' in the world by imitating the theological and ethical patterns which Christ has set.

ETHICS

The starting point for considering the ethical aspects of the letters from prison which I have chosen is the study of the independent units of tradition found in Colossians 3:18-4:1 and Ephesians 5:21-6:9. These sections are concerned with ethical conduct within the Christian household and, as such, have been termed 'household codes'. They can be analysed as follows:

Structure & Content	Colossians 3:18-4:1	Ephesians 5:21-6:9
1. Christological foundation Mutual respect to be grounded on reverence for Christ		**'Be subject to one another out of reverence for Christ'** (Eph 5:21)
2. Wives & Husbands	Wives – be subject to husband	Wives – be subject to husband **Husband is the head of his wife, just as Christ is the head of the Church**
	Husbands – love your wife (Col 3:18-19)	Husbands – love your wife **As Christ loves the Church** **Marriage as a profound mystery within the order of creation** (Gen 2:4) (Eph 5:22-33)

3. Children & Parents	Children – obey parents	Children – obey parents **Basis: First Commandment** (Deut 5:16)
	Fathers – do not provoke children (Col 3:20-21)	Fathers – do not provoke children (Eph 6:1-4)
4. Slaves & Masters	Slaves – obey your master in obedience to to the Lord	Slaves – obey your master in obedience to the Lord
	Masters – treat your slaves fairly in obedience to your Master in heaven (Col 3:22-41)	Masters – treat your slaves fairly in obedience to your Master in heaven (Eph 6:5-9)

Given that the household was the first unit of social identity within Graeco-Roman society and that these sections represent a Christian presentation of the rules of household management what is apparent is that Paul, in Colossians, is using an existing ethical code. This code has been utilised in Ephesians with distinctive features added; first, the integration of Christian marriage within a wider Christological and ecclesial order and secondly, a more obvious dependence is placed upon Jewish *Torah* ethics. This dependence can be seen by the author's use of quotations from Genesis 2:24 (in Eph 5:31); Exodus 20:12 (Eph 6:20) and Deuteronomy 5:16 (Eph 6:3). At the same time, because Ephesians is based upon Colossians, a synthesis is produced between Jewish ethics and the conventional ethical patterns found in the writings of Graeco-Roman authors. This latter aspect is revealed in Colossians with its emphasis of behaviour in terms of what is 'fitting' (3:18) or 'pleasing' (3:20), a characteristic of Stoic ethics. Paul, however, develops the Christian aspect of the traditional ethical form by adding (in Col 3:18-4:1) a seven-fold reference to 'the Lord'. From these observations three points emerge:

1. Pauline ethics developed from a careful synthesis of both the established Jewish (*Torah* and wisdom traditions) and Graeco-Roman ethical patterns. Paul had no wish to divorce Christian ethical conduct from society at large

but rather to present a Christian version of conventional ethical mores. In this sense Paul (and the developing Pauline tradition) is not offering new rules for ethical conduct but reinterpreting those rules which exist already in Graeco-Roman society, including their interpretation within Judaism. The key to understanding Paul's ethical reinterpretation is to be found within his Christology: the way in which faith in Christ defines both Christian identity and Christian ethics.

2. Paul's ethics developed from those presented on marriage, for example, in 1 Corinthians 7. His views expressed in that chapter reflect, first, the particular situation within the Corinthian church and secondly, his perspective regarding the end of the world order and the return of Christ in judgement. The understanding of Christian theology within what is considered to be an eclipse of this imminent return (*parousia*) of Christ is very difficult to determine given the problems related to chronology and perception. What is clear is that Christian ethics are in part motivated by the conception of the future coming of God's reign and the promise of the return of the glorified Christ. This eschatology provides a heavenly perspective.

3. Although in the letters from prison a 'prison ethic' is presented, it is also clear that a future for the newly established Christian communities is envisaged. Thus, household codes, desired both for the strengthening of the Christian community and also for continuing involvement of Christians within society, are deemed necessary. In this respect all four letters from prison deal with the concept of slavery. In Philippians Paul declares that Christ took the form of a slave (Phil 2:7) and, on this basis, the Christian ministry is to be conceived in terms of being slaves of Christ Jesus (Paul and Timothy, Phil 1:1; Epaphras, Col 4:12). The household codes of Colossians and Ephesians speak of the 'right' relationship of slaves and masters in terms of obedience from slaves and just treatment from masters (Col 3:22-4:1; Eph 6:59). To

Philemon Paul requests that he receives Onesimus 'no longer as a slave but more than a slave, as a beloved brother' (Philem 16). In this statement the basic tension within early Christianity is revealed. On one hand, Paul declares that all Christians (including both slaves and free men) are 'one in Christ Jesus' (Gal 3:28); on the other, the social conventions between slaves and masters are maintained. While the household codes, for example, provide an important window into different areas of life in Graeco-Roman society; with regard to slavery, however, one important question remains: how did belief in Christ change, modify or refine the relationship between master and slaves given that the basic institution of slavery is unchallenged?

A note on the issue of Pauline authorship

Now that the four Letters from Prison have been considered it is necessary to enlarge upon and summarise the discussion presented in the Introduction to this chapter on the issue of authorship. Scholarly literature on the subject uses the technical concept of **Pseudonymity** (false identity). This concept can appear misleading. What is *not* meant is that subsequent authors within the Pauline tradition were being deceptive. On the contrary they were showing deep respect for Paul and the Pauline tradition helping to project his memory and reinforce and develop his teaching.

In this regard I speculate that Ephesians is part of the Pauline tradition whilst the other Prison Letters represent Paul's own position. This position is based upon an evaluation of specific aspects of the textual data. In the case of Ephesians these aspects concern: (i) uncertainty regarding the destination of the letter; (ii) its literary style and vocabulary and (iii) the theological, Christological and ecclesial features found in the letter. These features point to 'developments' within the Pauline tradition.

It could be argued, therefore, that Colossians demonstrates the transition from the 'age of Paul' into the situation initiated by Paul himself as to how his thought could be interpreted authentically. Colossians probably formed the basis for the post-Pauline writer of Ephesians to begin this literary and theological process (Dunn, *OBC*, 1165).

In the next chapter I shall be considering the Pastoral Letters. With these letters to Timothy and Titus it is apparent that Pauline theology, ethics and ministry are being interpreted in a 'new' context (maybe linked to Ephesus, 1 Tim 1:3 and Crete, Titus 1:5, representing an ecclesiological situation in the 80s) by the use of 'new' (for Paul) linguistic and theological conceptions. Although I remain uncertain as to the placing of 2 Timothy in this regard, I speculate that the author of the Pastoral Letters is reproducing some of Paul's ideas within his own framework and context.

Two further points need to be made. First, I reiterate my argument that the Pauline tradition is an authentic development from Paul himself and the movement between Paul and his tradition should be seen as one primarily of continuity rather than discontinuity. Secondly, a distinction should be made between Paul's letters and his interpreters (see my chapter 7) and in this regard to note that the Pauline tradition reflected in Ephesians and that reflected in the Pastoral Letters are variable. Thus, both in tradition and interpretation, Paul's inspirational approach to theology opened rich veins for new approaches for reflection upon Paul's ideas while remaining faithful to their central core: the delivering of God's free given grace through Christ.

CHAPTER 6

TO TIMOTHY AND TITUS

Paul's two letters to Timothy and his letter to Titus are known generally as the 'Pastoral epistles'. Given that all of Paul's letters can be said to be 'pastoral' the application of this term demonstrates later interpretation regarding their purpose and contents. St Thomas Aquinas (1225-74) referred to 1 Timothy as 'a pastoral rule which the apostle [Paul] committed to Timothy' (quoted by Hultgren, *CCSt.P*, 141). By this description St Thomas may have perceived this letter as a forerunner of Pope Gregory the Great's *Pastoral Rule*: a manual for Christian leaders as to how they were to exercise the Christian ministry. The first use of the term 'pastoral epistles' to describe all three letters has been attributed to Paul Anton (1661-1730) in lectures delivered at Halle in 1726-7. Again the intention is clear: the pastoral epistles are to be used to demonstrate the qualities needed in Church leaders and how they should exercise the ministry of pastoral care (shepherd – sheep metaphor) to Christian congregations.

In my youth these Pastoral letters, or at least sections of them (not the denunciation aspects, e.g. Titus 1:10-16), were seen to be important manuals in relationship to the exercise of the Anglican ministry. During my years working in the field of vocations to the ministry of the Church of England I commended them to prospective ordinands. Incumbents offered them to curates as fine examples of pastoral practice. Newly appointed Bishops were encouraged to imitate the pastoral maxims which they offered. On these grounds the Pastoral epistles were viewed as being quintessentially Anglican. On one hand, they refer to the three-fold Catholic order of ministry: bishops (*episkopoi*, 1 Tim 3:1-7; Titus 1:7-9); elders [later priests], (*presbyteroi*, 1 Tim 5:17-19; Titus1:5), who formed a ministerial council (*presbyterion*, 1 Tim 4:14) and deacons (*diakonoi*, 1 Tim 3:8-13). On the other hand, these ecclesiastical office holders could be married (1 Tim 3:2; Titus 1:6), they were to be moderate in their life style and well behaved (Titus 1:8), good at teaching and management (1 Tim 3:4) and preserve sound teaching (e.g. Titus 1:9); in short, model Anglican clergy. Thus, many of the phrases found in the letters have passed into the prayers and injunctions to be found in the Ordinal of the Book of Common Prayer (Ziesler, *DBI*, 519).

Yet, however worthy these exhortations to pastoral work seemed to be, and whatever might be said about the interpretation of the Pastoral epistles along these lines, the question remains as to the function and purpose of these texts in their original setting. The recovery of this setting is not easy. It is clear that the Pastoral letters were concerned with succession: the handing on of the apostolic ministry of Paul to the next generation symbolised by Timothy and Titus. On Paul's authority Titus was commissioned with the task of appointing new elders (Titus1:5) thus providing a succession of church pastors for future generations. What the Pastoral letters demonstrate is the new context and the new perception in which this 'ministry of succession' occurs.

Before we proceed the following three points need to be noted. First, it should be recognised that the Pastoral letters need not have been written in the order in which they are to be found in the New Testament, 1 Timothy, 2 Timothy and Titus. This canonical order is produced by arranging the letters in descending order of length. It is possible (but not certain) that Titus was written first (Brown, *INT,* 640). Second, given the reasonably close relationship between the letters (2 Tim probably stands somewhat apart) I shall present the structure and lines of argument of each letter in turn in their canonical order and then make observations about the theological, pastoral and hermeneutical issues which they raise at the end. Third, at this stage I am making no judgement about authorship as to whether the letters (or some of them) are Pauline, partly Pauline or post-Pauline. On this basis I shall use the name 'Paul' to describe the author (not 'the Pastor' as does Drury, *OBC*, 1224) of these letters. I believe that it is important, first, to research their structure and the lines of argument which they present before any judgements are made regarding authorship or dates of composition.

1 TIMOTHY

SECTION 1 – STRUCTURE

A. OUTLINE

1:1-2   Opening address and greeting

1:3-20   Paul's instruction to Timothy – introducing the
           main themes of the letter

2:1-3:13   Worship and Leadership in the Church

3:14-4:10 Theological perspective: Household and Creation

4:11-6:2   Teaching for different groups within the Church

6:3-6:19   Summary: false teachers, Timothy's role

B. LINES OF ARGUMENT

Opening address, 1:1-2

As with other Pauline letters 1 Timothy contains an opening
address and greeting. Paul describes himself as usual as an
apostle but affirms that this ministry occurs as the result of
a 'command' from God. This command, a new term in the
Pauline vocabulary, illustrates that Paul is acting under divine
instruction rather than human inclination (cf. Gal 1:1).
Salvation is a basic theme in these letters, especially Titus.
Here, in 1 Timothy 1:1, God is perceived as 'Saviour'. This
language is important both in terms of theology and of the
position of Christianity within the Roman Empire where
the Emperor was viewed as saviour. In this context 'mercy'
is added to those virtues which can be received from God.
Timothy is described as a 'true child in the faith' (1:2), thus
making him a legitimate and worthy successor to Paul in the
apostolic ministry.

Paul's instructions to Timothy, 1:3-20

Paul instructs Timothy to remain in Ephesus now that he is
travelling to Macedonia (Acts 20:1-5). It is likely that Paul

had given him authority over the Ephesian church. With this authority Timothy is to confront what Paul believes to be false teaching. In this confrontation Timothy is to demonstrate love (cf. 1 Cor 13:4-8 and 13) and sincere faith which arises from a good conscience (1:6) which is seen in comparison to the teachers who promote merely 'myths and endless genealogies' (1:4), an expression for useless speculation as used polemically in contemporary philosophical debates. There is also a Jewish element within this false teaching but these teachers do not have sufficient understanding of the interpretation of Jewish *Torah*. Returning to a theme used in different ways in Galatians and Romans (e.g. Gal 4:4 and 5:3; Rom 3:31) Paul argues that the law (*nomos*) is good (1:8) because it offers a moral framework for indicating the nature of immoral behaviour. A list of vices follows (cf. 1 Cor 6:9-10) indicating, not those categories of behaviour where those who practice them will not inherit the kingdom of God (1 Cor 6:10) but modes of conduct which are contrary to sound doctrine (1 Tim 1:10) which is enshrined in God's Gospel (1:11).

Paul illustrates this point by utilising his personal testimony. On the face of it this illustration is strange. Being a zealous Jew (Gal 1:14) it is highly unlikely that he committed the vices which are indicated in 1 Timothy 1:9-10. Rather it appears that he is making a general point about Christ Jesus' redemptive power in offering salvation to sinners (1:15). Paul had blasphemed against God by persecuting the Church (cf. Gal 1:13; 1 Cor 15:9) but, as a result of Christ's divine intervention, Paul was called by grace (1:14) into ministry (1:12). If Christ had given him this opportunity, in the same way those who had committed acts of vice could likewise receive salvation through belief in Christ and receive eternal life (1:16). Of this salvation Paul became a minister as he represents the 'longsuffering' of Jesus Christ which forms a pattern which other sinners might follow (1:16). Paul's reflections on this theme conclude with an acclamation of praise to God which contains the expression 'the King of ages', probably inherited from the synagogue and now becoming a part of Christian liturgy. Here is another example of how Paul has included items used in the Christian worship of the churches to enforce his particular argument (e.g. 1 Cor 8:6; Phil 2:6-11).

Timothy is addressed directly in 1:18 in which three statements are made. First, he is to rely on the Spirit-filled prophetic utterances about which Paul has spoken. These utterances, and the way in which they are to be delivered, have been set out in 1 Corinthians 14:1-5. In the Ephesian church, as in Corinth, this Spirit-filled ministry is designed for the edification of the faithful (1 Cor 14:12). Secondly, Timothy's ministry is to be seen in terms of warfare (Eph 6:10-11) which operates positively, battling for the faith with a good conscience (1 Tim 1:19) and, negatively, in vigorously opposing false teaching and its teachers. Thirdly, in this latter regard, Timothy is warned against Hymenaeus (2 Tim 2:17) and Alexander (as 2 Tim 4:14?) whom Paul has excluded in order that they might learn not to blaspheme (1 Tim 1:20), a state of life in which Paul himself was formerly guilty (cf. 1:13).

Worship and Leadership in the Church, 2:1-3:13

Beginning at 1 Timothy 2:1 Paul places his charge (1:18, cf. 1:5) on Timothy regarding his ministry within the broader context of society within the Roman Imperial world. Prayers should be offered for political leaders because, as a result, the lives of Christians will be peaceable on the grounds that, by such intercession and conduct, they will have demonstrated respect and piety (*eusebeia*, 2:2). I shall discuss this concept more fully in Section 3 as the use of *eusebeia* (taken from Graeco-Roman religious language) influences how the Pastoral letters understand the nature of practising the faith. This perception leads forward to explain how Paul understands here both theology/Christology and his own ministry. At the centre of his theology is salvation which is seen both as a characteristic of God (our Saviour, 2:3) and a state of life into which all humanity are invited to enter. This invitation is made possible through the unique mediatorial role (2:5) of Christ Jesus whose sacrifice as a ransom offering (2:6 cf. Rom 3:24 and 8:23; also Titus 2:14 and in the synoptic tradition,

Mk 10:45 and Mt 20:28) was effective for the redemption of all humanity. Paul is here utilising language used in connection with the redemption of captives and slaves for which payment had to be made. Theologically, the concept was also applied to God's redemption of Israel from slavery in Egypt at the time of the Exodus. Here, in 1 Timothy 1:6, this concept is used to explain the means whereby all humanity is able to become acceptable (2:3) before God through the sacrificial activity of Christ. On this basis Paul is able to communicate the truth about his own ministry. He is Christ's herald (2:7; also 2 Tim 1:11); his apostle (standard Pauline claim, e.g. Gal 1:1 and numerous other references) and teacher (for himself here, 2:7; also 2 Tim 1:11) of the non-Jewish people (the Gentiles) in faith (in the sense of 'good faith') and truth (used twice in 2:7 to emphasis Paul's claims against those who doubted them).

These claims allow Paul the authority to request (2:8) certain codes of conduct from the Christian congregations under Timothy's charge. First, prayer should be undertaken without quarrelling (2:8; also Col 3:12-17) and secondly, together with a longer explanation, injunctions as to how women should behave. Paul had already given instructions to the Corinthians (cf. 1 Cor 14:33b-36) as to the silence that women should demonstrate during Christian worship. Here, in 1 Timothy, he considers the wider status and actions of women. This consideration operates, within the Pastoral letters, on three inter-related levels: (i) women in the home and their role as wives, mothers and widows; (ii) women within the general context of society and the call (by men) for them to be modest and (iii) the role of women within the church community.

In presenting these issues Paul utilises two particular sources. First, the general tradition of Graeco-Roman moral philosophy in which women were exhorted to behave with modesty and not to be indecorous by wearing precious stones. Within this general context there was the issue of educated women. In Alexandria, for example, the presence of Jewish women philosophers is recognised. The Jewish philosopher, Philo (c. 20 BC – c. AD 50), himself a native of that city, grudgingly accepts the work of these women but with the proviso, that they must act modestly. Likewise, the philosopher, Plutarch (c. 50-120) offers this advice to women in terms of their behaviour within marriage. Secondly, the Jewish interpretation of the Adam and Eve narrative in Gen 2:18-25 was said to demonstrate the respective roles of the male and the female (Gen 3:16b, for the superiority of the male) given that the woman, Eve (used and explained, Gen 3:20), was the means by which Adam was beguiled (1 Tim 2:14 from Gen 3:13); who, as a result of the serpent's action, disobeyed God, ate the forbidden fruit and was able to know the difference between good and evil (Gen 3:8-24). The pain of childbearing which God inflicted upon the woman (Gen 3:16a) now begins, for Paul, the means for her salvation providing that she demonstrates the ethical virtues of faith, love, holiness and modesty (1 Tim 2:15). This teaching could represent a development of the Pauline tradition on the subject which began with 1 Corinthians 11:2-16 (cf. 1 Tim 2:13-14 and 1 Cor 11:8-9). References to both Graeco-Roman and Jewish sources (sometimes together, given that Philo, for example, attempts to combine Jewish and Greek thought patterns) assist the twenty-first-century reader of the Pauline texts to place his attitude to women in 'context'. Many of the views expressed in the Pastorals reflect the conventions of the time. As we shall see with other references to women, part of our contemporary hermeneutical skill should be to determine the teaching that is valid for all time and that which was relevant only to a particular situation in the past. Thus, such texts as 1 Corinthians 14:33b-36; 1 Timothy 2:8-15; 2 Timothy 3:6; the household codes of Colossians 3:18-19 and Ephesians 5:22-33 should be considered alongside the fundamental Pauline declaration that '…there is neither male or female; for you are all one in Christ Jesus' (Gal 3:28). When this process is undertaken is it right to describe either Paul, and/or the Pauline tradition, as misogynist?

It is on the basis of this understanding of gender relationships that Paul now turns to consider the qualities needed in those who aspire to ministerial office in the Church. To illustrate that he is setting forth a point of doctrine (concerned either with Christology or ministry) Paul uses the expression, 'the word (is) faithful' (*pistos ho logos*) which he does also at 1 Timothy 1:15 and 4:9; 2 Timothy 2:11 and Titus 3:8. At 3:1 the expression opens Paul's injunctions for those seeking episcopal (or oversight) ministry (3:1-7; Phil 1:1). These injunctions for the ministry of a bishop (*episkopos*) are divided into four sections: (i) those traits of character which are necessary for episcopal ministry (3:2-4); (ii) the question which is to be asked relating to his competence at household management; if there is failure in this area how will the candidate for episcopacy be able to have effective oversight over various churches? (iii) The danger of recent conversion (called a neophyte, 3:6) to Christianity is highlighted as those in this category might be filled with personal ambition and so become an instrument of evil. For the emphasis on humility and identification with Jesus' sufferings as a qualification for Christian ministry, see for example Mark 8:31-33 and the numerous Pauline texts on the subject (e.g. Phil 3:7-11). (iv) The candidate must also have a good report from outsiders (non-Christian leaders of civic society? 3:7) in order that he might operate effectively the mission of Christianity (based on Christ's offer of salvation to all, cf. 2:4 and 2:6) within society at large (like Paul has done? 2:7).

In 1 Timothy 3:8-13 Paul considers the ministry of deacons. The precise relation between bishops and deacons is unclear as some of the same characteristics are demanded for this ministry as for that of bishops. Deacons are to be high-principled (3:8) and irreproachable (3:10). They should be able to organise effectively their household (3:12, cf. 3:5), with their wives exhibiting the same good aspects of character as their husbands (3:11, cf. 3:8) and their children being also of upright conduct (3:12). Deacons also should be; first, in terms of faith, able to adhere to its principles with a 'pure conscience' (3:9) and proclaim its contents with boldness (3:13). Secondly, in a verse (3:13a) which is difficult to translate, it appears that the deacon (like the bishop, 3:7) should be acceptable to the wider civic society.

Household and Creation, 3:14-4:10

In 1 Timothy 3:14 Paul reverts to personal matters (cf. 1:3). He is hoping soon to visit Timothy in Ephesus. For the moment, however, in case of delay he offers instructions to Timothy as to how he should behave in the household (3:15 cf. 3:5 and 3:12) of God. The analogy is here made between the 'domestic household' and the 'church household', with the implication that the same order and good management should be a familiar feature in both establishments (given that for Christians they carried the same space). First, though, the household of God in the Christian sense needs to be defined. It is described in terms of an architectural metaphor as being the pillar and bulwark of the truth (3:15). This metaphor would have been easily recognisable in any ancient city which would have possessed numerous temples dedicated to the gods. The author may have even seen the Church in terms of the replacement for the Jerusalem Temple (destroyed AD 70, see also Jn 2:13-22). In order that the metaphor cannot be used to imply that the Church is 'static' its dynamic quality is maintained by its description as being 'of the living God', given that the truth about him and his manifestation in Christ is timeless. The timelessness of this truth is now expressed in the form of a liturgical, Christological, confession of faith the subject of which, Christ Jesus, relates the confession cf. 3:13, who (*hos*, cf. Phil 2:6) was:

1. manifested in the flesh;
2. justified in the Spirit;
3. seen by angels;
4. preached among the nations;
5. believed in throughout the world;
6. taken up into glory (3:16).

The purpose of this six-fold confession is to unite the missionary proclamation of the Church (4. Paul's own evangelistic ministry is implied here; e.g. Rom 15:19, to which Timothy is both co-worker and successor) to the ministry of Christ. This unity is provided by the concept of universality

(4 and 5). The confession proclaims Christ's incarnation, and thus his humanity (1); his divine status (2); recognised by God's messengers (3); his return to God in glory (5, see also Acts 1:9) and the 'evidence' for the truth (1 Tim 3:15) of this claim being seen in the dynamic, evangelisation ministry of the Church which this truth ought to manifest. In this context this confession could be seen as (i) a statement of 'Christian orthodoxy' against the Gnostic(?) and docetic(?) claims of the false teachers whom Timothy is to avoid (1 Tim 1:3 and 4:7) and (ii) as how it demonstrates the religious (*eusebeia*, see later discussion in Section 3) truth of Christianity.

Paul now examines this false teaching in more detail (4:1-5). The context for this discussion is the false teaching and its teachers who will arise prior to the arrival of the final, eschatological, age (see 2 Thess 2:9-10). This age, and the activity associated with it, has been prophesied by the Spirit (4:1). At its heart the goodness of God's creative activity (Gen 1:31) is being denied (4:4). This situation is reflected by the forbidding of marriage and the abstinence from certain foods (4:3). Given this challenge Timothy's role as a good minister (*diakonos*, 4:6; cf. 3:12-13), as instructed by Paul, is to proclaim both the faith and teaching of the Church (4:6). Using the language of religion (*eusebeia*, 4:7; cf. 3:16), he is to shun the profane and train himself (athletic metaphor; see also 1 Cor 9:25) in godliness. The earlier Christological confession has linked the human, divine and eternal aspects of Christ's ministry (3:16); on the same basis, Timothy's ministry links the contemporary to the eternal (4:8). This truth is confirmed (4:9, 'the word is faithful') by the declaration that the apostolic ministry is based on the declaration of God as Saviour offering the hope of salvation to all (4:10).

Teaching for different groups within the Church, 4:11-6:2

Paul begins this section by offering Timothy a series of maxims as to how the apostolic and pastoral ministry is to be conducted. In this ministry both his youthful zeal is to be respected and, at the same time and in a reciprocal manner, he is to set a pattern (4:12) of virtue (love, faith and purity) both in conduct and speech (4:12). The functions that he is to perform are now listed: (i) the public reading and interpretation of Scripture (the Jewish Bible, together with the exhortations sent by Paul?); (ii) the offering to the worshippers of the gifts of Spirit-filled prophetic speech (cf. 1 Cor 14:1-5 and 26-33, also Col 3:16) and (iii) the recalling of his original commissioning for ministry as a result of the laying on of hands (the reinterpretation in Christian liturgy of the Jewish form of commissioning, Num 8:10 and 27:23-33, also Acts 6:6 and 13:3; 2 Tim 1:6, Paul to Timothy) by the council of the elders (4:14, cf. 2 Tim 1:6). Both on the basis of virtue and function Paul exhorts Timothy to progress in his ministerial life through his teaching and by focusing on the purpose of the ministry: to offer salvation (4:16; cf. 2:3-4 and 4:10) in relation to God and through Christ.

These pastoral maxims are now focussed in three particular groups: older men (5:1a); younger men (5:1b) and widows (5:3-16). In offering injunctions to Timothy as to how each group is to be treated Paul is mindful of the Church's family obligations (5:1-2); in this context the longest section and the most detailed instructions are given to the treatment of widows (5:3-16). This length indicates that the issues relating to widows were of considerable pastoral importance (note James 1:27, helping orphans and widows as the basis of true religion) and complexity within church communities from which particular insights can be gained from the situation both in Ephesus (1 Tim 1:3) and in Jerusalem (Acts 6:1). Here, as a result of the pastoral problems resulting from community divisions, the ministry of the seven 'deacons' was initiated (Acts 6:2-3) to deal with the issue (Acts 6:1). In the ancient world widows were often subject to poverty. In Jewish communities, however, the charitable support of them was considered as essential, especially by their own family (perhaps including now their wider, church family?), because of God's command in the *Torah* (1 Tim 5:1-2; background, Ex 20:12). Failure to care for family members was considered to be a denial of faith (5:8). In 1 Timothy reference is made to 'real widows' (5:3) and the need for younger widows (under 60) to be enrolled (5:9). The issue may have been that some widows (especially younger widows, 5:11-14) were living for pleasure (5:6; 5:13) whereas 'real widows' will exercise faithfully familial and religious duties (5:4-5).

In 1 Timothy 5:17-22 Paul returns to the consideration of issues relating to the exercise of ministerial order, this time in relation to the elders (*presbuteroi*, 5:17; cf. 4:14, also Titus 1:5-6). In their duties of preaching and teaching these elders are entitled both to 'double honour' and payment for their work (cf. 1 Cor 9:15-18). This injunction is based on two sources. First, the scriptural quotation from Deuteronomy 25:4 with the image of the ox (employed earlier by Paul in 1 Cor 9:9 surrounded by comments, 1 Cor 9:8-12 concerned with his own apostolic work) is used to justify the financial support of the church's ministers by their respective congregations. Secondly, a proverbial saying found in the teaching of Jesus (Mt 10:10; Lk 10:2, from Q?) relating to a labourer deserving wages also is utilised to establish the same principle. Yet this support cannot be accepted without obligation. If an elder is deemed to have sinned (5:20, been guilty of misconduct) he is to be examined impartially (5:21); the charge, however, must be brought, in the Deuteronomic manner, by two or three witnesses (5:19; based on Deut 19:15, also Mt 18:16). In this context it should be noted how, in the understanding of its life and ministry, the churches both use Jewish patterns set out in the Jewish scriptures but also reinterpret them in a Christological context (5:21). Timothy is advised to avoid disciplinary situations by choosing elders with care (5:22a). He is also reminded of the need for purity in his conduct and to avoid harmful associations (5:22b; cf. 1:18-20 and 4:12). Two general sets of maxims follow (5:23-24). First, that relating to Timothy's personal life-style, in which he is advised, on health grounds, to take a little wine and not to drink merely water (5:23). In this injunction the theme of moderation is renewed (cf. 3:2), both excess and asceticism are to be avoided. Secondly, maxims relating both to evil and to good and their manifestation, are considered (5:24). Whether these maxims refer to the elders (cf. 5:20) or to the believers in general is difficult to say. The section concludes with reference to the role of slaves (6:1-2). We have seen from Philemon and the household codes in Colossians and Ephesians how the slave-master issue presented pastoral challenges for early Christianity (also on the basis of the Christological, baptismal statement in Gal 3:28). The aspect of the challenge considered in 1 Timothy is the issue as to whether the Christian slave has a Christian or non-Christian master. In both cases the slave must give honour (6:1) to their masters. Those slaves with Christian masters must not presume on their Christian relationship but should work all the harder (6:2).

Summary: false teachers, Timothy's role, 6:3-6:19

Paul now returns to the subject of Timothy's personal role in teaching and exhortation (6:2b which links 6:3ff back to injunctions given in 5:1ff). In 6:3-8 a contrast is made between Timothy, who preaches the 'healthy words of our Lord Jesus Christ' in godliness (*eusebeia*, 6:3), and the false teachers who are engaged in fruitless disputes about the meanings of words and who believe that godliness (*eusebeia*, 6:5) can be obtained by requesting payment. This contrast leads to another: that between satisfaction with life (6:6; 6:8) and the unbridled pursuit of wealth which is 'the root of all evils' (6:10). This pursuit has meant that some have forsaken the Christian community for what they consider to be (wrongly, 6:10b; the image of the 'pierced heart' is used) a fuller life (6:10).

Timothy is advised to flee from this attitude to life and to reconsider his ministerial calling (6:11; cf. 1:3). In the course of this reconsideration a number of injunctions are offered and observations made: (i) he should aim to manifest virtue (six are mentioned, 6:11). (ii) The image of warfare is used to describe his continuing journey of faith (6:12; Eph 6:10-11). (iii) This journey reaches both, forward to eternity and, back to his original confession of faith made within the church community. This occasion could have been either Timothy's Baptism or commissioning for ministry (2 Tim 1:6-7). (iv) Timothy's confession is based on that of Jesus made before Pontius Pilate (6:13). In this way Timothy's ministerial life has to be demonstrated clearly to be Christologically based, rooted in Jesus' own historical ministry set here (6:13) in the context of the occasion of his Roman trial in Jerusalem (e.g. Mk 15:1-5 and parallels) which resulted in his crucifixion. Timothy's ministry must be rooted in, and reflective of, these events. (v) Resulting from them Timothy must be undefiled in preparation for the eschatological return (the word, *epiphaneia*, epiphany is used) of Christ. Thus, Timothy's ministry must be exercised always in relation to the coming eschatological day of Christ. What Christ will do on that day follows. His task will be to manifest God (6:15) who is then described in terms of kingship and light (6:15-16) and to whom eternal honour will be given and from whom eternal might will be manifested. As with 1 Timothy 2:5-6 a Christian liturgical declaration of God's greatness has been introduced into the letter. Many of the theological phrases used would have originated in the Jewish synagogue. Here they are interpreted Christologically and into their framework Timothy's ministerial understanding is to be placed, which is concerned primarily with the salvation of humanity, which is both the will of God and an attribute of his nature (cf. 4:9-10). The Semitic affirmation 'Amen' completes and confirms this doxology.

What has been said already about wealth (6:9-10) is renewed in 1 Timothy 6:17-19 but with a softer tone. The theological nature of riches links the concept back to what has been said about God's nature (6:17, cf. 6:15-16) and the rich are exhorted to be liberal and generous which will ensure for them a promising future (6:19, cf. 6:9).

Concluding remarks, 6:20-21

In these concluding remarks Paul both summarises the contents of the letter and returns to his earlier charge in 1:18. Timothy is to guard the deposit of faith (2 Tim 1:12), the contents of which, together with the practice of, have been outlined. He is again reminded to be watchful against profane utterance and false knowledge (4:7) by being reminded of what he ought to be doing (cf. 4:11-15). The letter concludes with the offering of Paul's 'grace' (6:21).

2 TIMOTHY

2 Timothy contains an outline similar to other Pauline letters with an opening address and concluding blessing. There is no mention of Church officers and the tone is that of a farewell letter with personal instructions to Timothy.

SECTION 1 – STRUCTURE

A. OUTLINE

1:1-2	Opening address and greeting.
1:3-7	Thanksgiving and recollection of the past.
1:8-18	Paul's prison reflections.
2:1-26	Paul's exhortations to Timothy.
3:1-9	False teachers and teaching in the eschatological days.
3:10-4:5	Further advice to Timothy.
4:6-4:18	Farewell and concluding information.
4:19-4:22	Concluding information, blessing and greeting.

B. LINES OF ARGUMENT

Opening address, 1:1-2

This opening address follows a traditional Pauline type structure. Paul acknowledges his apostolic ministry which is exercised according to God's will which also contains within it the promise of life based presumably upon the fact of Christ's resurrection and the Christian hope of eternity based on that resurrection. Timothy is addressed as in 1 Timothy as 'my beloved child' (2:1; 'true child' in 1 Tim 1:2) thus reinforcing the spiritual father – son relationship between Paul and Timothy and the idea of him receiving Paul's spiritual and apostolic inheritance. This intimate tone is continued throughout the letter. The attributions of God and Jesus are also communicated: grace, mercy and peace.

Thanksgiving and recalling the past, 1:3-7

Paul's fatherly declaration to Timothy begins with the hope of a meeting (2 Tim 1:4). He is reminded first of his maternal parentage: mother Eunice and grandmother Lois. It is to be implied that Timothy is here to recall his upbringing in Lystra (Acts 16:1) and the devotion of his Jewish mother (and grandmother?) in preparing him to receive Christianity through the following of their Jewish life and practice. It was Paul who completed this process and who now, in 2 Timothy 1:5-7 reminds Timothy of his consecration to ministry through the laying on of hands and the receiving of the gifts of the Spirit (cf. Acts 13:2-3). These divine gifts, including power, love and self control, are to be rekindled (1:7). The giving of them should result in Timothy's dynamic action for the Gospel. He has received the life-imparting Spirit which calls for a ministry of divine strength and not timidity. The binding force between Timothy's apostolic work and his familial relationships is his sincere faith. Thus 2 Tim 1:5-7 forms both a fitting context for, and transition to, the main body of the letter.

Paul's prison reflections, 1:8-18

Paul's task is now to offer advice to Timothy on the proper understanding and action in the ministry. Given that Paul is in prison and likely to face death (1:8; 4:6-8), these reflections represent Paul's attempt to hand on this legacy. In doing so familiar concepts are to be found:

(a) the tension between ministry exercised by grace and not works (1:9);

(b) this ministry is to be seen against the panorama of the totality of God's action focussed supremely in 'Christ Jesus before the ages' (1:9-10);

(c) thus, Paul emphasises the centrality of the ministry of Christ in whose suffering (1:12) he now shares as a prisoner (1:8), on account of being called by Christ as a preacher (lit. herald), apostle and teacher (1:11).

These reflections are to be seen within the context of the final arrival of the eschatological age (Day of the Lord theme, cf. 1 Thess 5:2). It is in this hope that Paul feels secure (1:12). On this basis Timothy is to: (a) follow Paul's words and (b) guard the deposit of faith and teaching entrusted to him by the Holy Spirit (1:14).

Paul now connects these reflections to the practical realities of the ministry. On one hand, he reminds Timothy of those believers who have turned away from him (from the faith?) in Asia including Phygelus and Hermogenes (1:15); while on the other hand, Paul praises Onesiphorous and his household, who ministered to him at Ephesus (1:18), but who also cared for him in Rome, the place of Paul's imprisonment (1:16-17).

Paul's exhortations to Timothy, 2:1-26

The idea of Timothy as Paul's 'spiritual son' is renewed in 2:1. The earlier Pauline theme of the apostolic ministry being exercised under grace (*charis*) is both emphasised and transmitted to Timothy (2:1, cf. Gal 1:15 and 1 Cor 15:10) who, by implication, is to transmit it, in turn, to those men whom he appoints as church leaders. The qualifications for this ministry are faithfulness and the ability to teach (2:2). Timothy is exhorted also to share in Christ's suffering in the way in which Paul has done (2:3; back, for example, to 2 Cor 5:11). Three metaphors are used in order that Timothy might understand fully the implications of exercising the ministry: military service (2:3-4; Timothy is a soldier of Christ, note imagery at Eph 6:10-17); athletics (possibly wrestling, 2:5; cf. 1 Cor 9:24-27) and farming (2:6; echoes of 1 Cor 4:5-9?). These metaphors, all found in some shape or form in the Pauline tradition, are utilised to demonstrate both the attitudes and actions necessary for the effective exercising of the ministry.

Paul now compares his own imprisonment to the unfettered way in which the 'word of God' operates in the evangelistic ministry (2:9). This word is based on Christ's resurrection, which in turn is the fulfilment of God's promises to David (2:8; cf. Rom 1:3-4, note also Acts 2:25-31). The purpose of the resurrection and its continuity with Israel's past is to demonstrate that through faith in God's promises the elect (2:10, the new Christian, chosen race formed out of Israel) receive the salvation which Christ offers and with it eternal glory (cf. Rom 8:18 and 30). In this context four conditional sayings follow. Their structure is: (i) If we do X or Y now; two sayings are positive (2:11; 2:12a) two are negative (2:12b; 2:13); in consequence, (ii) Christ will, in future (note verb tense), perform the action appropriate to the condition.

This 'theory' is given practical application in 2:14-26 in what Paul instructs Timothy to do or not do in the ministry. He is (i) to avoid empty talk (2:16) and not to enter into fruitless arguments about the meaning of words or unnecessary controversies (2:14; 2:23). He is also (ii) to 'shun youthful passions' and aim for the higher virtues in purity of heart (2:22). He must also confront false teaching especially that associated with the resurrection and linked to the views of Hymenaeus (see also 1 Tim 1:20, an important rival church teacher?) and Philetus (2:17-18; cf. 2 Tim 2:8 and 1 Cor 15:12). Into this scenario for Timothy's ministry two building metaphors are used to describe the Church: the foundation (2:19; cf. 1 Cor 3:10-15) and the house (2:20). In 2 Tim they are used to indicate; first, that the house must be built upon the solid foundation of the true faith based upon a traditional understanding of the resurrection of Christ and the believers and secondly, this house, for the time being at least, contains those who believe and teach this faith (Paul and Timothy = gold and silver) and those who teach the contrary (Hymenaeus and Philetus = wood and earthenware).

False teaching and eschatology, 3:1-9

The context for the exercise of Timothy's ministry is to be the difficult (3:1) times which will arise prior to the imminent coming of the eschatological age (see 2 Thess 2:1-11). Those who will cause these difficulties are categorised by a conventional list of vices (3:2-5; see also, 1 Tim 1:9-10 and Titus 3:3). These lists, which have their foundation in Jewish literature (e.g. Wis 14:25-26), are an important feature in Pauline literature (e.g. Gal 5:19-21; 1 Cor 6:9-10; Rom 1:29-31). Timothy is to avoid them (2 Tim 3:5). 2 Tim 3:6 raises again the question of the role of women (cf. 1 Tim 2:8-15) and here, in connection (probably) to their education. It could be that the issue at stake is not necessarily sexual but relates to the convention of the private education of women at home by young male teachers. The situation in 2 Timothy 3 appears to be that those whom Paul regarded as false teachers were ingratiating themselves into the household of the members of the 'orthodox' congregation.

To illustrate the uselessness of these teachers Paul uses the example of Jannes and Jambres, magicians at Pharaoh's court during the time prior to the Exodus (Ex 7:11). For all their miraculous powers, which had similar manifestations to those of Moses, they were unable ultimately to withstand the power of God in his desire to free Israel from Egypt. In the Christian era Timothy, inheriting them from Paul (2 Cor 3:7-16), has (by implication) been given apostolic authority greater than the power given to Moses. With this authority Timothy should be able to withstand the false teachers.

What Timothy is to do, 3:10-4:5

In this section Paul lists the ways in which Timothy is to imitate his ministry, not only in following his teaching, but also his manner of life (3:10). Within this ministry there is to be found persecution and suffering. Paul illustrates this point by reminding Timothy of the persecution that he endured in Antioch, Iconium and Lystra (3:11; Acts 13:50; 14:5-6 and 14:19). It is to be assumed that Timothy would have been familiar with these events given his home was in the Lystra region (Acts 16:1). The purpose of this reminder was 'memory recall' (2 Tim 3:11, cf. 1:3-7) in order that Timothy might perceive further the providence of God together with the injunctions of Paul within his own ministry. General statements follow in 2 Tim 3:12 and 13. These statements highlight the contrast between: (i) the fact that all godly (*eusebos*) Christians should expect persecution while (ii) their persecutors will continue in their wickedness and deception. In 3:14 Paul returns to offering direct injunctions to Timothy. On this occasion these injunctions concern the use of the Jewish scriptures (most likely in their Greek translation). Given that he has been acquainted with these writings since infancy (through the influence of his mother and grandmother? Acts 16:1; 2 Tim 1:5; 3:15) Timothy is to continue to learn from them especially in connection with their interpretation of the Christ event and the salvation which emanates from that event. A general statement about the scriptures follow. Not only are they sacred in that God has breathed his life into them (3:16, *Theopneustos*, trans., inspired) but they are the principal means by which Christian instruction (*paideia*, a Greek educational term) can be imparted both in terms of theology and ethics. The purpose of this study is to enable Timothy (and all Christian leaders) to be equipped for the effective exercise of their ministry (3:17).

The urgency behind Paul's injunctions relates to the appearing of the glorified Christ in order that humanity may be judged. Although here the concept is framed in epiphany language (4:1) in essence it is a restatement of the earlier eschatological message relating to the coming Day of the Lord (cf. 1 Thess 5:1). The context in 2 Timothy relates both to the zeal with which Timothy is to exercise the ministry (4:2) and to the presence, within church communities, of false teachers. The presence of such teaching signifies that the eschatological day of Christ will arrive shortly. In this context Timothy is commanded to undertake four things: (i) to be steady, not to be taken off course by these false teachers; (ii) to share in the suffering which the ministry brings (e.g. 1 Cor 4:9); (iii) to continue fervent missionary activity and (iv) to accomplish, to be overflowing in, the ministry with which he has been entrusted (cf. 1:8-10).

Farewell and concluding information and blessing, 4:6-18

The final section of the letter is composed of two, inter-related parts. First, Paul signals his impending martyrdom (4:6-8). The metaphors used are from the language of religious sacrifice and from athletics. The former metaphor has been used already in Philippians 2:17 and may have been Paul's way of identifying his martyrdom with that of Christ and on the Church's subsequent reflection upon his death in terms of the 'theology of the cross' (e.g. Mk 14:24). The latter metaphor is intended to show Paul's journey to martyrdom and the 'justification' of his ministry in terms of it. The future hope expressed in 4:8 is couched in royal terms, which are both theological and ethical. The 'crown' that Paul will receive is qualified by the genitive 'of righteousness' which, in turn, will be offered to him by the 'righteous' Lord. The earlier 'Day of the Lord' (cf. 1 Thess 5:2) terminology, now seen in terms of epiphany, forms the framework into which both Paul's sacrifice and race are to be conceived (see also, Phil 3:12-15). This activity is corporate to all believers who are united by loving the epiphany of Christ, probably implying a reference both to his incarnation and also to his future epiphany. It could be that the royal, epiphany language is deliberately couched in order to create a difference between adherence to Christ, the righteous One, and to the Roman Emperor and the unjust Imperial system and with it the tensions raised for Christian believers. What is more difficult is the historical reconstruction of events relating Christians to Roman persecution, especially that of Nero. An added complication in this area is the scholarly disagreements over both the dating and the identity of the author of 2 Timothy.

Given the intensity of this portrait of martyrdom it may be surprising that Paul requests Timothy to visit him (it can be assumed that Rome is the place) shortly (4:9). This verse forms the link between the two parts: 4:6-8 and 4:10-18. The reason for such a visit is unclear. Why should Timothy be requested to leave his 'settled' ministry in Ephesus (1:3)? Was there a time-gap between Paul's trial, death sentence and his execution, on account of his Roman citizenship? Was it because the other disciples who were with Paul had left him with the exception of Luke and, therefore, strengthening and fellowship were needed? However this request may be interpreted, Paul now embarks on the second part of this section: information relating to individuals in relation to him.

Some of the names may have been familiar to Timothy and to his Ephesian (1 Tim 1:3) congregation as they had been named already by Paul in Colossians and Philemon. A note of caution must be registered, however, in any attempt to construct a chronology of missionary activity and relationships on the evidence provided, given that the order and the dates when these various letters were written remains an area of both uncertainty and disagreement.

2 Timothy 4 provides the occasion on which we can summarise the information given elsewhere:

4:10   Demas – known as a fellow worker with Paul and others, Philemon 24; Colossians 4:14. Has he now deserted the ministry and returned to Thessalonica, in order to return to his previous Graeco-Roman 'secular', civic adherence?

4:10   Crescens – known only from this text. He may have been sent by Paul to consolidate his earlier missionary and ministerial activity in Galatia (the reading Gaul offered by some manuscripts is doubtful).

4:10   Titus – was already well known (see summary in Section 2) may have been sent by Paul (away from Crete, Titus 1:5) in order to prepare for, or to strengthen, the existing ministry in that province (Rom 15:19?).

4:12   Tychicus (Acts 20:4; Col 4:7; Eph 6:21; Titus 3:12) is sent to Ephesus. Given his closeness to Paul it may be that Tychicus was sent in order to assist Timothy in the strengthening of the Ephesian church or to deputise for him when he leaves for Rome to visit Paul.

Two points emerge thus far: (i) Paul is portrayed as continuing to organise ministerial activity amongst the churches. Depending on the view taken of the authorship of 2 Timothy this organisation could represent either Paul himself at the conclusion of his ministry, or be seen in terms of reflection on the ministry in some of the Pauline churches by a later author reflecting the Pauline tradition. (ii) Given that Luke is seen as Paul's sole companion in his imprisonment (4:11; Col 4:14; Philem 24), a series of requests follow: Mark's presence is requested (Col 4:10; Philem 24; also, Acts 12:12; 12:25; 15:37; 15:39; note in addition, 1 Pet 5:13 but is this the same Mark as named in 2 Tim 4:11?) on the grounds that he is useful (cf. 2 Tim 2:21 and Philem 11) in the ministry. In addition Timothy is requested to bring Paul's cloak and books; again, given the circumstances, why? (4:13). Another warning (1 Tim 1:20) is issued regarding the activities of Alexander the coppersmith who appears to be acting against Paul and his companions. This warning highlights the opposition which Paul encountered (and which we have seen throughout his letters) from various quarters: from within the Christian movement, from Judaism and, at certain times, from the Roman political system. In this regard Paul mentions his 'first defence' (4:16). I shall be referring to the diversity of the evidence relating to his trial and martyrdom in a later section, in the meanwhile it is clear that, in whatever circumstances Paul finds himself, he is anxious to affirm the Lord's protection of him and the furtherance of the Gentile mission to which he had been called (4:17; cf. Gal 1:16). The section ends with the doxology (4:18).

Concluding information, blessing and greeting, 4:19-22

Timothy is exhorted to greet Prisca (her Greek name, its Latin form, Priscilla is used by Luke, Acts 18:2; 18:18; 18:26) and Aquila. They have had an important role in Paul's ministry (1 Cor 16:19; Rom 16:3; 2 Tim 4:19) given that they shared a similar occupation (Acts 18:3), were of Jewish background (Acts 18:2) and gave Paul considerable support in his ministry (1 Cor 16:19). Timothy is also to greet Onesiphorus who, with his household, has helped Paul pastorally (2 Tim 1:16). Paul names Erastus who has the most influential role of being the city treasurer of Corinth (Rom 16:23) where he is remaining (2 Tim 4:20) having worked with Timothy in assisting Paul in his ministry (Acts 19:22). Trophimus, the Ephesian (Acts 21:29), who assisted Paul in his ministry around the Aegean Sea (Acts 20:4) and accompanied him to Jerusalem (Acts

21:29) is now ill at Miletus (2 Tim 4:20). In the midst of these greetings Timothy is asked to visit Paul before winter, again in the light of 4:6 and 4:13, why? (4:21). In turn Timothy receives greetings from Eubulus, Pudens, Linus, Claudia and all the believers. Nothing else is known about these believers with the exception that Linus appears in episcopal lists as the second bishop of Rome after Peter. The value of lists of greetings at the conclusion of letters ascribed to Paul is that the theological and ethical content of them is rooted in the reality of pastoral and human experience.

The letter concludes with the offering of the Grace (4:22).

TITUS

SECTION 1 – STRUCTURE

A. OUTLINE

1:1-4   Opening address and greeting.

1:5-2:15 Organisation of the Church
- 1:5-9   Organisational structure for the Church in Crete.
- 1:10-16 False teachers and their teaching.
- 2:1-10   Christian duties within the household.
- 2:11-15 Salvation and Ethics.

3:1-11   Christian duties and controversies.
- 3:1-8   Christian duties within society.
- 3:9-11   How controversies are to be avoided.

3:12-14 Paul's requests to Titus.

3:15   Concluding blessing and greeting.

B. LINES OF ARGUMENT

Opening address, 1:1-4

Other than perhaps that to the Romans (Rom 1:1-7), the single sentence greeting contained in Titus 1:1-4 is the most formal to be found in the Pauline corpus of letters, certainly in comparison with the other Pastoral letters (1 Tim 1:1-2; 2 Tim 1:1-2). Paul begins, as he does in Romans (1:1), with the declaration of his ministry in terms of being a slave and apostle of Jesus Christ (1:1). He continues to describe the purpose of this ministry: (i) to further the faith of the Christian chosen (the elect) and their full knowledge of the truth. This task accords with true piety (*eusebeia*); (ii) to proclaim God's promise of eternal life; (iii) to preach, on the basis of God's command, the manifestation of Christ (later, 2:11-14).

Titus is greeted as Paul's 'true child' (1 Tim 1:2) and their common faith is emphasised (1:4). The greeting from God and Jesus in terms of grace and peace follows with the qualification that God is Father and that Jesus is Christ and Saviour. Thus, it is the salvation theme which, not only binds God and Jesus, but also provides the purpose for which Christian preaching from Paul and Titus is necessary. Also, it provides the apostolic and ecclesiological basis on which Paul is able to give authoritative injunctions to Titus as to how the church in Crete is to be organised.

Organisation, 1:5-2:15

Although nothing is known about Paul's foundation of Christianity in Crete (Luke records that the ship on which Paul was sailing to Rome as a prisoner sailed close to Crete, Acts 27:7-15), it can be assumed that when he left the island the organisational operation of the church was left to Titus. On the part of the Cretan Christians they could claim, like other churches, a Pauline foundational heritage. Titus is to appoint elders (*presbuteroi*) who would be given pastoral oversight over local city congregations (1:5). These appointments would enhance the Paul – Titus continuity within the church. In Titus 1:7 Paul speaks of bishops (*episkopoi*, overseers). It is difficult to know if bishops and elders form the same office or whether the bishops have oversight over groups of churches. The qualifications for ecclesial office are similar to those found in 1 Timothy 3:1-7 (for bishops), it could be that, in certain churches (e.g. Crete, Ephesus), an agreed traditional list existed.

One of the functions of these elders is to protect the faithful from harmful theological and pastoral influences. This was also Timothy's function in Ephesus (1 Tim 1:3-7). In Crete Paul speaks of those who heed 'Jewish myths' (1:14). Exactly to what these myths refer is difficult to determine. From what Paul says, however, it is likely that Jewish converts to Christianity, 'the circumcision party' (1:10) were either encouraging Gentile Christians to adhere to Jewish mores (perhaps circumcision and keeping the Sabbath that had been attempted in Galatia, cf. Gal 4:10 and 5:2-3), or attempting to construct a Jewish-Christian synthesis of religion. Whatever the problems may have been, Paul is clear that the faithful are being unsettled in their faith. To make matters worse the Cretans themselves are unreliable as far as the truth is concerned. They will be corrupted easily and readily accept anything other than the 'pure' (cf. Rom 14:20) doctrine. The Greek philosopher, Epimenides, whom Paul describes as their (a Greek) prophet, had, in the sixth century BC, made a similar judgement that the Cretans are liars (1:12). Paul is here then repeating, and expressing agreement with (1:13), a well established proverbial view regarding the Cretans.

In this situation Titus' role (as bishop of Crete?) is to teach sound doctrine (2:1; cf. 1:9, for the bishop and 1 Tim 1:10). This teaching is both theological and ethical. There follows instructions from Paul as to how older men (2:2); older women (2:3); younger women, especially in relation to their husbands and children and the management of the domestic aspects of the household (2:4-5), and younger men (2:6) are to be instructed. Titus is also given instructions as to his conduct as a church leader (2:7-8). He is to set a pattern of behaviour for the faithful to emulate and to conduct himself in the ministry with the proper seriousness. These measures will ensure a 'Pauline succession' through Titus in the Cretan ministry. In this context slaves are to be submissive to their masters (2:9, cf. Col 3:22). This action, in conjunction with that suggested in 2:2-8, will ensure that the church finds a fitting and useful place in, and can make a harmonious contribution to, civic society. It is likely that Paul (as has been done in Colossians and Ephesians) is utilising existing regulations relating to conduct within households which includes guidance for their role in society. Yet, here (2:10), and elsewhere (e.g. 'in the Lord theme', Col 3:18-24) these regulations are, for Christians, given theological under-girding. In Titus it is the doctrine of God as Saviour (2:10) which provides the basis for this theology. The ability to practise Christianity in this way is provided by God's grace (2:11). A different perspective is placed upon this concept from that found in Paul's earlier letters (e.g. Gal 1:15 and 2:21). In Titus grace is concerned with 'training' (2:12). The purpose of this educational metaphor is two fold: negatively, in order that irreligion and passion might be removed; while positively, an education in grace provides godliness and justice. The aim is for believers to live honourably in society. Yet in this present-day living, however, the distinctive eschatological, ethical and salvation aspects of Christianity must not be lost. The manifestation of God and Jesus are seen in terms of both glory (the traditional term) and epiphany (*epiphaneia*, the newer term). The Christological implications of this theological understanding are now stated, given that Jesus Christ was the one who (2:14, note use of *hos* to introduce Christological statements, cf. Phil 2:6; Col 1:13 and 1:15): (i) gave himself for the salvation of humanity (note the idea of offering, e.g. Rom 4:25 and 8:32). (ii) The reason for this self-giving was to ransom or redeem humanity from iniquity. The implications of this action are that: 1. God has created his own cleansed, renewed people. This idea for the Christian community is based on the notion of Israel as God's possession and his holy nation (e.g. Ex 19:5-6). 2. This community will, as a result, be zealous ethically for the doing of 'good works'. The section concludes with Paul's declaration that Titus is responsible, and has the authority (from Paul, Titus 1:5), to proclaim these truths and not to be distracted by opponents (2:15).

Christian duties and controversies, 3:1-11

Titus 3:1-8 returns to the theme of Christian duties within Graeco-Roman society. Respect for the ruling authorities is commanded (3:1; 1 Tim 2:1-2; Rom 13:1-7) as are the virtues of hard work, courtesy and gentleness. In turn the practice of these attributes by Christians will mean that they will be respected within society (Titus 3:2). Paul provides the rationale for this conduct by returning to the life-style of the pre-conversion days marked by malice, hatred and envy but, into this scenario, God intervened. Thus, the ethical patterns of conduct which Paul has presented are based on theological precepts: God's kindness, salvation and righteousness. A reminder of entry into the Christian people (cf. 2:14) through Baptism is included (3:5). A glimpse is provided into the increasing manifold interpretation given to this rite of initiation. Baptism (see also, Gal 3:27; Rom 6:3-11; Col 2:11-15; Mt 28:19-20) is seen in terms of regeneration (3:5, re-birth), renewal in the Holy Spirit, the means of being 'in the right' before God and as granting the hope of eternal life (3:5-7). The understanding of Baptism always provides the basis for the quality of ethical life which should be the hall-mark of Christian people (3:8; cf. 3:12). This position is acclaimed (the usual way in the Pastoral letters) by the confirmatory statement 'faithful (is) the word' (3:8). This understanding of Christian living ought to provide the community with the basis for unity. Titus is shown how to avoid quarrelling (about the understanding and exercise of Christianity). If, however, there is continual argument he, as leader of the community, is to issue two warnings (see Mt 18:15-17); then expulsion should result (3:9-11).

Paul's requests to Titus, 3:12-14

As before (2 Tim 4:10-21, although note the issue about the order in which the Pastoral letters were written) Paul imparts information, makes requests and offers greetings. This information is not always easy to interpret. In 3:12 Paul promises to send either Artemas (named only here) or Tychicus (see comment on 2 Tim 4:12) to Crete while he encourages

Titus to visit him in Nicopolis (in northern Greece) where, it can be inferred, Paul was engaged in continuing missionary activity. Zenas (the lawyer, named only here) and Apollos (the same person as named in 1 Corinthians and in Acts?) are to be well provided for and sent on their way. Maybe the letter to Titus was to form a letter of recommendation for them? Again, Paul recommends the ethical maxims of good works and charity towards the poor (3:14; cf. Gal 2:10).

Concluding blessing and greeting, 3:15

The letter concludes with the offer of greetings for Paul and his companions to the believers in Crete (cf. 1:5) and with the grace.

SECTION 2 – CONTEXT

GENERAL REMARKS

The way in which the Pastoral letters are to be conceptualised within the ministry of Paul is difficult to determine with certainty. Much is dependent on the particular views taken regarding the authorship of the letters. Those who argue for non-Pauline authorship do so on grounds of: (i) the historical issues which arise in the attempt to reconstruct the ministry of Paul in relationship both to Timothy and Titus and the other literary sources, Paul's earlier letters and Luke's Acts; (ii) the fact that the letters reveal a particular style and contain vocabulary which is not found in the earlier letters but which has resonance to later works such as Acts and 1 Clement and (iii) that the nature of the teaching given on theology; Christology; ecclesiology and the location of the false teachers/ teaching found in letters reflects a period in the 80s and 90s rather than during Paul's ministry.

The matter of authorship is complicated by: (i) the different styles which exist between the three letters and (ii) that some 'genuine' fragments of Paul's letters may have been included in the letters by their later author. Certainly confessional, perhaps liturgical, statements of faith have been included (1 Tim 1:15; 2:5; 3:16; 2 Tim 2:11-13 and Titus 3:4-8a) in the text. Implications, however, of the Christology which they contain is not applied in the same way as similar statements in the earlier letters are wedded to their context (e.g. 2 Cor 8:9, to the context of the collection; Phil 2:6-11, on the need for humility).

It is not possible to consider in detail all the arguments relating to authorship and date. For our purpose it is sufficient to observe that: (i) if the letters were written before Paul's martyrdom than they reflect a picture of certain aspects of church life in the 60s. If, however, (ii) they form part of the Pauline tradition and were written in the 80s then they portray how the ministry was perceived at that time. On this basis the Pastoral letters become part of Pauline interpretation and should be seen in relation to Acts. Whichever view is accepted it is clear that the Pastoral letters either look forward to, or are reflecting upon, the nature of the Pauline tradition and succession as mediated through two of his most important colleagues: Timothy and Titus. I remain uncertain as to where the Pastoral letters are to be placed within the context of Paul and the Pauline tradition. I think that the most likely explanation is to place 1 Timothy and Titus, in their final form, as having been edited by one of Paul's disciples c. 80 in which some of Paul's original material has been retained. 2 Timothy has the form of a prison letter (2 Tim 1:8 and 1:16), almost (the hope of future release? 2 Tim 4:9 and 4:13) a last will and testament (2 Tim 4:6) and therefore could be placed either c. 64-67 or as a 'reflective' letter composed c. 80. Whether c. 60s or c. 80s the Pastoral letters are moving Christianity, and Christian ministerial organisation, from one age to another.

As such they should be seen as erecting a bridge in order that Christianity might respond to new circumstances. The ministerial tension which is presented, for example, is between that form of ministry which is itinerant (of which Paul is a supreme example) and that which is settled, as indicated by the qualifications for church leadership as indicated in 1 Timothy and Titus. Titus, for example, appears to have been given, by Paul, a settled ministry in Crete in order to give the church there organisational structure (Titus 1:5) yet, at the end of the letter, Paul requests his presence in Nicopolis, in the Roman province of Epirus, western Greece (Titus 3:12) where Paul is to spend the winter. Titus is also depicted as undertaking pastoral work in Dalmatia (2 Tim 4:10). Although it is difficult to reconstruct any of these movements with certainty two points are clear. First, Timothy and Titus both act, in their different ways, as Paul's representatives, form part of the Pauline succession and ensure that Paul's influence is felt and is maintained (with others, e.g. Luke, Clement) over a wide canvas of the churches, both for its own sake (note: geographical references, 1 Tim 1:3; 2 Tim 4:9-13; Titus 1:5 and 3:12) and against opposition named (1 Tim 1:20; 2 Tim 2:17; 3:10 and 3:14) and unnamed (e.g. 1 Tim 1:3-7). Secondly, this activity indicates that Timothy and Titus form a bridge between the early Christian apostolic ministry (c. 30-c. 60/70?) which was largely itinerant (as reflected by Luke's portrait of Paul) and that which developed later and was largely concerned with a settled (post 70? note: 1 Tim 1:3, Timothy and Ephesus, Titus 1:5, Titus and Crete) location.

By the time Eusebius composed (c. 325) *The History of the Church* the tradition of the settled, episcopal ministry had gained ground; thus, Timothy is said 'to have been the first bishop appointed to the see of Ephesus, as was Titus to the churches of Crete' (Book 3:4). In this attempt to establish the continuity in apostolic, episcopal ministry from the apostles in the fourth century, it should not be forgotten that Timothy and Titus were also (as portrayed in the Pastoral letters) itinerant ministers of the Gospel whose task it was to encourage and support other churches; in particular, as far as they were able, in the Pauline image.

TIMOTHY AND TITUS
WITHIN THE MINISTRY OF PAUL

At this stage it is necessary to reconstruct what is known of Timothy and Titus in relation to Paul. For the readers of the Pastoral letters such background would have provided important information on which their understanding of the letters, in particular with regard to apostolic teaching and authority, should be based.

Timothy is portrayed as Paul's co-worker (2 Cor 1:19) whom he describes as his 'fellow worker' (Rom 16:21) and 'brother' (Col 1:1, Philem 1). Timothy is sent by Paul on a variety of missions (1 Thess 3:2; 3:6; 1 Cor 4:17; 16:10; Phil 2:19; 2:23) and appears as co-sender of five letters (1 Thess 1:1; 2 Thess 1:1; 2 Cor 1:1; Phil 1:1; Philem 1). Paul rightly praises Timothy seeing him as his 'son' (Phil 2:22) in the work of the Gospel. This sonship motif is continued in the Pastoral letters (1 Tim 1:18) where he is also described both as Paul's 'true child' (1 Tim 1:2) and 'beloved child' (2 Tim 1:2).

It is also clear that Timothy is envisaged as a young man (1 Tim 4:12) and encouraged by Paul not to engage in 'youthful passions' but to aim for the higher virtues (2 Tim 2:22). According to Luke (Acts. 16:1-3) Timothy was born of mixed Jewish and Greek parentage. His mother was Eunice and grandmother Lois (2 Tim 1:5). Timothy begins to follow Paul after his evangelistic campaign in Timothy's hometown of Lystra. Luke also portrays him as Paul's companion during the evangelistic mission in Greece, Macedonia and Asia (Acts. 17:14 and 17:15; 18:5; 19:22 and 20:4). From the various shafts made into the traditions of early Christianity it is clear that Timothy emerges as a significant figure within his own right in the church's leadership from the 60s onwards.

Titus emerges as a Greek convert of Paul (Gal 2:3) who accompanies him to the apostolic conference in Jerusalem recorded by Paul in Galatians 2:1-10. Paul describes Titus as 'partner and fellow worker' (2 Cor 8:23) and as such played an important role as Paul's envoy to the Corinthians mediating in the disputes which Paul had with that church (2 Cor 7:13-15; 12:18). He delivered a letter to them (2 Cor 2:4; 2:13; 7:6; 7:8) and was active in promoting the collection for the Jerusalem church (2 Cor 8:16-18). According to 2 Tim 4:10 Titus was in Dalmatia (on missionary service?) and according to Titus 1:5 he had been appointed by Paul to organise the system of church elders in Crete. In which order these events occurred is now impossible to say. Perhaps surprisingly, unlike

Timothy, Titus is unknown to Luke (the link to Titius or Titus Justus in Acts 18:7 is unlikely). Another interesting feature is that while Luke records that Paul had Timothy circumcised in order to please local Jews (Acts 16:3, on the grounds that his mother was a Jew?), Paul himself notes that, being a Greek, Titus was not compelled to be circumcised (Gal 2:3). It could have been that, by the time of the writing of the Pastoral letters, Timothy represented a Christian leader from a Hellenistic Jewish background with joint parentage while Titus was ethnically Greek. They might even have symbolised Paul's missionary maxim offered to the Romans (Rom 1:16) that he evangelised first Jews (Timothy) and then Greeks (Titus)? Would such a combination in Church leadership illustrate also Paul's insistence that the exercise of the ministry, being based on the call of Christ Jesus, be above ethnicity and social class?

SECTION 3 – THEOLOGICAL, PASTORAL AND HERMENEUTICAL ISSUES

In this section I shall highlight two areas in which I believe that the Pastoral letters raise important hermeneutical and historical issues.

1. NEW CONTEXTS LEADING TO NEW LANGUAGE AND PERCEPTIONS

In this section I indicate two important language concepts: one theological, the other concerned with the right Christian 'attitude'. Both concepts are prominent in the Pastoral letters and both have their roots in conventional religious vocabulary.

First, there is the concept of epiphany. The noun (*epiphaneia*) is used at: 1 Timothy 6:14; 2 Timothy 4:1 and 4:8; Titus 2:13 (note also: 2 Thess 2:8) and the cognate verb (*epiphaino*) at Titus 2:11 and 3:14 (note the use of the verb in different ways; Lk 1:79 and Acts 27:20; also, the prayer for the 'appearing' of God's peace, 1 Clem 60:3). In Graeco-

Roman culture these terms referred to the manifestation of the gods in the world accompanied by the appropriate signs of their power and authority. Thus, in Ephesus, for example, both in relation to Artemis and to the Imperial cult, 'epiphany language' would have been readily recognisable. In the Pastoral letters this language is used Christologically. The ministry of Christ is embraced by two epiphanies: one, incarnational (first epiphany; e.g. 2 Tim 1:10 and Titus 2:11); the other pointing to the final judgement (second epiphany; e.g. 1 Tim 6:14). In this regard Paul's earlier '*parousia* language' for Christ's return (e.g. 1 Thess 4:15) is exchanged, in the Pastoral Letters, for 'epiphany language'. This change is not easy to explain. I offer merely three questions. Was it that, in Christian theology, the earlier emphasis on Christ's return was, by c. AD 80, being shifted towards incarnation (e.g, 1 Tim 3:16 and John 1:14)? Or that, in terms of metaphor, to describe Christ in terms of divine manifestation (*epiphaneia*) was more convincing than seeing him as a visiting Emperor (*parousia*)? Or that, in terms of the readers, the language of epiphany was more familiar (and acceptable) than that of *parousia*?

Secondly, there is question of the right Christian 'attitude'. In the presentation of the answer the Pastoral Letters utilise the language of 'godliness'. There are 13 uses of this concept in the letters: the noun (*eusebeia*; e.g. 1 Tim 2:2); the verb (*eusebeo*; 1 Tim 5:4) and the adverb (*eusebos*; 2 Tim 3:12; Titus 2:12). These expressions are not found in Paul's earlier writings but are used by Luke in Acts (e.g. 3:12) and in 2 Peter (e.g. 1:3). In the Graeco-Roman setting, however, they occur often in politico-religious speech. They referred to the necessary homage that should be given both to the gods and to earthly rulers, embracing both outer and inner attitudes: the homage paid in worship which ought to be reflected by an inner consciousness. In this way they become a much prized virtue. This 'godliness language' was also used by Jewish writers to explain Hebraic concepts of God. For Jews it embraced theology: understanding the knowledge of God and ethically: living in a godly way according to his commandments (note the use in Prov 1:7; Isa 33:6 and Sir 49:3).

The writer of the Pastoral Letters, therefore, had a rich

treasure of the cultural and religious use of godliness from which he could draw in order to reveal to Timothy and Titus how they might apply the concept in their respective ministries. As with the Jewish usage both theology and ethics were involved, yet, in the case of the Pastoral Letters, it was the Christological aspect (1 Tim 3:16; 2 Tim 3:12) which gave the concept Christian meaning and displayed what the right Christian 'attitude' should be. The practice of godliness was rooted in the knowledge of God and in the content of the Christian Gospel (1 Tim 6:3; 5:11; Titus 1:1). Furthermore godliness is an 'attitude' to life which can be pursued and in which training can be given (1 Tim 4:7-8; 6:11; Titus 2:12). This particular 'attitude' is displayed through specific 'right' ethical actions such as children and grandchildren honouring their widowed mother (1 Tim 5:4). The writer of the Pastoral Letters, therefore, has found, within the language of the Graeco-Roman world (which had already been utilised in Judaism) an overarching concept (godliness, *eusebeia*) which embraces both theology and ethics. Used hermeneutically this concept is surely 'good news for today' as it enables us to both perceive and practise the inter-related elements of godliness and to contain these elements under the umbrella of a single, unifying philosophical concept and to explore contemporary attitudes and activity in the light of that concept.

In these two language concepts (*epiphaneia*, *eusebeia*) the Pastoral Letters demonstrate: 1. the development of the Pauline message in the first century and 2. provide for the twenty-first-century Church a model of how the reinterpretation of its preaching and ministry might be achieved in order that our contemporary needs might be met.

2. PAUL'S FINAL WORDS, JOURNEY, TRIAL AND MARTYRDOM

Given their emphasis upon 'succession' and new perceptions the Pastoral letters raise questions as to how the conclusion of Paul's life and missionary activity might be reconstructed. Although much weight is given rightly to Paul's martyrdom (and also to Peter's) the reconstruction of events is extremely problematic. With regard to Paul's succession to Timothy and Titus it is the understanding of this concept which both enhanced Paul's vocation in his latter years and defined the 'vocational shape' of Timothy and Titus. This definition gave them the necessary authority by which they were able to exercise the ministry both as envoys of Paul during his life, but perhaps more significantly, after his martyrdom. There are two important concepts in this regard: first, 'the Pauline succession' originates from 'Christ Jesus' (1 Tim 1:12; 2 Tim 1:13) and secondly there is the concept of the tradition itself: its meaning and implications for Gospel ministry. These concepts also define the ministerial tasks to be performed (e.g. 2 Tim 4:2; Titus 1:5) and the beliefs (e.g. 1 Tim 1:3-5) and character (e.g, Titus 1:5-11) necessary in those appointed to exercise them. These observations, however, ought to be seen in the context of a wider framework.

First, the question arises as to the final words which Paul wrote. The answer depends on the judgements made regarding Paul's 'authentic' letters and the order and the date on which they were written. The possibilities are: 2 Timothy 4:6-22; Ephesians 6:10-23; Colossians 4:7-18; Philippians 4:8-23; Romans 15:14-33; 16:17-23 and 16:25-27. The texts in which Paul speaks of his imminent death are: Philippians 4:17 and 2 Timothy 4:6-8. The interpretation of these passages is difficult. 2 Timothy could have been written after Paul's death and be a 'reflection' upon it while the location of Paul's writing of Philippians in Rome has been questioned. We have also seen that, in both Philippians and 2 Timothy, Paul envisages the possibility of release from prison and the continuation of missionary activity.

Secondly, Luke leaves the question of the outcome of Paul's Roman trial unresolved. He concludes his Acts narrative with Paul preaching Christ in Rome 'openly and unhindered' and 'at his own expense' (Acts 28:30-31). Is the reader of Acts to suppose that Paul was released after his first trial in c. 62 and able to continue with missionary activity either in Spain (Rom 15:24), in Dalmatia (2 Tim 4:10) or in Nicopolis (Titus 3:12)? In 2 Tim 4:16 Paul writes of his 'first defence'. Is the reader to imply that Paul was released in c. 62 and, if 2 Timothy is post-Pauline, that he was re-tried and executed in either 64 or 67/68? There is no way that these questions can be answered satisfactorily except to note (as indicated in chapter 7) that Paul's theology (as reflected through the Pauline tradition or Paul's interpreters) became influential in large areas of the Church.

Thirdly, the first Christian writer to refer to Paul's martyrdom is the author of 1 Clement (I discuss the author, date and the interpretation of Paul offered by this author in chapter 7). Clement's comments are to be found in chapter 5 where he uses the example of Peter and Paul both to encourage the Corinthian Christians to remain steadfast in the faith and to illustrate how Peter and Paul were subjected to 'envy and jealousy' (1 Clem 5:2). It is the first occasion in the Christian tradition in which the ministries of Peter and Paul are seen together (cf. Gal 2:11; Acts 15:6-21) in terms of being 'the greatest and most righteous pillars of the Church' and who, as a result, were persecuted and martyred. The reward for such endurance and suffering is eternal, heavenly glory which Clement describes in terms of Jerusalem Temple language as the glorious or Holy place (1 Clem 5:4 and 5:7). Clement also provides details concerning the world-wide (in Roman terms) nature of Paul's missionary activity (5:6-7). Like the readers of 2 Timothy, are Clement's readers to suppose that Paul's martyrdom took place after this activity in c. 64 or 67? Also, were they to imply that Peter and Paul were not martyred at the same time or in the same way? This latter point is confirmed by Eusebius who maintained that: 'It is recorded that in his (the Emperor Nero's) reign Paul was beheaded in Rome itself, and that Peter likewise was crucified, and the record is confirmed by the fact that the cemeteries there are still called by the names of Peter and Paul, and equally so by a churchman named Gaius, who was living while Zephyrinus was Bishop of Rome.' (*The History of the Church*, 2:25.5-6). Eusebius' purpose is both to demonstrate the unity of these principal apostolic figures in faith and martyrdom but also to highlight that, as a Roman citizen, Paul died by beheading while Peter suffered (like Jesus) the penalty of crucifixion. Clement places the united testimony of the principal apostolic

271

figures, Peter and Paul, at the head of a more extended account of Christian witnesses who were prosecuted, tortured and executed by Nero c. AD 64-68 (cf. 1 Clement chapter 6). The circumstances surrounding the persecution of Christians by Nero is narrated by the Roman historians, Tacitus (*The Annals of Imperial Rome*, 15:44) and Suetonius (*The Twelve Caesars, Nero*, 16).

In the light of the diversity of this evidence how are we to assess the circumstances relating to Paul's martyrdom? It is likely that he arrived in Rome, c. 60, having appealed, as a Roman citizen (Acts 22:25-29), to the Emperor on charges (Acts 24:2-9) brought against him originally by the Jews of Judaea (Acts 25:10-12). Paul's activity (if any) after his 'first defence' (2 Tim 4:16) is a matter for speculation. If he was freed he may have undertaken some of the missionary and ministerial work (with his companions) which he had intended. This activity was based on God's eschatological plan of salvation through Jesus, which involved the in-gathering of the nations (advanced in Rom 15:15-21). On this basis, at some stage, c. 64/67, Paul would have returned to Rome. On this occasion he would have become embroiled in the political, cultural and religious activities of Nero against the Christians together with the unstable government which existed in both the city of Rome and in parts of the Empire (recounted by Tacitus, *Annals*, 15:48ff). Of the events of this period probably the most powerful is that which Tacitus records of the suicide of Nero's former tutor, the Stoic philosopher, Seneca (*Annals*, 15:60-64), ordered to be poisoned by the Emperor on account of his role in the 65 plot. The martyrdom of Paul, therefore, ought to seen against the wider context of Nero's misrule and the political instability from 64 onwards and in terms of the 'Christ or Caesar' argument. If Eusebius is correct in recording that Paul was beheaded (the usual form of execution for a Roman citizen) then it can be supposed that he underwent some form of trial. What were the charges on this occasion? Again, we can speculate that they involved belonging to an illegal organisation and treason against Rome and its Emperor, the Jewish accusations having become a thing of the past.

Eusebius records information provided by Gaius that he

can 'point out the monuments of the victorious apostles. If you will go as far as the Vatican or the Ostian Way, you will find the monuments of those who founded this church' (*The History of the Church*, 2:25.7). Whatever the value of this evidence (Gaius is mistaken about Paul being the founder of the Roman church, Rom 1:10-12) both the traditional sites for Paul's martyrdom on the Ostian Way: Tre Fontane Abbey and St Paul's Outside the Walls form a fitting symbolic conclusion to Paul's life and vocation. Not only does this symbolic conclusion unite Peter and Paul in the apostolic ministry based at Rome, where the church continued to expand despite Nero's activities, but illustrates also how Paul's influence continued. This influence can be conceived in two ways. First, in terms of Paul's theology regarding the resurrection (e.g. 1 Cor 15:12-58) and eternal life (e.g. Phil 3:20) in which he, and all Christian believers, share and secondly, the progression, extension and development of Pauline thought manifested both by the missionary expansion of the Church and the production (Hebrew, Ephesians?, the Pastoral Letters?) and the interpretation of the Pauline writings. Continuing evangelisation and the developing interpretation of Paul's life and activity based on these writings is surely good news for today.

CHAPTER 7

PAUL'S EARLY INTERPRETERS

LUKE

1. Understanding Luke's method and purpose

To understand Luke's aim in presenting his portrait of Paul in the way he does it is necessary first to ask about Luke's overall purpose in writing and then secondly, to enquire how he achieved this purpose as Paul's first interpreter. Luke wrote two volumes now known as the Gospel of Luke and the Acts of the Apostles, probably in the 80s of the first century. These volumes cover the period of the Christian movement from the annunciation of the birth of John the Baptist to his father Zechariah in the Jerusalem Temple (Lk 1:5-25) until the arrival of Paul in Rome as a prisoner (Acts 28:16). Luke's narrative concludes with Paul arguing with the local Jews (Acts 28:23-25) and reproving their hardness of heart for not accepting the Messiahship of Jesus as revealed in the Jewish scriptures (Isa 6:9-10 quoted in Acts 28:26-27). Luke, perhaps deliberately, leaves his readers in suspense over what happened next regarding Paul's trial, instead concluding his narrative with Paul preaching the Gospel of Jesus 'openly and unhindered' at the heart of the Roman Empire (Acts 28:31).

In Luke 1:1-4 Luke explains to his patron Theophilus (Lk 1:3; cf. Acts 1:1), his reason for compiling a narrative which, by beginning in the Jerusalem Temple and concluding in Rome, enshrines the origin and subsequent development of Christianity. Luke realises that he is not the only writer to present the Christian story (Lk 1:1) and justifies his attempt by returning to tradition. Thus, the Christian message and activity was performed both by 'eyewitnesses', the original apostles (Acts 1:21-22) and subsequently by 'ministers of the word' in which category Luke places himself. His aim is to present a narrative which demonstrates how Christianity can be both proclaimed and practised. His theme is continuity: the way in which early Christianity reflects the life and teaching of

Jesus and how these two phenomena are inter-connected. This observation has led to much discussion in modern scholarship as to how the two volumes should be conceived of as a unity (Walton, *FNTS*, 236). In this context I suggest that Luke is asking his readers to consider the relationship between Jesus' ministry in Galilee, Samaria and Jerusalem with that offered in, for example, Jerusalem, Samaria, Antioch, Corinth, Ephesus and Rome in the post-Ascension age Church (Acts 1:8). The common theological thread is provided by the activity of the Holy Spirit who acts as both the motivating force in the life of Jesus (e.g. Lk 4:1; 4:14 and 4:18, quoting Isa 61:1) and that within the early Church (e.g. Acts 1:2; 1:5; 1:16 and 2:4). Because of both the diversity and the inter-connectedness of the Christian tradition Luke is anxious to offer 'an orderly account', one in which the various currents and trends within the Christian movement might be followed easily.

Luke's purpose is achieved by the method he employs to present his material to Theophilus and his readers. Luke claims reliability (*asphaleia*, Lk 1:4) for this material. This claim refers to Luke's text in all aspects: historical, theological and pastoral. In contemporary scholarship numerous labels have been utilised to characterise Luke's form and method. In my judgement the clearest and most accurate is 'apologetic historiography'. By using this label it can be shown that Luke is presenting a 'case', perhaps a series of different cases, maybe to different audiences, Jewish and Gentile. His 'case' is to demonstrate the purpose (Lk 1:4) and nature of Christianity (e.g. Acts 2:41-47) within the Roman environment of which Judaism forms part.

2. Luke as historian

Three facets of Luke's historical approach are worthy of further comment. First Luke acts as a 'theological historian'. His narrative is a description of God's power in action principally evidenced through the Messianic ministry of Jesus, and the subsequent missionary endeavours of his apostles (e.g. Peter and Paul) and the early Christian communities they evangelised. The purpose of Luke's narrative, therefore, is to demonstrate the expansion of Christianity, the nature of its message and practice together with its reception within Graeco-Roman society of the eastern Mediterranean as part of God's plan and the result of God's revelation in Jesus, the Messiah (e.g. Acts 2:22-24; 13:27-31).

Secondly, Luke acts as a 'biblical historian'. This activity operates in a number of ways, but is especially evident in Luke's imitation of the style and content of the Greek Bible, the Septuagint (LXX). Luke introduces numerous biblical quotations into his narrative (e.g. Acts 13:33 quoting Ps 2:7), and utilizes biblical characters as archetypes; for example, Abraham (e.g. Acts 7:2-8) Moses (e.g. Acts 7:35-44), Hannah (unnamed but forms the background to Mary's song, Lk 1:46-55), David (e.g. Acts 2:25-35), Elijah and Elisha (e.g. Lk 4:25-27), to illustrate both their fidelity to God and their fulfilment in Christ. In this way Luke's account of Jesus and the Church is based on God's dealing with Israel.

Thirdly, Luke utilises the conventions of Graeco-Roman historians (explicated especially in the prologue to each volume addressed to his patron, Theophilus [cf. Lk 1:3, Acts 1:1]). In this area it is important not to claim too much or to overstate the argument. Many suggestions have been made as to the classical authors upon whom Luke is relying. I find that reference to the fifth century BC Greek historian, Thucydides, remains one of the most convincing patterns for Luke to have followed. In book 1 of his *History of the Peloponnesian War*, Thucydides reveals the research basis upon which this account is based (sections 20-23). There is not sufficient space here to justify the patterns in detail except to note: (i) a common desire to present the closely researched truth; (ii) to utilise the most reliable sources in order to project this truth and (iii) on occasions where the characters in the narrative make speeches to remain '...as closely as possible to the general sense of the words that were actually used, to make the speakers say what, in my opinion, was called for by each situation' (Thucydides, 1:22).

Both Thucydides and Luke in their different contexts and by variant methods, are apologetic. They are commending, explaining and justifying. Luke's task was to present the worth of Christianity to Theophilus, its origin within Judaism and Jesus and its subsequent, post-Ascension development through the apostles; in particular, Peter. Yet, for Luke it is the Pauline strand that he wishes to emphasise. It is the strand with which he is most closely involved and it is the one which takes the reader to the heart of the Empire, Rome. Furthermore, both Thucydides and Luke are reflective, hindsight, historians. They look back on events and attempt to interpret them. For Luke, writing in the 80s, he attempts to interpret, for example, the Christian experience against the background of the destruction of the city and Temple of Jerusalem by the Romans in AD 70. Against this event how is the ministry of Jesus and Paul to be perceived for both Jews and Romans?

3. Understanding Luke's view of Paul; insights gained from Luke's use of his sources

In the composition of his two-volume work Luke utilises a variety of sources; for example in his Gospel, Luke employs the existing written Gospel(s) (certainly Mark), oral tradition relating to Jesus' activity and in Acts, information compiled by the Antiochene church (Acts 11:19-27; 13:1-3; 14:26-28; 15:22-23; 15:30-35; 18:22-23) and that supplied by Paul's companions. Although with regard to Acts sources are less clearly defined than in the Gospel and more carefully woven into the narrative. In terms of 'the Acts source category', however, sections where Luke writes in the first person plural ought to be emphasised. These sections are commonly known as the 'we passages'. They are found in:

1. Acts 16:10-17 – preaching in Macedonia, Troas and then Philippi.
2. Acts 20:5-8; 20:13-15 – activity in Troas, Paul's other companions are named at 20:4 (including Timothy) and the subsequent journey to Assos, Mitylene, Samos and Miletus.
3. Acts 21:1-18 – journey from Miletus to Caesarea and eventually to Jerusalem.
4. Acts 27:1-28:16 – final journey to Rome, 'we passages' at 27:1-8; 27:15-20; 27:27-29; 27:37?; 28:1; 28:11-16.

There is little agreement as to how these passages are to be evaluated in literary and historical terms. Their purpose is clearly for the narrator, Luke, to present himself as involved in the narrative rather than recording events second-hand. He may have had access to his own, or another traveller's, diary or he may have been using a traditional literary convention of writing himself into the text at certain points in order to authenticate its testimony. The extent to which Paul's perception of Luke as one of his 'fellow workers' (Philem 24); 'the beloved physician' (Col 4:14) or his lone supporter (2 Tim 4:11) can be related to his role as the author of Acts or as a way of reconstructing the progression of Paul's ministry in relation to Luke, remains speculative.

4. Insights gained from Luke's presentation of Paul

With regard to Luke's presentation of Paul in relationship to the progression of Christianity he emerges as a result of the martyrdom of Stephen. In terms of character Paul (called by his Jewish name, Saul until Acts 13:9) is compared unfavourably to Stephen who is described as being 'full of grace and power' (Acts 6:8); of having a face like that 'of an angel' (Acts 6:15); of possessing great powers of wisdom and oratory and of accepting death as Jesus had done (Lk 23:34 and 23:46) with a spirit of serenity and forgiveness (Acts 7:59-60). Saul, on the other hand, is portrayed initially by Luke as a zealous murderer and persecutor of the Christian community (Acts 7:58; 8:1; 8:3; 9:1). Through this portrayal Luke is offering, through the medium of an 'apologetic narrative', his interpretation of Paul's own statements found in his letters (cf. Gal 1:13-14; 1 Cor 15:9; Phil 3:6).

Similarly with the conclusion of Luke's narrative where Paul has arrived as a prisoner in Rome (Acts 28:16-31). Paul's preaching in Rome is to be seen in terms of the fulfilment of the command of the Risen Christ to the apostles that they are to be his witnesses 'unto the extremity of the earth' (Acts 1:8) which clearly includes Rome, symbolically the capital at the centre of the earth. Luke records that Paul's preaching in Rome has a two-fold aspect: (i) proclaiming the kingdom of God and

(ii) teaching about the Lord Jesus Christ (Acts 28:31). Luke uses this two-fold perspective both as a conclusion to Acts and also as the finale to his two volume work, Luke and Acts. Paul is seen to be both summarising and forming the continuity with Jesus' own proclamation on the subject of 'the kingdom' which began at Lk 4:14 and was reiterated by the Risen Christ in Acts 1:3. At the end of Luke's second volume none of the original apostles to whom the Risen Christ conferred in Acts 1:1-8 are present in Rome. Instead the burden of the commission in Acts 1:8 relating to the 'extremity of the earth' is being executed by Saul/ Paul of Tarsus, the preacher of salvation 'to the Gentiles' (Acts 28:28). It is Luke's intention to explain how, between Acts 7:58 and 28:30-31, these ironies arose.

For Luke, the clue to understanding these ironies is to be found in the observation of God's supernatural activity in relation to Saul/Paul. In this regard Luke records three accounts of Paul's call, conversion and commission. These accounts explain and enlarge in narrative form what Paul has said in his letters (cf. Gal 1:16-17; 1 Cor 15:8-11; 2 Cor 12:1-2; Phil 3:7-11). Luke's three accounts are:

(i)   Acts 9:1-22 which is a sophisticated composition by Luke in which the narrative is formed as a result of the combination of voices: the divine voice of the glorified Lord Jesus; the human voice of the would be disciple, Saul; the voice of the existing disciple, Ananias and the voice of the narrator, Luke.

(ii) Acts 22:2-21 which is Paul's defence speech in Hebrew to the Jewish crowd, 'brethren and fathers' (22:1), after his arrest in Jerusalem. Paul's explanation is rejected.

(iii) Acts 26:2-23 which is another defence speech but on this occasion before the Roman procurator, Festus and king Agrippa (Marcus Julius Agrippa II) and his sister, Bernice, who believed that Paul had done nothing to deserve death or imprisonment and, if he had not appealed to Caesar, he would have been a free man (Acts 26:31-32). Thus, the unfavourable attitude of the Jews in Acts 22 is to be compared to the reasonably sympathetic attitude of the Roman officials in Acts 26.

It is not possible to comment in detail upon these three accounts or upon their implications for Luke's interpretation of Paul except: (i) To note that throughout the narrative Luke perceives that the supernatural action of God is at work (e.g. Acts 16:10) and that what Paul was doing was to respond constantly to what God was asking of him in terms of mission and ministry. (ii) To observe 'the new features' which Luke has included in order to explain Paul's 'life journey' and to account for the nature of his activity.

First, Luke informs his readers that Paul was born at, and in the early part of his ministry returned to, Tarsus (Acts 9:11; 9:31; 11:25; 22:3) which he describes as 'no mean city' (Acts 21:39). There is no good reason to doubt the accuracy of this information which Luke has provided as it accounts for some important elements in our evaluation of Paul's thought. Tarsus was the capital of the province of Cilicia and, under the Romans, became a city of cultural and political importance (details, *BSGT*, 322-325). For Luke it explained how Paul was able to be 'cross-cultural': a Hellenistic Jew and, as such informed about both Judaism and aspects of Greek intellectual life, while, at the same time, being born into Roman citizenship (Acts 22:28) and, as far as his Judaism allowed, shared in Roman civic life.

Secondly, Luke states that Paul was educated in Jerusalem by Gamaliel according to 'the strict manner' of interpreting the Jewish *Torah*. In this exercise Paul became zealous (Acts 22:3, also 21:20 and Paul's statement in Gal 1:14) for God and 'the traditions of my fathers' (Gal 1:14). Gamaliel, being a descendant of the Jewish sage, Hillel, was one of the most respected Jewish teachers of his time, c. 25-50 (see also Acts 5:34-40, an attitude not shared by his pupil, Saul of Tarsus). The fact of Paul's education under Gamaliel would account not only for Paul's use of the Jewish scriptures in furthering his particular arguments, but also of the way in which he deals with detailed issues of interpretation. Paul's Jewish education is apparent from his letters. What Luke provides is a personal focus by which the particular form of this education can be identified in Gamaliel and through him to locate the superiority of the teaching which Saul/Paul received.

Thirdly, Luke records that, with Aquila and Priscilla, Paul worked as a tentmaker (*skenopoios*, Acts 18:3). This occupation would have involved a number of skills including working in linen and leather. It has been suggested that the building of theatre stages and props for the plays were also included. This trade had two particular implications for Paul's ministry. First, he used it as a means of supporting himself and his mission rather than relying on the financial support of the local church (1 Thess 2:9; 1 Cor 4:12 and 9:3-18). Secondly, given Paul's education as mentioned above, there would have been a certain contradiction between learning and manual labour which would have identified Paul with the poor and made him, in some circles, the source of derision. Again Luke focusses what Paul had already said about labour in the specific trade of tent-making.

Fourthly, Luke informs us that Paul claimed that he was a Roman citizen (Acts 16:37; 22:25-29). Again there is no reason to doubt this claim (even given Paul's record of his beating in 2 Cor 11:25) and might go some way to explain Paul's political attitudes as stated, for example, in Romans 13:1-7. In this context it should be observed also that there were numerous different ways of understanding what being Roman meant and what this status meant in practice. This fact is illustrated by the conversation between the Roman tribune, Claudius Lysias and Paul in Acts 22:25-29, the difference between being born a Roman citizen and paying for citizenship.

Thus, three innovative features can be detected in Luke's presentation of Paul: (i) Luke offers new insights into Paul's intellectual activity; (ii) by reference to the Roman authorities and unreceptive Jews, the chronological and evangelistic scope of Paul's mission is broadened (iii) Luke offers his own (favourable) appreciation of Paul's character; on occasions, more sympathetic than Paul's appreciation and justification of himself (e.g. 2 Cor 12:7-10?). The 'new features' of information which Luke offers in relation to Paul provide a framework, above all an over-arching chronological framework, into which

Paul's missionary activity can be situated. Luke follows Paul's missionary movements in roughly the chronological order in which they occurred in order to systemise these movements from what he can glean from the account of Paul's journeys from other sources.

Paul becomes the focus in the 'case' in which Luke is making to Theophilus. In doing so Luke is unable to give an over-view of the total movement of Christianity, instead he presents the progression of Christianity from the broad canvas of the command of the Risen Christ (Acts 1:8), the empowering for this ministry being given by the Spirit on the day of Pentecost (Acts 2:1-13) and gradually narrowing in focus until Paul arrives in Rome as a prisoner (Acts 28:16) and preaches 'openly' in that city (28:31).

6. Understanding Luke's interpretation of Paul today

In some areas of contemporary biblical scholarship the interpretation of Luke's view of Paul is a matter of intense debate. To what extent does Luke present an accurate historical picture of Paul? Has Luke understood Paul's theology? In actuality these questions are complex as they involve multi-levels of understanding relating to the development of early Christianity and various literary forms in which these developments were communicated. In this context I offer two perspectives of my own. First, I believe that it was Luke's intention to offer a multi-sided 'case' to Theophilus by presenting Paul within the totality of the Christian experience through the medium of narrative (Acts). The result (in terms of Luke's two volumes: Luke and Acts) should be seen as a considerable achievement not least because of both the continuity and the development portrayed between the activity of Jesus and the progress of Christianity concluding with Paul's arrival in Rome. This view of Luke was accepted within the Church as evidenced by Eusebius (*The History of the Church*, book 3, ch. 4).

Secondly, there has been an unfortunate tendency to present the tension between Paul and Luke as a contrast between the 'authentic' or 'real' Paul seen in his letters (or at least in those claimed to be 'undisputed') and the 'imagined' Paul as interpreted by Luke. A good example of a significant point of discontiuity concerns the apostolic identity of Paul. Luke is doubtful that the category should be applied to Paul (contrast 1 Cor 9:1-2; but cf. Acts 14:4, 14) as he believed that apostleship was invested supremely with the twelve who were called by Jesus at the beginning of his earthly ministry (Lk 6:13-16) and who witnessed his resurrection (Acts 1:21-22, Peter's statement at the election of Matthias). Paul could not claim to be an apostle on these grounds but argued for his apostleship on the basis of God's direct call and intervention (e.g. Gal 1:1 on the basis of 1:15-17).

I should wish to present this tension differently, as between the way in which Paul presents himself in his letters and the interpretation of Paul as offered by Luke. If Luke is writing in the 80s then the context in which Christianity operates, certainly in relation to Jews and Romans and their relationship to each other, has changed from Paul's time. It is in this context that Luke is presenting to Theophilus how the Church ought to be perceived in terms of its founder, Jesus and his followers, including Paul; how the nature of its faith ought to be explained; its understanding of community, both within itself and in terms of civic responsibility and the trials which are confronting it. In this scenario Luke's interpretation of Paul is of great importance. That is why, in addition to the researching of Paul's letters, a study of Luke's Acts is also good news for today.

HEBREWS, 1 PETER, 2 PETER

1. Hebrews

The issue before us is how can these New Testament writings be said to be interpreting the Pauline tradition. In the case of Hebrews it is now considered that this epistle is non-Pauline (Attridge, *OBC*, 1236) given its genre, structure, vocabulary and contents. This non-Pauline position results, for example, from the fact Hebrews does not use the central Pauline terms and has a wider vocabulary than used by Paul. The Christology of the work is distinctive, as is its form, which is presented in the shape of a homily. The structure of the work is also unlike any known Pauline letter. The question arises as to the degree to which the author, being highly skilled in ancient rhetoric, utilised this skill to a greater extent than is manifest in other Pauline letters. Yet the reference to Timothy in the conclusion (Heb 13:23) may have suggested a connection with Paul and his pastoral ministry (Heb 13:22), despite the lack of explicit reference to Paul as author.

As a result the early Church Fathers dealt with this 'mixed' picture in various ways. Some unease emerged over the question of its Pauline authorship and, on this basis, its place within the Church's canonical scripture as an authentic Pauline document was questioned. The Syriac church, for example, did not accept the letter as canonical until the sixth century.

Clement of Alexandria (c.155-220) accepted Pauline authorship in a modified sense: Paul wrote a hypothetical original document in Hebrew which Luke translated it into Greek (noted by Eusebius in *The History of the Church*, Book 6:14). It was therefore in this process of translation and scribal reinterpretation that the differences in style between Hebrews and the other Pauline letters were alleged to have occurred. In the same vein Eusebius (Book 6:25) quotes Origen (c. 185-254) who believed that, although the contents were worthy of Paul, the style came probably from either Clement (Bp. of Rome) or Luke. Origen is uncertain and declares that the identity of the author 'is known to God alone' thus becoming the first biblical exegete to place Hebrews within the Pauline tradition. Athanasius (c. 296-373, Bishop of Alexandria from 328) in his 39th Easter Letter of 367 first argued for a fourteen letter Pauline corpus in the New Testament, which includes Hebrews.

Hebrews begins with a four verse (Heb 1:1-4) single sentence prologue, which is a comparison between the two ages: the fragmentary age of Israel's past and the totality and finality of the Christian era manifested by the person and activity of the Son who is superior over all creatures, in particular the angels. Pauline letters have no hint of such a form, opening rather with the traditional letter greeting, declaring the apostolic author(s) and intended destination. The author of Hebrews calls his work 'my word of exhortation' (*ho logos tes parakleseos*, Heb 13:22) an expression which he shares with Luke where Paul declares that his Pisidian Antioch Synagogue homily is a 'word of exhortation' (Acts 13:14). By designating his work in these terms the author of Hebrews demonstrates both his genre and his purpose, a homily to exhort his readers not to return to Judaism but to hold on steadfastly to their Christian calling (e.g. Heb 3:11 and 6:4-6). It could be that, given the form but not the content of the prologue and the author's stated purpose of 'encouragement', perhaps it is the Lucan tradition (as perceived by both Clement and Origen, cf. Lk 1:1-4; Acts 13:14) which is being interpreted or even the Pauline tradition as mediated by Luke rather than Paul himself, with which the author of Hebrews is engaging.

The three major issues with which Hebrews is concerned: (i) Christology, (ii) pilgrimage and (iii) Judaism, are all Pauline themes but the author of Hebrews interprets them differently from Paul.

(i)   In terms of Christology Hebrews retains Paul's 'Sonship' Christology (e.g. Heb 1:2 and 2:5; cf. Gal 1:16; Rom 1:3) but then interprets Jesus in terms of high priesthood (Heb 3:1), combining Sonship and high priesthood (Heb 5:5, by means of Ps 2:7 and 110:4), and using the ancient figure of Melchizedek (Heb 7:1-3, by means of Gen 14:17-20) to demonstrate the superiority of Jesus' priesthood to that of the Jewish priests (e.g. Heb 7:4-10). Some aspects of this Christology of high priesthood are to be found also in 1 Clem 36. While relating the superiority of Jesus over the angels and affirming his Sonship and Lordship (Ps 2:7-8; Ps 104:4; Ps 110:1) Clement uses his own expression in that experiencing Jesus 'the peerless perfection of the face of God' is perceived. It is likely that Hebrews and Clement are drawing upon the same Christological traditions in order to advance their particular arguments (1 Clem 36:1- Heb 2:18; 3:1; 1 Clem 36:2- Heb 1:3; 1:4;

1:7; 1 Clem 36:4- Heb 1:5; 1 Clem 36:5- Heb 1:13). The background to this high priestly language might be found in the conjunction between Jesus as high priest and Jesus as the sacrifice offered. In 1 Corinthians 5:7 Christ is seen as the Passover sacrifice, so it could be that the author of Hebrews is building upon this idea and combining it with priesthood.

(ii) For the author of Hebrews the Christian faithful are the pilgrim people who have no abiding city in the world (Heb 13:14) but whose destiny is the heavenly city to come (Heb 12:22). To this city Jesus has gone already (Heb 4:14) as pioneer and perfecter (Heb 12:2). Both these terms are unknown to Paul. Faithfulness is the prerequisite for the believers to enter into this heavenly rest (Heb 4:1); if they commit apostasy they will become like Israel of old and never enter the promised rest (Heb 3:15 and 4:3 interpreting Ps 95:7-8 and 11 regarding Israel entering the promised land).

(iii) For Hebrews Judaism, the old covenant is obsolete (Heb 8:13 by means of Gen 31:31-34). This observation confirms the author's view that Christianity is superior. Like Paul, Hebrews frequently uses the Jewish scriptures to enhance his arguments. Their use though, for him, is two fold. First, to demonstrate the need for steadfastness and discipline in the practice of Christianity (e.g. Prov 3:1-12 used in Heb 12:5-6) and secondly to show the superiority of Christ over other mediators (e.g. Ps 8:4-6 used in Heb 2:6-8).

It is in the concluding greetings and blessing (Heb 13:18-25) that the closest resemblance to the Pauline literary form can be seen:

13:18   Request for prayer for us, the apostles (?) in their ministry linked to the idea that they have a clear conscience (used by Paul, 2 Cor 1:12);

13:19   'I' (presumed to be Paul's) injunction for the believers to act honourably in order that he might visit them (cf. 2 Cor 13:1 and 13:11 where both the name of the apostle (Paul) and the church (Corinth) are indicated clearly);

13:20-21   The concluding blessing which emphasises: The God of peace (note found in many Pauline opening greetings, e.g. 2 Thess 1:2; Gal 1:3; 1 Cor 1:3; 2 Cor 1:2; Rom 1:7 and in the concluding blessings, 2 Cor 13:11; Rom 15:33).

Hebrews 13:22-24 contain injunctions of personal intent:

13:22   The author makes an appeal for his readers to endure his 'word of exhortation'

13:23   Timothy was Paul's companion and often sent on missionary work by him (1 Thess 3:2; 1 Cor 16:10; Phil 2:19 and the Pastoral letters). Timothy's named involvement gives the homily a personal perspective, although his imprisonment is not known. It is, therefore, the 'Paul – Timothy link' which historically places the homily within the 'Paul – Pauline tradition' axis.

13:24   Has two parts: (a) an injunction to greet the faithful (saints) and the leaders and (b) a greeting from 'those from Italy'. This observation has led to the speculations that those addressed were also Italian, maybe Roman (Rom 16:21 where Timothy greets the Roman Christians).

13:25   The homily concludes with the offer of grace.

Any consideration of Hebrews is beset by imprecision with regard to its location and date. Equally no clear picture emerges as to how the author is interpreting Paul. Even in Hebrews 13 it is possible that Pauline maxims and circumstances are being utilised but also the author of Hebrews could be interpreting Paul alongside other Christian traditions. When Hebrews was considered to be Pauline by the collector of the manuscript corpus of Pauline letters, P 46 (with eight other Pauline letters) the perspective changed; an attempt to integrate Hebrews into Pauline thought was necessary. Rather than providing a contrast between the Christology of Hebrews and Paul's earlier letters, the editor of P46 would have seen Hebrews' Christology in terms of development, thus broadening the horizons as to how Paul's thought should be conceived. Both Clement and Origen observed the difficulty of this attempt and tried to account for it by posing 'second revisors'. From the contemporary, historical – critical perspective, if Hebrews is relating any of Paul's thought he is doing so in a particular way. The terms of Christology, however, the amalgam of high priesthood, Sonship and 'divine hero' produces an unique understanding of Christ. The question remains as to whether Paul would have recognised, or even agreed with the amalgam. What the study of the epistle to the Hebrews illustrates is the creative possibilities which the interpretation of Paul and other Christian writings can produce.

2. 1 and 2 Peter

If Luke is seen as Paul's interpreter in narrative form and the author of Hebrews as his interpreter interwoven with other Christian traditions in homiletic form of the apostles and the 'I' of Paul assumed to be entering the text at the epistle's conclusion (Heb 13:18-25), then the Petrine epistles in their various ways illustrate the influence of the Pauline letter – structure; some aspects of Paul's thought and his influence (2 Pet 3:15-17) upon other Christian (now canonical) literature.

The question remains as before; how can 1 and 2 Peter be seen to be interpreting Paul? To which question there is no specific answer, although some general observations can be attempted. The way in which this literature interprets the relationship between Paul and Peter is instructive. From Paul's perspective he exposes his disagreements with Peter (Cephas, Gal 2:11 and 2:14) within the context of Paul's ambivalent relationship with the Jerusalem apostles (Gal 2:9) and his tumultuous relationship with the Galatian churches. Luke, however, portrays the corporate activity and united theological purpose of Peter and Paul (e.g. Acts 15:7-12) while the author of 2 Peter exalts his readers to follow 'our beloved brother Paul' by imitating the wisdom found in his letters (2 Pet 3:15-16).

The difficulty in relating these perspectives with each other is one of dating and context. Although Paul's reflections relating to Peter in Galatians and 1 Corinthians (1:12; 3:22; 9:5; 15:5) can be given a reasonably precise context: Luke is probably writing in the 80s, while both the authorship and dating of the Petrine epistles remains both uncertain and controversial. Luke and the Petrine epistles probably reflect the 'martyr traditions' which developed round Paul (2 Tim 4:6) and Peter (Jn 21:18-19) following their death during Nero's persecution in the 60s (1 Clem 5). Their martyrdoms acted as a unifying factor whereby subsequent generations could perceive their death in terms of united witness to Christ and the Gospel.

The work of the Petrine authors in terms of being interpreters of Paul can be seen in two ways: first (i) the use of the Pauline letter structure and secondly (ii) through the theological and pastoral issues which are raised.

(i)   1 Peter 1:1-2 declares Peter to be an apostle and to be writing to the numerous churches to be found in the Roman provinces of Pontus, Galatia, Cappadocia, Asia and Bithynia. Both on his own admission and also according to Luke's narrative in Acts, Paul had founded some of these churches (see Map 4). Yet for Peter to have addressed such a large area illustrates the development of the letter form to include regional (2 Cor 1:2), multi-provincial communities (1 Pet 1:1) and to have application for all churches in addition to specific local issues (e.g. 1 Thess 1:1; 4:1; 5:1). Peter uses a theological formula in which to address these churches and like Paul offers them grace (*charis*) and peace (*eirene* 1 Pet 1:2 cf. 1 Thess 1:1). Peter adds, however, the observation developed from the Jewish diaspora that the Christians addressed are 'exiles of the dispersion'. This idea develops that of Paul where he writes of the Philippian Christians as having their 'commonwealth in heaven' (Phil 3:20). The Christians' true home therefore is in heavenly glory, their ministry in the world being seen in terms of exile or of anticipating the return of Christ (1 Thess 4:16; Phil 3:20). The author of 2 Peter, following this tradition, universalises the message of his letter in order that all believers might share in the righteousness of God and Jesus (2 Pet 1:1) which develops Paul's idea on this theme (e.g. Rom 1:17). In order to authenticate the contents as Petrine, the author has added Peter's Jewish name, Simeon (cf. Mk 3:16). This procedure is designed to link the letter (note also 2 Pet 1:16-18 in relation to Mk 9:2-8 and parallels) to Peter's role as one of Jesus' original disciples. In exalting Peter in this way the author knew that he could not do the same for Paul (cf. Gal 1:15-16; 1 Cor 15:3-10). Paul, therefore, has been grafted into this ministry as a result of God's subsequent calls to him and through Paul's writings Peter is given the wisdom to confront the false prophets (2 Pet 2:1-3) within the church community.

1 Peter 5:12-14 contains a concluding exaltation and blessing similar to that found in Paul's letters (e.g.,1 Cor 16:19-24) which illustrates the attempt to imitate Pauline concluding greetings. Individuals are mentioned (Silvanus and Mark), the purpose of the letter stated – to exhort and declare what is the true grace of God and to offer the greeting of peace (cf. 1 Thess 5:23-28). Babylon (1 Pet 5:13; Rev 16:19) is likely to be a code-word for Rome. If this is so, 1 Peter contains the tension between Rome, the persecutor of Christians (1 Pet 4:12-19) and its Emperor who is to be honoured (1 Pet 2:13 and 2:17). 2 Peter does not have a concluding greeting along this pattern but rather an exaltation for those addressed to 'grow in the grace and knowledge of our Lord and Saviour Jesus Christ' (2 Pet 3:18). This universal statement and the doxology which follows fits well with the generalised nature of this letter (cf. 2 Pet 1:1). Given that the Petrine letters are difficult to date (suggestions range from AD 60-120) it can be seen that in terms of structure the Pauline letter form remained an important vehicle for Christian communication. It is likely that the author of 1 Peter is utilising the Pauline letter form and into that form places his particular synthesis of Christian theology addressed to numerous churches in four/five Roman provinces.

(ii) What is less certain is the Pauline texts upon which the Petrine authorship are drawing. In the case of 2 Peter, although Paul's letters are mentioned and their wisdom praised (2 Pet 3:15), it is not clear upon which Pauline texts (1 Thess and Rom?) or what of Paul's ideas he intends his readers to note. The clue to this issue is probably to be found in 2 Pet 3:10 where the coming of 'the day of the Lord' is said to be 'like a thief' an image which Paul has used in his earliest letter, 1 Thessalonians (5:2 and 5:4). Peter's purpose therefore, is to demonstrate that he and Paul are united both in their eschatological teachings and in their prophetic utterances (2 Pet 1:20-21). True, Paul's writings are difficult to understand and, as a result, open to misinterpretation (2 Pet 3:16). If they are interpreted, however, in the light of God's true prophetic spirit their contents reveal that both Simeon Peter and Paul are slaves and apostles of Jesus Christ (2 Pet 1:1; Rom 1:1) and in the light of this united apostolic witness teach the same truth relating to Christ's return as judge and of the upright ethical behaviour which is to be demanded from the believers (2 Pet 3:11-13). Paul's letters then are being utilised in 2 Peter as a vehicle against false teaching.

The contents of 1 Peter are said to bear similarities to Romans and Ephesians. This observation, however, raises difficulties. As 1 Peter does not mention Paul by name the question arises as to the interpretative value of similarities.

On one hand it could be argued that 1 Peter demonstrates literary dependence upon the letters or, on the other, that they represent a more general affinity to the catechesis offered by the churches. Here are some examples by which the options might be tested:

1 Peter 1:6-7	–	Romans 5:3-5
1 Peter 1:14	–	Romans 12:2
1 Peter 2:6-8	–	Romans 9:32-33
1 Peter 2:13-17	–	Romans 13:1-7
1 Peter 3:8-9	–	Romans 12:16-17
1 Peter 4:10-11	–	Romans 12:6-7

In addition literary affinities have been found with Ephesians (e.g. 1 Pet 1:3; Eph 1:3; 1 Pet 1:10-12; Eph 3:5); with the Jesus tradition (e.g. 1 Pet 3:9; Lk 6:28); Acts, the Pastoral letters and 1 Clement. Yet the acknowledgement of such affinities raises questions relating to authorship, date, genre and purpose and still leaves us with our central question: how does 1 Peter interpret Paul? It is possible here only to offer pointers to how this question might be answered:

1. In enquiring about Pauline interpretation in 1 Peter it is first necessary to ask about what this author intends. With the exception of the theology of the Holy Spirit, 1 Peter produced a balanced synthesis of the major elements of Christian theology. This work is primarily theological in that it seeks to present Christianity within the framework of God's action in terms of him being the faithful Creator who brings the new creation to birth and who acts as impartial judge (e.g. 1 Pet 1:3-5; 2:9-10; 4:19; 5:6). 1 Peter may have the intention of offering both baptismal catechesis (1 Pet 3:21-22) and encouragement in time of persecution (1 Pet 4:12-14). In presenting these aims 1 Peter is drawing upon already formulated statements of theology and Christianity found in the church's catechetical tradition. 1 Peter interprets Paul, along with other traditions, to further the intentions of the letter. By making this observation we look first to the interpreter's purpose and context.

2. This point goes some way to explaining why 1 Peter clearly affirms some aspects of Paul's thought whilst other aspects are absent. Given that one of the groups of churches which 1 Peter addresses is in Galatia (1 Pet 1:1) there is no hint of the theological and pastoral argument which Paul had in Galatians relating to justification by faith in Christ performing the 'works of law' and the theology of grace (e.g. Gal 2:16; 2:21). Yet by the time 1 Peter was written these issues may have been resolved or, being a letter and having a specific context they may not have been relevant to the author's purpose. Thus, 1 Peter

'uses' Paul in the way in which he is needed to enhance the arguments presented in 1 Peter.

3. Whatever its date it is clear that 1 Peter stands within the Pauline tradition, but how? I speculate that the author of 1 Peter gives Paul an honoured place within the developing Christian tradition but places him alongside other traditions and interprets what he knows of Paul's writings (certainly Romans) in terms of his own purpose and within the wider context (1 Pet 1:1) of the developing Church and the circumstances forced upon it by 'Babylon' (1 Pet 5:13).

1 CLEMENT, IGNATIUS, POLYCARP, MARCION

1. Setting the Scene

The aim of this section is to offer, in outline form, the ways in which Paul's letters and teaching were interpreted from the late first century into the middle of the second century AD. Clement (d.c. 96); Ignatius (c. 35-107) and Polycarp (c. 69-155) are described as 'Apostolic Fathers' on account of their orthodox and Catholic interpretation of Christianity. Marcion (d.c. 160) on the other hand, a native of Sinope in Pontus, who arrived in Rome c.140, formed a Christian philosophical system of his own which attempted to exclude Judaism and the Jewish *Torah* from Christian theological understanding and to establish Christianity in terms of a Gospel of Love, thus marginalising the legal framework of *Torah*. On these grounds Marcion was excommunicated from the Roman church in 144 and declared to be heretical. Marcion's writings have now been lost and much of what is known about him can only be gleaned from the Church Fathers, especially Tertullian (c.160 – c.225) and Irenaeus (c.130 – c.200) who sought to refute his ideas. My purpose in comparing the thought of Marcion to that of Clement, Ignatius and Polycarp is to demonstrate that alternative interpretations of Paul are one of the ways in which the profound disagreements between the different groups arose. These disagreements focussed fundamentally on different doctrines of God. For Marcion, the concept God and Father of Jesus Christ needed to be separated from the manifestation of God found in the Jewish scriptures, while for the Church Fathers it was essential that continuity be maintained between the two concepts, Jesus' manifestation of God being the fulfilment of what had been revealed to Israel. In this context it was important that, in terms of ethics, the Jewish *Torah* be seen to have been both accepted, and also fulfilled and re-interpreted by Jesus, Paul and ongoing Christian teaching.

I have simplified these different approaches in order to illustrate: (i) that during the second century, Paul's thought was open to a variety of interpretations and for us to understand the basis on which they are based and (ii) through my outline description to offer the incentive for the reader to engage in further research.

2. 1 Clement

Clement mentions Paul on two occasions:

1. 5:3-7 where he speaks of the martyrdoms of Peter and Paul. I have referred already to this text in the attempt to reconstruct the outline of the circumstances of Paul's martyrdom. Clement also records here Paul's other trials on behalf of the faith: imprisonment, exile and stoning. These trials were on account of 'jealousy and strife' (5:6) and, as a result of them, Paul won 'the prize of endurance' (5:5). He was also a herald of the faith in both 'the East and the West' and through this ministry 'taught righteousness to the whole world' (5:7). Clement's purpose is to demonstrate that in his time (c.96) Paul's example of both evangelisation and endurance is to be emulated by Christians and their leaders.

2. 47:1-3 where the Corinthian Christians are exhorted to read and act upon Paul's letter – presumably 1 Corinthians – which he wrote to them in an earlier age,

c.54. In this way 1 Clement is to be seen in continuity with 1 Corinthians. The same 'personality centred' attitude to church leaders (3:3; 44:6) and disunity within the church was occurring in c.96 as it did in Paul's time. In 47:3 Clement quotes 1 Cor 1:12 regarding the Corinthians' habit of causing disunity by linking themselves to particular church leaders; for example, Apollos and Cephas. In c.96 they seem to be still adopting this unhealthy attitude. The reading of 1 Corinthians, therefore, should encourage the few troublemakers (47:6) to repent (51:1) and to respect those who have been duly appointed as their Church leaders (44:3-6; 46:4; 47:6; 48:1). It appears that some of the younger men have deposed the more senior elders (3:3), for Clement an act of disrespect given that these leaders had exercised a blameless ministry (44:6). Their behaviour has been harmful to the 'image' of the church, both within other churches (including Rome) and within wider Roman society ('those who do not share our faith' 47:7).

It is important, however, not merely to recognise Clement's use of Paul in cases where there seems to be literary dependence. The analysis of this alleged dependence is not easy to gauge and there are disagreements as to how many of Paul's letters (with the exception of 1 Corinthians and Romans) that Clement actually knew. Here are some examples:

1 Clem 24:1	1 Cor 15:20	1 Cor 15:23
1 Clem 24:4-5	1 Cor 15:36-37	
1 Clem 35:5-6	Rom 1:29-32	
1 Clem 37:5	1 Cor 12:12 & 12:14	1 Cor 12:20-28

I have shown already the possible allusions between 1 Clement 36:1-5 and Hebrews 1:3-17, yet the substantial point in this context is that Clement is presenting (and reminding) the Corinthians that both the ministry of Paul and his teaching is to be seen as a 'model' for their attitudes, ministry and behaviour and a 'model' to be imitated by them in their contemporary context.

Yet Clement has utilised his perceptions about Paul in

order to relate them to the particular church situation with which he was confronted. Although I have referred to the letter as 1 Clement, and followed the convention of naming Clement as the author, it is important to stress that the letter was written from the Roman church, rather than from a church leader, to the Corinthian church. It is a community product, written in the first person plural. Although the opening greeting (1:1-3) is similar to that found in some of the Pauline letters, nevertheless, unlike these letters, the author is not named. In every surviving manuscript however Clement's name appears in the title. Numerous suggestions have been made as to Clement's identity. Although he does not name him as the author, Irenaeus dates 1 Clement from when Clement was Bishop of Rome who is named as the fourth in line of Episcopal succession: Peter, Linus, Anacletus, Clement. Eusebius also makes this connection but names Clement as the third Bishop of Rome and as a companion of Paul. If this connection is correct then, behind the letter is the authority of the Bishop for whom succession to Peter and Paul is claimed and under whose guidance Clement acts and, with the congregation of the Roman church, requests that the Corinthians do the same (1 Clem 5:3).

If the authorship of 1 Clement has been questioned so has the date on which the letter was supposed to have been written. The c. 96 date is based on a particular interpretation of 1:1 where Clement speaks of 'our recent series of unexpected misfortunes and set-backs' (Louth trans. 23). These misfortunes are said to be connected to the persecution of Christians which took place under the Emperor Domitian in 93. This persecution is said to have generated memories of the persecution of Christians by the Emperor Nero thirty years before in 64 (6:1-2; 7:1). The extent, form and geographical location however, of Domitian's activity are now difficult to reconstruct. It could be that 1 Clement should be dated earlier say to the 70s or 80s. Despite the difficulties relating both to authorship and date I believe that this earlier date is unlikely and traditional scholarly opinion of arguing that Clement (third or fourth Bishop of Rome) was the author and that c.96 was around the time when the letter was written remains the most plausible suggestion given that the persecution mentioned in chapters 5 and 6 seems to have been in the distant rather than the recent past and that the Corinthian church is described as 'ancient' (47:6).

My purpose has been to demonstrate Clement's interpretation of Paul. This interpretation goes beyond the questions of verbal parallels and literary dependence. It includes the call to imitate Paul as an ethical 'model' and guide. In this regard this imitation is interpreted by Clement in terms of the particular ecclesial situation which is being addressed. Although it is true that the conflict in Corinth with which the Roman church is confronted has similarities to the situation which Paul encountered in the 50s (recognised in 1 Clem 47:3 by quoting 1 Cor 1:12). Nevertheless in the intervening forty(?) years the context has changed. Peter and Paul have been martyred (1 Clem 5:3-5), together with other Christians (1 Clem 6:1-2; 7:1), now the persecution of the Church has recently resurfaced (1:1). Thus, 1 Clement provides insights into both the Roman and Corinthian churches in which, given the practical situation, unity amongst themselves, both within and between churches is essential.

If the historical context has changed so has the environment from which the respective writers, Paul and Clement have emerged and so has also the literary forms in which they are communicating. Paul arose from 'zealous Judaism' (Gal 1:14) into Christianity in the mid-30s while Clement, as a Greek, encountered Christianity in the 50s or 60s. Given the external events related to the first Jewish war and the destruction of the Temple (70) the issues which Paul confronted in the 50s relating to the retention of Jewish religious practice for Christian believers has now faded into the background. Both Paul and Clement operated within a Graeco-Roman environment yet, as the study of the respective use of rhetorical conventions illustrates, by the time Clement wrote these conventions were both used more widely and in a more sophisticated manner. This sophistication may have been due to Clement's Roman education. This tendency is to be discerned in both the form in which Clement writes and in the vocabulary which he utilises. Clement's sixty-five chapters, with their opening greeting, go beyond what is known of Paul's literary texts. 1 Clement emerges as a sophisticated literary treatise which is formed through the medium of persuasion or advice. Clement avoids the use of the command, rather his aim is to encourage his readers in Corinth to accept the suggestions he is making and to act upon them in order that the status quo might be restored. Also Clement supplements Paul's vocabulary. Clement uses the notion of peace (used by Paul both as an attribute of God; e.g. Gal 1:3; Phil 1:2 and as a virtue which believers should demonstrate; e.g. Rom 14:19) but adds to it the concept of harmony (*homonoia*, e.g. 63:2). Did Clement employ this additional concept in order to make the idea of peace better understood by the Corinthians? By the time of the writing of 1 Clement were the Corinthians themselves a church which had become more familiar with this additional civic and literary vocabulary? Does the way in which Clement presents his argument indicate a more sophisticated church membership who, in the intellectual life, were not only familiar with the Jewish scriptures but also edging towards the culture of what has become known as the 'Second Sophistic'? Was the 'not in lofty words or wisdom' strategy of Paul being overtaken by events?

I raise these questions in order to generate discussion as to how Clement interpreted Paul. For Clement Paul is the basis, both on grounds of teaching and martyrdom on which the ministry of the church and its leaders is to be founded. In doing so Clement provides an important continuity between his writings and the earlier Pauline letters. Into Pauline thoughts and actions however, Clement offers a new interpretive framework which is provided by the ecclesial, civic and intellectual environment in which he is operating.

3. Ignatius

Ignatius' sole reference to Paul occurs in his Letter to the Ephesians, 12.

Using Paul's earlier technique of contrast (1 Cor 4:10) 'I am in danger, you are established in security' (I Eph 12:1) Ignatius declares that Ephesus is the gateway through which he will pass on his way to execution in Rome. In this passage Ignatius and other Christian martyrs, are:

I   fellow initiates with Paul,
II   who was sanctified, gained a good report and was blessed.
III Ignatius is imitating Paul who is described as 'saintly and renowned'.
IV   After his death Ignatius believes that, like Paul he will be united fully with God.
V   Paul remembered the Ephesian Christians (in Christ Jesus) 'in every letter' he wrote (I Eph 12:2).

This latter comment is difficult to interpret. Was Ignatius exaggerating the point – certainly Paul did not mention the Ephesians in every letter – or, is Ignatius referring to the four Pauline letters (as he believed them to be) of which he has knowledge: 1 Corinthians; Ephesians; 1 Timothy and 2 Timothy?

It is clear that Ignatius makes reference to these Pauline letters elsewhere in his letters. Here are some examples:

I Eph 16:1	1 Cor 6:9-10
I Eph 18:1	1 Cor 1:18 and 20
I Magn 10:2	1 Cor 5:7-8
I Rom 5:1	1 Cor 4:4
I Eph introduction	Eph 1:3-14
I Poly 5:1	Eph 5:25
I Eph 14:1	1 Tim 1:3-5
I Eph 20:3	Rom 1:3

Having noted these references and allusions the question remains as to how and why Ignatius was imitating Paul and was encouraging other Christians to do the same.

Before attempting to answer these points it is important to place Ignatius in context. First, Ignatius was Bishop of Antioch in Syria (perhaps the second or third line of succession). He was condemned as a 'Christian' and transported to Rome where he faced martyrdom (I Eph 21:1-2; I Rom 2:2). This event occurred during the reign of Trajan and dated around 107. It must be stressed that the historical reconstruction of events is far from clear as Eusebius (*The History of the Church*, Bk. 3, 22) provides no details of the actual time of Ignatius' death. Antioch had been established as an important centre of Christianity (e.g. Gal 2:11; Acts 11:19; 13:1; 14:26; 15:22, 18:22).

This establishment was of strategic importance given that Syrian Antioch was one of the three largest and most important cities in the Roman Empire (the others being Rome and Alexandria; for historical and archaeological details see *BSGT*, 143-152). Peter and Paul (Gal 2:11) had both been resident in the city and it had been assumed (by Origen and Eusebius) that Paul had been the first Bishop. It was the city from which Paul and Barnabas were sent on their missionary journey (Acts 13:1) and to which, on occasions they returned (15:22; 18:22). The point is that Ignatius would have regarded himself as being (both personally and through his office) in the succession of Peter and Paul.

Secondly, Ignatius, who also called himself Theophanous (God-bearer) wrote seven letters on his way to martyrdom. This point represents the generally accepted view of the extent of Ignatius' correspondence there being also a longer and a short list.

The seven letters are:

To the Ephesians	(= I Eph)
To the Magnesians	(= I Magn)
To the Trallians	(= I Trall)
To the Romans	(= I Rom)
To the Philadelphians	(= I Phild)
To the Smyrnaeans	(= I Smyr)
To Polycarp	(= I Poly)

Like Paul writing to Philemon, Timothy and Titus, Ignatius writes to Polycarp who was Bishop of Smyrna and whom we shall meet in the next section. Also like Paul, Ignatius wrote to the churches of Ephesus and Rome and to other ecclesial communities in Asia Minor: Magnesia, Tralles, Philadelphia and Smyrna. Ignatius' letters follow the pattern of Paul's and are of similar length to the shorter ones. There is:

1. An opening greeting and blessing.

2. The Body of the letter which deals with matters of theology, ethics and ecclesial organisation. Travel plans and the personalities involved in them are revealed. Opponents of Ignatius and those who hold 'false teaching' are criticised.

3. The letters conclude with a farewell blessing in praise of God and Jesus Christ.

Having set the context we must now return to our consideration of how and why Ignatius (c. 35 – c. 107) was imitating Paul (c. 8/9 – c. 67). Here are some comparisons between them: both were leaders of churches; they worked in similar geographical areas; both emphasised similar aspects of theology and Christology; both faced opposition; both were condemned to death and both suffered martyrdom in Rome. Throughout, therefore, Ignatius was conscious of following Paul's life and faith both actually (journey to Rome as a prisoner) and metaphorically. On the basis of Paul's earlier authority Ignatius claimed his own, both as a Bishop (which Paul did not claim or was not given) but also as a slave and disciple of Jesus Christ (I Rom 4:2) who, like Jesus, faced death in order that Ignatius might identify with his suffering (I Magn. 5:2). It is this tension which lies at the heart of the issue as to how and why Ignatius imitated Paul; on one hand ecclesial authority over churches and in judging opponents on the grounds of having been called by God to exercise this authority (I Phild 7:1-2) and, on the other, as Paul had done, to follow completely the path taken by Jesus Christ. Ignatius knows that until he has achieved martyrdom he would not have fully imitated Paul or Peter (I Rom 4:3) nor shared completely in Christ's resurrection (I Eph 3:1; I Phild 1-3).

Yet, as with Clement, Ignatius' imitation of Paul ought to be seen within the new perspective of the later second century. It is not possible to elaborate on all the details of this 'new perspective', except to highlight one area, that of the ministry. Like 1 Timothy and Titus, Ignatius argues for the threefold pattern of ministry: bishops, presbyters and deacons.

This arrangement is of apostolic foundation. In Ephesians Ignatius praises the bishop, Onesimus (I Eph 1:3) and the deacon Burrhus (2:1) and encourages the Ephesian church to be united in their submission to them and to the other clergy (2:2). This submission will increase the full measure of their holiness (2:2). Why then does Ignatius emphasise so strongly this attitude to this ministry? First, because of the need for ecclesial unity, in describing this unity Ignatius uses the (new) image of the orchestra playing in harmony and the harp playing in tune (4:1-2). Secondly, this unity is necessary because of the challenges being made to 'orthodox' belief relating to Christology (7-9). Only a united church and ministry can counter fully 'heterodox' belief which maintained, among other things, that Christ only appeared to suffer (I Trall 10:1). Thirdly, a church united under Episcopal authority is best equipped for mission as unbelievers should be given an opportunity to learn, (and to become disciples) from Christians (I Eph 10:1).

Ignatius is sometimes said to be advocating a 'monarchical (from the Greek for one, *monos*, ruler, *arche*) episcopacy'. The use of this term is to misunderstand his position as there is nothing 'monarchical' about his explanation of the ministry. Rather Ignatius argues: (i) that the bishop must be regarded 'as the Lord himself'. In this regard Ignatius is building upon Paul's view that the true apostolic ministry is identification with Jesus as Lord through his suffering and resurrection (e.g. 2 Cor 4:5; 4:10-11). That is why, for Ignatius, the Episcopal ministry ought to be respected as those who exercise it reflect (and their lives illustrate this fact) Jesus. (ii) Ignatius compares the bishops to a head of household (I Eph 6:1). 1 Timothy also shares this view (1 Tim 3:4-5). Despite persecution this identification of episcopacy with household management indicates that the bishop now has a 'settled place' within Graeco-Roman society.

In these two particular ways Ignatius' interpretation of Paul can be discerned. Paul is presented as a 'model' of life and ministry which should be followed both by clergy and lay faithful. At the time Pauline principles are being applied to the 'new perspectives' facing the Church in the early second century which relate to the need to find unity and focus within the diversities of theological understanding and church ministry.

4. Polycarp

In his Letter to the Philippians Polycarp mentions Paul on four occasions:

3:2   'For neither am I, nor is any like me, able to follow the wisdom of the blessed and glorious Paul…'

9:1   'I appeal now to every one of you to hear and obey the call of holiness (found in…) Paul himself and the other Apostles.'

11:2   'Do we not know Paul teaches us, that it is God's people who are to judge the world.' (Latin text)

11:3   '… you with whom the blessed Paul laboured, and who were his letters of commendation.' (Latin text)

In the course of this letter Polycarp alludes to a greater range of Paul's letters than do either Clement or Ignatius. Polycarp uses: 1 Corinthians (note a favourite of Clement and Ignatius); [cf. Polycarp Philippians 3:2-3; 1 Corinthians 13:13; Polycarp Philippians 5:3; 1 Corinthians 6:9-10] and Ephesians [cf. Polycarp Philippians 12:1 (Latin text); Ephesians 4:26].

He probably used 1 and 2 Timothy and perhaps Romans, Galatians and Philippians. In the latter case Polycarp refers to letters in the plural (Phil 3:2). How this fact is to be interpreted in the light of what is known about Paul's Philippians is difficult to say. Again Polycarp utilises the Pauline letter framework.

1.   Opening greeting, in his case from himself and the church elders to the Philippian church with the declaration of the mercy and peace of God.

2.   The body of the letter with chapters 11, 12 and 14 surviving only in Latin.

3.   The final greetings with the commendation of the bearer of the letter, Crescens, and the traditional farewell.

It is clear also that Polycarp sees himself as bearing the Church's tradition which stretches from Paul through Clement and Ignatius to himself.

These observations must now be contextualised within Polycarp's own situation as Bishop of Smyrna. Although it is known that Polycarp suffered martyrdom in c. 155, as recorded by the *Martyrdom of Polycarp*, it is likely that his letter to the Philippians was written c. 130-140. The letter comes in the form of exhortation and advice to Philippian Christians on questions of which they have asked (3:1; 13:1). In this area Polycarp offers three major themes which have their base in Pauline thought. First, salvation, which God has accomplished through the ministry of Jesus Christ: his death (1:2; 8:1; 9:2) and resurrection (2:2; 5:2). This resurrection has an eschatological dimension; it is a state of life which Christians will share in the future (5:3; 8:1; 12:2). Salvation, therefore concerns gift and achievement, a life which God offers and which can be obtained through faithful obedience. Secondly, righteousness, which Polycarp allies with the call of holiness (9:1). Building on Paul's idea that righteousness is both a characteristic of God's nature and the means of entering a right relationship with God, for Polycarp 'righteousness' has an ethical function. Thirdly, imitation, a life of endurance by following Jesus' sufferings which Paul, Ignatius, Zosimus, Rufus and others of the faithful have manifested.

It can now be seen how Polycarp is an interpreter of Paul, c. 115-155, a period in which Paul's individual letters are beginning to be established as having relevance over a wide geographical area of the church. The Philippians are exhorted to return to them and the 'wisdom' (3:2) which they offer. They should also perceive that they themselves are Paul's letter (11:3), living witness to the maintaining of his original ministry in Philippi. Paul, together with other faithful church leaders, are to be imitated, not merely through what they have written but in the manner of their living in Christ (9:1).

5. Marcion

Eusebius, quoting Irenaeus, relates how on one occasion when Polycarp was visiting Rome, he met Marcion by chance. Marcion apparently asked Polycarp if he recognised him, to which he replied 'I do indeed: I recognise the firstborn of Satan!' (*The History of the Church*, Bk. 4:14). This event illustrates the depth of feeling and division relating to Pauline interpretation between the orthodox bishops: Clement, Ignatius and Polycarp and the heretical leader, Marcion.

According to Tertullian, Marcion formulated a list (the *Apostolikon*) of Pauline letters (c. 140). This list contained Galatians, 1-2 Corinthians, Romans, 1-2 Thessalonians, Laodiceans, Colossians, Philemon and Philippians. In recording this list Tertullian makes two other points. First, that the letter to the Laodiceans is a version of that to Ephesus and secondly, that Marcion consciously rejected the Pastoral letters from his list. In making this list Marcion's particular interpretation of Paul becomes manifest. It might be presumed that Marcion's rejection of the Pastoral letters was because they were thought to be too Jewish (e.g. 1 Tim 1:8) and by placing Galatians at the head of his list Marcion was arguing that, in this letter, the reader encounters Paul at his 'purist'. In Galatians, and probably sections of Romans, Marcion discovered the 'purist' Gospel which focussed on Christ's love and mercy towards the Gentiles (Gal 1:16; 2:2; 2:14-15). In the exercise of this ministry Marcion believed that, in particular Peter, misunderstood Paul's position, preferring rather to cling on to the older conception of the Jewish 'lesser' creator God who offered salvation only on the grounds that the demands of the *Torah* should be accepted (Gal 2:7; 2:14-15). Paul, according to Marcion, found Peter's position unsatisfactory because it was based on Law rather than on the Gospel of the 'new' God the Father of Jesus Christ, who offered justification by faith (Gal 2:16 and 21). For Marcion, Paul maintained continuity with the teaching of Jesus as 'rightly' understood (a form of Luke's Gospel, a disciple of Paul, was used as evidence for this argument). Jesus desired to separate himself from the 'Jewish' God by demonstrating that the 'new' God showered blessings on the poor rather than the rich – an authentic sign of the new Gospel. It is likely that, from this understanding of the Jesus – Paul tradition, Marcion commended celibacy rather than marriage and child bearing as a means of freedom from the 'evil' world. In this regard Marcion could be regarded (at least in some areas) as 'Gnostic' and that his Christology was 'docetic' in that he thought Jesus only appeared to suffer and that his role was to liberate humanity from the power of the 'Jewish' God.

Following his excommunication from the Roman church in 144, Marcion promoted his views vigorously and formulated a Marcionite church on the strength of them with its own ecclesial and sacramental life. Tertullian testifies (in c. 207) to the success of the Marcionite movement which he believed might 'fill the whole world'. Certainly Marcion's interpretation of Paul could appear attractive. It stressed 'newness', grace, faith, Gospel, freedom, salvation, continuity with Jesus together with the egalitarian nature of the Christian community in terms of both membership (Gal 3:27-28) and common life. Yet, at the same time, Marcion's interpretation of Paul was flawed. By combining his understanding of the new Christian Gospel found in Paul with aspects of Gnosticism and Docetism, Marcion confused and complicated matters. By denying both Paul (and Jesus) their rightlful continuity with the Jewish background and by postulating ' a two Gods theology' Marcion robbed Christianity of its antecedents, especially the theological language needed for its definition. Marcion's interpretation of Paul (and Jesus) could only operate by removing or changing the evidence. Marcion's new Christian philosophy system is unworkable even on the basis of this 'canonical' list of Pauline literature.

I have sketched Marcion's interpretation of Paul in order to illustrate that in the second century, there was a diversity of ways in which Paul's thought might be understood. It must be accepted that there is always a certain 'open-endedness' to how Paul is able to be understood. Marcion's interpretation, however, comes through the lenses of others, namely Tertullian and Irenaeus, and in fairness to Marcion it must be accepted that our evidence relating to his interpretation of Paul is far from complete. The point of real importance is that in both orthodox and heterodox circles of second century Christianity Paul was a highly regarded and much respected figure.

PAULINE LETTER COLLECTIONS (P46) AND MANUSCRIPT DEVELOPMENT

1. P46

The papyrus collection of Paul's letters known as P46 contains the following: Romans (beginning at Rom 5:17), Hebrews, 1 and 2 Corinthians, Ephesians, Galatians, Philippians, Colossians and 1 Thessalonians. This manuscript, one of the Chester Beatty papyri collection acquired by A. Chester Beatty in 1931, was written probably around AD 200. It terminates in an awkward place and it is likely that more Pauline letters (perhaps the Pastorals?) were included but are now missing from the collection. It is estimated that about 86 leaves of the original 99 or 104 have survived. The significance of the contents of P46, which may reflect the situation in Alexandria, given that the letters were copied onto papyrus, illustrates that Paul's letters were beginning to be seen together as part of a canonical collection. This collection might be seen as the 'orthodox' challenge to Marcion's earlier collection. Letters originally designed for individual churches could now be given universal application. These letters were also beginning to be seen as 'canonical literature', thus taking their place alongside the Jewish scriptures, and probably the four Gospels, to form the sacred, apostolic scriptural texts of Christianity.

If the Muratorian Latin fragment (published in 1740 by L.A. Muratori) is to be dated to the late second century, then we can discern the same process occurring as with P 46, this time associated with the western church, probably Rome. The compiler of this fragment does not merely provide a list of Pauline letters, but also adds comments on why they were written:

Corinthians	–	forbidding the schisms of heresy
Galatians	–	forbidding circumcision
Romans	–	emphasising the rule of the Scriptures and Christ as their first principle.

Paul, like John (Rev 1:11) writes to seven churches in the following order: 1. Corinthians; 2. Ephesians; 3. Philippians; 4. Colossians; 5. Galatians; 6. Thessalonians; 7. Romans. To which should be added a second letter to both the Corinthians and the Thessalonians. In these letters to individual churches, however, the complier of this fragment observes that: 'Yet one Church is recognised as being spread over the entire world.' In addition the letters to individuals: Philemon, Titus and two letters to Timothy are recognised. Two other letters are also in circulation: to the Laodiceans and Alexandrians; but these are forgeries written in order to comply with the heresy of Marcion (text of the Muratorian fragment in *A New Eusebius*, 123-125).

However the comments of the Muratori writer are to be evaluated it is clear that both in terms of naming a canonical list of Paul's letters and also by the comments made, the work of interpreting Paul's intentions is becoming manifest.

2. Manuscript development

In addition to quoting from, and listing, Paul's letters, multiple manuscripts of them were being written. These multiple manuscripts are particularly apparent with regard to Romans in which there are fourteen different families of texts, many containing a variety of forms for the final chapters 14-16, (Jewett, *CCSt.P*, 91). These manuscripts ensured that the Pauline texts were widely available, not merely to be heard (1 Thess 5:27; Col 4:16 requiring a single copy) but also to be studied (multiple copies).

Numerous theories have been proposed as to how individual Pauline letters became formed into a body of Pauline writings (Marcion, P46, Muratorian fragment). Often these theories are based on insufficient evidence. It could have been that the desire for a collection of letters originated with Paul himself (Col 4:16) through an exchange between the churches. It is likely that Paul's immediate followers were involved in such a collection; for example, Luke, Timothy or even Onesimus (Col 4:9; Philem 10). Given their relatively close proximity it could be that various churches or regional groups of churches exchanged and collected Paul's letters (e.g. Corinth, Ephesus, Philippi). Whatever may have been the case, and from whatever prospect they were viewed, for Luke, Clement, Marcion and the compliers of P46 and the Muratorian fragment, Paul's life and thought was 'good news' for them in their time. This situation arose because Paul's writings generated a Pauline tradition which could be imitated and interpreted in subsequent generations.

Conclusion

The purpose of reviewing some of these later interpretations of Paul by a variety of writers (e.g. Clement, Ignatius, Polycarp, Marcion, P46) is to illustrate the diverse and multiple patterns which the interpretation of Paul's thought continued to generate. From them we can see the importance of Paul's position in the sense that the various sides of the theological, Christological and ecclesial debates within the second century churches and their leaders and thinkers were prepared to 'use' Paul in order to expound and justify their own theological standpoints. Whatever was thought of Paul it was impossible to remove him from the heart of the theological debates with which Christians were engaged. I believe that this situation was 'caused' by Paul himself. Through communication with churches and individuals (a method continued after his martyrdom as if he were alive) Paul confronted the major issues facing theology; for example, the understanding of God, Christ, salvation, sin, grace, faith, Church, ministry and living in the world and in the family. As the churches faced new situations (both within and without), is it surprising that they used Pauline thought as a source of 'Good News', given that they had different ideas as to how this 'Good News' should be conceived and lived?

CONCLUDING REFLECTIONS

This title is a misnomer. The whole purpose of this book is to advance rather than to conclude: to encourage the reader to pursue his/her own lines of enquiry either individually or as part of a community, the members of which wish to pursue the same objective. This objective relates to (i) rediscovering Paul, and the traditions emanating from him, in terms of their original setting and (ii) to investigate how the study of Pauline thought can be 'good news for today'. In this pursuit I am biased in the sense that I maintain that Paul is good news for today and that the study of his life, thought and traditions are improving: theologically, spiritually, intellectually, pastorally and socially. This improvement is due to the fact that Paul faces issues in order to find hope and life both in terms of the present and of eternity. In order to advance these claims by way of summary I have chosen to concentrate on four areas. These areas, both inter-relate with each other but, at the same time, do not encapsulate the whole of Paul's thought. I use them by way of example: categories upon which discussion might begin.

Before I summarise these categories two other points ought to be made. First, we must never lose sight of the fact that Paul wrote letters addressed to specific situations and individuals. These letters take a variety of forms within which a diversity of literary techniques are to be found; rhetoric (of various kinds); irony, tension and paradox. Secondly, it is sometimes said that Paul was not a systematic theologian. I have always been uncertain as to how this term should be defined and interpreted. What linguistic force, for example should be given to the adjective 'systematic' in this context? True, at later times, theologians discussed Paul's thought in terms of categories: for example righteousness, grace, apostleship and freedom. Was this exercise undertaken because they wished to appear 'systematic'?

In this context Paul was both systematic in the sense of ordered, and unsystematic. This 'system' resulted from a cosmological understanding of God's action through Jesus Christ in which Paul and all other believers were enveloped. The 'unsystematic' dimension results from Paul's desire to apply this 'system' to particular theological and pastoral issues which were confronting (in different ways) the earliest churches. Thus, whoever and wherever we are in the contemporary world Paul continues to speak to us with his original powerful voice in terms of proclaiming and living the Gospel. It is to this voice that we are encouraged to attend. What we have discovered from our study of the Pauline literature is that Paul was a creative genius of the highest order, always broadening and deepening the conceptual basis of his thought and practice and, at the same time, providing a dimension of thought with enormous interpretative interest for subsequent readers. I shall now present some ideas in relation to my four categories.

1. THEOLOGY THROUGH THE MIRROR OF CHRISTOLOGY

'The glory of God in the face of Jesus Christ' (2 Cor 4:6)

Paul's aim as a theologian is to project what God is doing. How in the 'fullness of time' (Gal 4:4) he sent his Son Jesus who, in his role as Christ (Messiah) and Lord offered salvation to all humanity. This 'fullness' represents continuity in God's action which began with his dynamic action in creation, including humanity represented by Adam (whose disobedience God reversed, 1 Cor 15:22) through Abraham (Gal 3:6), Moses (2 Cor 3:7-8) and eventually to Christ. In this continuity the role of Israel is critical. It is to Israel that the Gospel must be first preached, then 'to the nations' (Rom 15:27). Paul is clear that his Jewish past is important (Rom 9:1-5) but at the same time, through his call, conversion and commission (Gal 1:15-16), his Jewish theology and practice had been reinterpreted by using the old categories; for example, Israel, law, righteousness and covenant in new ways. Thus the Church is now the 'Israel of God' (Gal 6:16); law becomes a way of ethics rather than a way to salvation (Rom 3:27-31); righteousness before God is as a result of his divine grace received by faith (Gal 2:15-21) and circumcision, the way to enter Israel's covenant (Gen 17:9-14) is replaced by Baptism which is available to all humanity as a way of entering Christ's new community (Gal 3:27-28; Rom 6:3-11; Col 2:11-12).

Reference to Baptism highlights Paul's theme of believers being identified with and totally embraced by Christ. The greatest move which Paul undertook from Judaism was to acknowledge that Jesus the Son, the Crucified and Risen one, (1 Cor 15:3-5) was God's Messiah (note the issue presented at Rom 9:5) and shared his Lordship (1 Cor 12:3; Phil 2:6-11). Unlike the Jews Paul did not need to look for a future (Davidic) Messiah. The Messiah had arrived in the person of Jesus. What was necessary, however, was for Paul and the believers to watch for the return of Christ in glory (1 Thess 4:13-18) and to think and to behave accordingly (1 Thess 5:5-8).

In the light of this Christology, therefore Paul presents his theology and soteriology based on an eschatological understanding of time.

1. **The past** to be understood as being based upon the historical action of Jesus (1 Cor 15:3-5 see also 1 Cor 11:23-26). To understand this action theologically it is necessary to return both to God's original action in creation (Col 1:16) and to the history of Israel in general. Within this history, at the appointed time God sent his Son (Gal 4:4).

2. **The present** to be understood existentially as being 'in Christ', 'dead to sin and alive to God' (Rom 6:11). Yet our relationship with Christ in the present is not completed. Our salvation has not been fully realised. We are pilgrims moving towards our promised heavenly future (Phil 3:12-16).

3. **The future** to be understood as the consummation of the eschatological age which, in the present we can only glimpse (1 Cor 13:12). It is anticipated that on that day (1 Thess 5:2) the believers will share in the totality of Christ's salvation, not merely his incarnation and death

(Phil 2:6-8) but also his glory (Phil 3:21 cf. 2:9-11, also Rom 8:30). In this process we are granted both the 'first fruits' (Rom 8:23) and the seal (2 Cor 1:22) of the Holy Spirit as a guarantee of this glorious, heavenly future.

Paul believed, therefore, that Christ represented the culmination of God's plan for humanity on account of the fact that he portrayed perfectly God's image (2 Cor 4:6). This image is seen in terms of the light shining out of darkness and, as a result, the continuity between creation and redemption in God's plan through Christ's saving work is established.

2. MISSION AND EVANGELISATION

'How beautiful are the feet of those who bring good news!' (Isa 52:7 quoted in Rom 10:15)

Mission is a generalised concept. Schools, for example are asked to write 'mission statements' which tell of their aims, objectives and practice. I am not sure if Paul would have understood his work described as 'mission' or his status described as a 'missionary'. I suspect that he would have found the idea too vague and unfocussed. He would have understood, I maintain, his work in terms of 'evangelisation' and perhaps his status as an 'evangelist' (2 Tim 4:5). This is because he used the concept of Gospel (*euaggelion*) and to preach the Gospel (to evangelise) on numerous occasions throughout his letters, and with them their synonymous concept of the 'word'; 'proclamation'; 'preaching' and 'witness'. The 'sharp' and all embracing focus of this 'word' to which Paul 'witnesses' is God's good news as manifested through the saving activity of Jesus. The concept is developed from the Jewish scriptures (Isa 52:7 quoted in Rom 10:15). In the Isaiah passage (note also Isa 61:1) the Gospel refers to God's promised action to ensure the release of the Jewish people from exile in Babylon. For Paul it refers to the release of humanity from alienation with God and slavery from sin through the saving activity of God's Son, Jesus (e.g. Rom 1:3-4). Frequently, when Paul is confronting pastoral issues, he returns to the basic facts of the Gospel. I offer three examples:

1. 1 Thessalonians 1:9-10 – in the midst of the Greek religious culture of Thessalonica from which his converts have been 'converted' Paul restates the summary of his preaching.

2. 1 Corinthians 15:3-7 – in the midst of the doubting of the resurrection by some of the Corinthians, Paul restates the tenets of the Gospel concerning Christ's death and resurrection and their implications for faith and belief.

3. Galatians 4:4-7 – in the midst of his profound disagreements with the Galatians and with their Judaising teachers, Paul restates both the basis and the implications on which a right relationship with God can be constructed, not in terms of *Torah* but of grace.

These passages may be ones which Paul is adapting from the received Christian tradition (1 Cor 15:3a) or through the liturgy (e.g. Phil, 2:6-11) but which he makes his own. In doing so he raises important questions for the contemporary reader. Through the ministry of evangelisation, which issues are constant or which issues change in relationship to different contexts? Or to put the question another way, how can the unchanging facts of the 'good news' remain as recognisable and applicable 'good news' in contemporary society? How should the Church present and live the Gospel? What should the hallmarks be of the 'good news' in the variety of contemporary contexts? How should the Pauline categories of 'justification' (Rom 3:21-31) and 'reconciliation' (2 Cor 5:18-21) be interpreted by us?

3. CHURCH AND APOSTLESHIP

'For we are God's fellow workers; you are God's field, God's building' (1 Cor 3:9)

Converts to Christianity whether Jews or Gentiles, were baptised into the saving life of Christ Jesus (Rom 6:3-4) and incorporated into the community of the Church. This Church was, for Paul, both universal, the fellowship of all believers and local, in the sense that it was contextualised in particular places: in Paul's case, the urban cities of the eastern Roman Empire. Paul's letters were addressed to churches and to individual Christians and an examination of their contents reveals, for the contemporary Church, important questions about the identity, perception, internal life and organisation and its role as an agent for evangelisation in contemporary society. When we ask questions (such as those listed above) about the Church we should not expect automatic 'answers' from Paul, given that he worked in a different context, rather we should find fundamentals from which we can develop and perceptions which we can apply to various situations. Fundamentally, the Church embodies Christ's death and resurrection; through his death it should reflect weakness which, paradoxically, is the source of its power (1 Cor 1:18). Through Christ's resurrection the Church demonstrates its role as the community of believers who proclaim hope and glory (Phil 3:20-21 reflecting 2:9-11). The Church has also an ethical role to demonstrate: believers are to live a life of righteousness before God (Rom 6:13 and 6:18). Three more points need to be made about the Church. First, the Church ought to be seen against its background as the development and interpretation of God's Israelite community (Eph 2:12-13). Secondly, Paul uses metaphors to describe the Church's work and identity (1 Cor 3:6-9). Their purpose is to illustrate how the Church 'grows', its role as an inter-connecting family of communion and as a phenomenon to be 'built up' (1 Cor 14:26) through the ministry of the various parts of the Body (1 Cor 12:12-13; Eph 4:11-12). Thirdly, in the Pauline literature the understanding of the Church develops; this insight is particularly true with regard to Colossians and Ephesians where the mystical and cosmic unity between Christ and the Church is stressed (Col 1:18; Eph 1:20-23).

Paul's most deeply felt convictions, and the area where he experienced controversy and opposition (e.g. 2 Cor 10-13), concerned his ministerial status and identity. In the context of defining his ministry Paul uses three particular terms: first, apostle. The origin of this designation is found in an ambassadorial context. For Paul it is interpreted by him as 'being sent as an envoy'; not from any political agency or from the authorities of Judaism, or even from the Jerusalem apostles (Gal 1:18-19), but from Christ himself (Gal 1:1). It is a characteristic which dominates Paul's missionary theology and ministerial understanding and through it is identified with Christ's death and resurrection (e.g. 2 Cor 4:7-12). Secondly, slave: a person totally dependent upon another, his master. In this context Paul declares that he is Christ's slave (e.g. Rom 1:1; Phil 1:1) and, as such, shares in Christ's incarnational work towards humanity (Phil 2:7). Thirdly, minister: used for example in Romans 15:16 where Paul describes himself as God's 'priestly minister' being the grace given through accepting Christ's Gospel, especially in a Gentile context, in terms of a sacrificial offering.

Having noted these ministerial categories and the cultural and theological background on which they are based, it is then necessary to recognise (as was done with his theology of the Church above) how Paul's ministerial perceptions developed within the Pauline tradition. In this context I offer two examples. First, in Ephesians, Paul's ministerial understanding is placed within the overall cosmic framework of Christ's saving work (Eph 1:15-23; 3:7-13). Secondly, in 1 Timothy and Titus Church leaders become representatives of the Church within society and are expected to possess similar characteristics to those holding civic office. These Christian leaders have a 'settled' ministry (e.g. Titus 1:5), the missionary ministry is to be undertaken by others (e.g. Crescens, Titus and Tychicus; 2 Tim 4:10-12 and 3 Jn 5-8). Paul's 'second generation' leaders, Timothy and Titus are to appoint bishops, elders and deacons who possess particular virtues; one of these important virtues which church leaders are to demonstrate is that of self-control or moderation (1 Tim 3:2). The pursuit of this virtue was a common feature in Graeco-Roman society; in the Christian pastoral context (alongside other virtues, e.g. discipline, Titus 1:8) it must be demonstrated by Christian ministers in the exercise of their ministry.

Given the numerous questions, uncertainties, joys and sorrows concerned with the exercise of the ordained ministry in the twenty-first century, the task of returning to Paul and the Pauline tradition for guidance and reflection is imperative. In this tradition we learn first, the theological and Christological foundation on which the ministry ought to be based; secondly, the qualities needed in those who exercise it and thirdly, we gain insights into how it should be undertaken, in particular, in the circumstances of the various kinds of opposition. We should, like Paul, when dealing with difficulties, as he does in the pastoral sphere, return to the first principles of the Gospel (e.g. 1 Cor 4:8-13). In this way an invaluable hermeneutical 'bridge' is constructed between the twenty-first century and the first century. Aspirants to the ordained ministry who believe that they are called (the concept of vocation) by God to it should also immerse themselves in this process; so for them and us, we shall be identifying ourselves with what is truly 'good news for today'.

4. ETHICS

'If we live by the Spirit, let us also walk by the Spirit' (Gal 5:25)

Ethical questions and decisions are phenomena which effect all our lives both in our private and public 'space'. In turning to Paul's ethics, therefore, we discover a rich treasury on which ethical 'principles' are to be based and as a result, the foundation for how ethical decisions ought to be made. Although the term 'ethics' is not used by Paul, nevertheless it was clear as to the direction that behavioural mores ought to take. The aim of living ethically was, as he taught the Thessalonian Christians, 'how you ought to walk and to please God' (1 Thess 4:1). This Jewish image of 'walking' is continued throughout the Pauline literature; thus the recipients of Ephesians are instructed to 'walk worthily in (the way of) the Lord' in which they have been called (Eph 4:1). This insight highlights the roots of Paul's ethics, mainly found in Judaism (e.g. 1 Cor 13:34) but with hints also from Greek (e.g. virtue lists; 2 Cor 6:6 and Gal 5:19-23) and Stoic (note the endurance motif in Rom 5:3-4) sources. In the twenty-first century, therefore, we should be searching both for ethical principles and for the roots of these principles; for example, in the search for justice.

Paul's ethics however, are given a particular 'shape' as a

317

result of his context. First, there is the all important context of Graeco-Roman society and the political situation of Roman Imperialism (note Rom 13:1-7). Secondly, Paul's ethics must be understood as being part of his total theological and Christological framework; we must all live lives worthy of the Gospel (Phil 1:27). Thirdly, Paul's ethics are situational in that they are responding to particular issues which have arisen within the churches (e.g. 1 Cor 5:1). On our part we ought to note these contexts and react to them in the light of experience; not forgetting, however, the foundational and permanent concepts of love (e.g. Rom 5:5); the work of the Spirit (e.g. Gal 5:16-26); freedom and obligation (e.g. Gal 5:13) and 'the obedience of faith' (Rom 1:5) which are at the heart of Paul's ethics and which provides Paul's thought with 'ethical integration' (Rosner, *CCStP*, 213).

Out of ethical enquiry arises also the study of society. In this area there have been studies related to the social conditions in which Paul's ministry occurred; for example, the dynamics of the household, the role of the courts and other civic institutions and the notions related to patronage. These institutions operated within Graeco-Roman society; thus, a profitable form of research concerns the environment of the community of the city state, the 'place' of Judaism within it and the development of the 'community of Christians'. In these ways an 'ethic of society' develops together with its complex social relationships. The study of Paul's 'social ethics', therefore, is a reminder of the importance of our contemporary observations about society and the place and functions of the Church within it. In this area Paul challenges us to engage in two particular exercises. First, how a sense of community can be developed and secondly, how the Church and Christians can best minister within the context of the wider civic society. A rediscovery therefore, of both 'social community' and 'family' (e.g. Col 3:18-4:1; Eph 5:21-6:9) arising from our study of Paul is again surely 'good news for today'.

In offering these reflections I have touched only on some fragments of Paul's total impact. The analysis of fragments, however, runs the risk of losing the sense of coherence. This search for coherence is not easy when studying Paul given that he is writing 'occasional' letters. Yet the question ought to be asked, in this regard how, through this occasional literature, the main elements of Paul's thought can be included in a meaningful framework. In this I believe Pope Benedict XVI provides a vital clue when he says that 'the entire plan of life of the Christian can only be modelled on Christ, entirely with him, for him and in him, to the glory of God the Father' (from a homily preached on 14 December 2007 quoted in *Thoughts on St Paul*, Alive Publishing, 2008, 31). I should wish to argue that this Christological approach provides both the framework and the coherence into which Paul's thought can be interpreted. Christologically, his expression 'the Lord Jesus Christ' (1 Thess 1:1 and later in Col 1:3) summarises Paul's continual reflection of the matter both in terms of Christ's 'identity' (who he is) and in what he has achieved in terms of God's salvation which is now, through Christ, offered to all humanity. Thus, Christology becomes the vehicle by which paradox is understood:

'for the sake of Christ, then, I am content with weaknesses... for when I am weak then I am strong' (2 Cor 12:11);

the way in which our victory through Christ can be appreciated:

'...we are more than conquerors through him who loved us' (Rom 8:37)

and, to return to the point made by Pope Benedict, the way in which we should live our lives:

'only let your manner of life be worthy of the Gospel of Christ' (Phil 1:27).

In the end Paul confronts us with the great personal maxim that:

'... it is no longer I who live, but it is Christ who lives in me. And the life I now live in the flesh I live by faith in the Son of God, who loved me and gave himself for me' (Gal 2:20).

FURTHER READING

1. Biblical Commentaries/Dictionary Articles

J. Barton and J. Muddiman (eds.), *The Oxford Bible Commentary*, 2001, Oxford, Oxford University Press = *OBC*

R.E. Brown, J.A. Fitzmyer, R.E. Murphy (eds.), *The New Jerome Biblical Commentary*, 1989, London, Chapman = NJBC

R.J. Coggins and J.L. Houlden (eds.), *A Dictionary of Biblical Interpretation*, 2003, London, SCM Press = *DBI*

G.F. Hawthorne, R.P. Martin and D.G. Reid (eds.), *Dictionary of Paul and his Letters*, 1993, Leicester, InterVarsity Press = *DPL*

2. Introductions to Paul & Pauline Literature

Raymond E. Brown, *An Introduction to the New Testament*, , 1997, New York, Doubleday, = *INT*

James D.G. Dunn (Ed.), *The Cambridge Companion to St Paul*, 2003, Cambridge, Cambridge University Press = *CCStP*.

A. E. Harvey, *A Companion to the New Testament*, Second edition, 2004, Cambridge, Cambridge University Press = *CNT*

Scot McKnight and Grant R. Osborne (eds.), *The Face of New Testament Studies: A Survey of Recent Research*, 2004, Michigan, Grand Rapids, Baker Academic = *FNTS*.
(cf. Bruce N. Fisk (Paul: Life and Letters), James D.G. Dunn (Paul's Theology))

3. More Detailed Studies of Pauline Literature and Theology

Jouette M. Bassler, *Navigating Paul*, 2007, Louisville, KY., Westminster

Morna D. Hooker, *Paul: A Short Introduction*, 2003, Oxford, One World.

David G. Horrell, *An Introduction to the Study of Paul*, 2006, London, New York, T & T Clark

Jerome Murphy-O'Connor, *Paul His Story*, 2004, Oxford University Press, Oxford

N.T. Wright, *Paul: Fresh Perspectives*, 2005, London, SPCK

John Ziesler, *Pauline Christianity*, Revised edition, 1990, Oxford, Oxford University Press

4. Archaeology/Geography

Amanda Claridge, *Rome*, Oxford Archaeological Guides, 1998, Oxford, Oxford University Press

Adrian Curtis, *Oxford Bible Atlas*, Fourth edition, 2007, Oxford, Oxford University Press

Glyde E. Fant and Mitchell G. Reddish, *A Guide to Biblical Sites in Greece and Turkey*, 2003, Oxford, Oxford University Press, = *BSGT*

Giacomo Perego, *Interdisciplinary Atlas of the Bible: Scripture, History, Geography, Archaeology and Theology*, 1999, St Pauls.

APPENDIX

1. CHRONOLOGY

We need to understand the overall chronology of Paul's activity which can be divided into five periods.

Period 1   Early Life

c. AD 7   Born in Tarsus in Cilicia (Acts 22:3).

c. 20   Educated as a strict Pharisee (Phil 3:5) in Jerusalem.

30-34   Persecuted the new Jewish Messianic movement.

34   Experienced a conversion-experience on the way to Damascus, called into Christian ministry and given a commission (Gal 1:15-16).

Period 2   Preparation for ministry

34-37   Preached in Arabia and Damascus (Gal 1:17), returned to Jerusalem.

37-48   Preached in Syria and Cilicia (Gal 1:21), settled in Antioch, returned to Jerusalem for an apostolic conference (Gal 2:1-10).

Period 3   Itinerant Evangelistic ministry

48-49   Preached in Cyprus and southern Galatia = first journey.

49-52   From Antioch revisited the Galatian churches, preached in Asia, then in Macedonia and Achaia (1 Thess 2:2; 3:1-5), settled in Corinth for eighteen months, brought before the proconsul Gallio, returned to Jerusalem (Acts 18:22) = second journey.

53-56   Revisited the churches, settled in Ephesus for two years and three months, returned to Macedonia and Asia.

Period 4 To Jerusalem and then to Rome

57	Returned to Jerusalem with the collection (2 Cor 8-9; Rom 15:26; Acts 21:16) = third journey.
57-59	Arrested in Jerusalem, appealed to Caesar, journeys to Rome as a prisoner, shipwrecked on Malta.

Period 5 To Rome, Spain(?), Rome, martyrdom

60-62	Paul seemed to be under house arrest in Rome (Acts 28:16). It is uncertain if he preached in Spain as was his intention (Rom 15:24).
64	Christians blamed by the Emperor Nero for starting the great fire and many were persecuted (recorded by the Roman historian Tacitus, *Annals*, 15:44.2-3). St Peter was martyred.
c. 67	St Paul martyred (1 Clem 5:5-7) by beheading (Eusebius, *The History of the Church*, 2:25.5) as he was a Roman citizen (Acts 22:25-29) as opposed to Peter who was crucified.

At this stage, two points need to be made: first, as with point 2 below, there are differences of opinion both as to the precise chronology and to the number of letters which Paul composed. The main arguments over non-Pauline authorship concern 2 Thessalonians, Ephesians and 1 and 2 Timothy and Titus. Secondly, Paul's life ought to be set within the expansion of Christianity as a whole, its context within Judaism, and of the authority of the Roman Empire.

2. LETTERS

We need to study Paul's letters to the churches and to the individuals Philemon, Timothy and Titus, in order to gain access to Paul's theology and ethics. There are thirteen Pauline letters in the New Testament (excluding Hebrews) and it is most likely that they were written in this order and approximately on these dates:

c. AD 50   1 Thessalonians and (probably) 2 Thessalonians.

52   Galatians.

54 -56   The Corinthian correspondence.

57   Romans (Paul had not founded this church).

c. 60- 65? The prison letters: Philippians, Philemon, Colossians, Ephesians.

c. 65- 80? The pastoral letters: 1 and 2 Timothy and Titus.

c. 80   St Luke wrote the Gospel of Luke and the Acts of the Apostles to the Roman official Theophilus in narrative form to explain the origin and development of Christianity (Lk 1:1-4; Acts 1:1). Saul (Hebrew name)/Paul (Greek name) features in this narrative from Acts 8:1 and is the principal character from 15:36.

Map 1

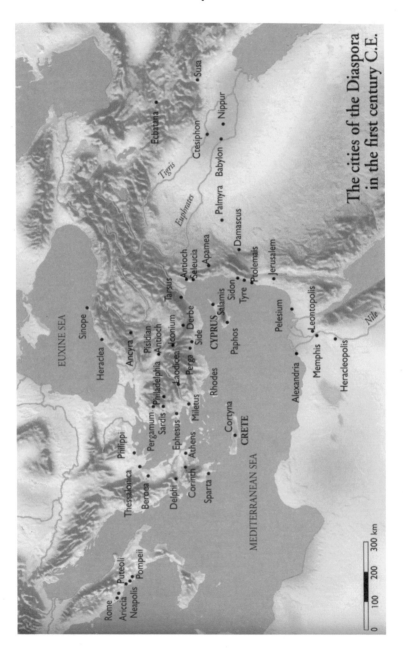

The cities of the Diaspora in the first century C.E.

Map 2

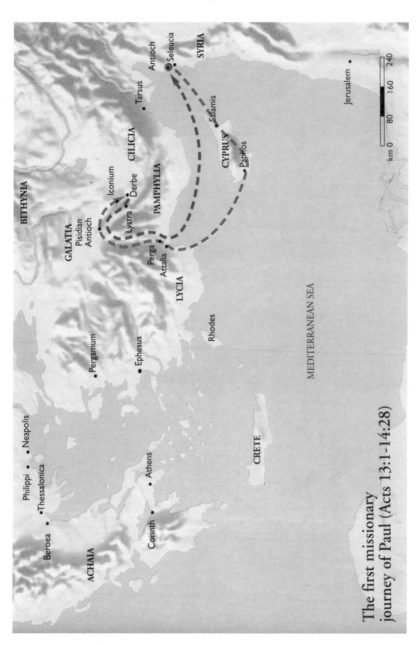

The first missionary
journey of Paul (Acts 13:1-14:28)

Map 3

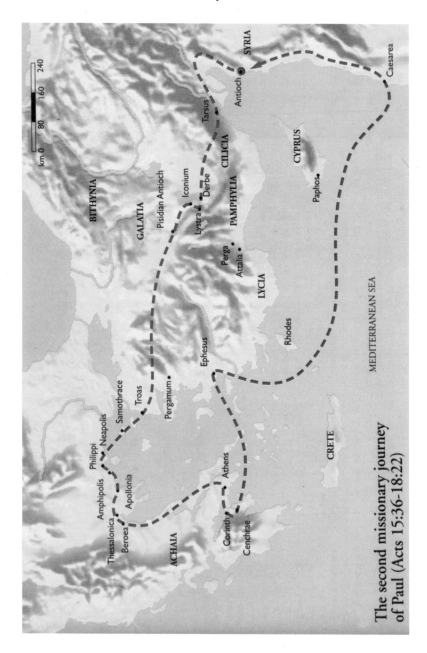

The second missionary journey of Paul (Acts 15:36-18:22)

Map 4

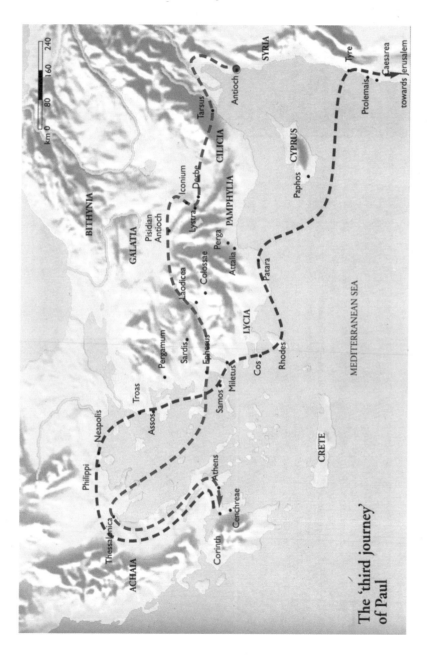

The 'third journey' of Paul

Map 5

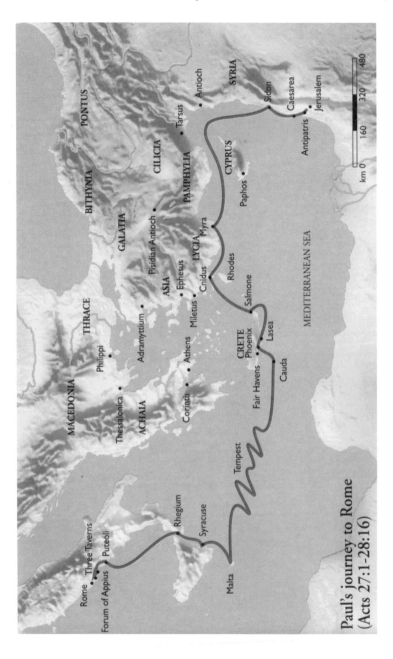

Paul's journey to Rome
(Acts 27:1-28:16)

Earliest surviving collection of Pauline letters
(Papyrus P46, c. 200 AD)
(Two leaves from the letter to the Colossians)

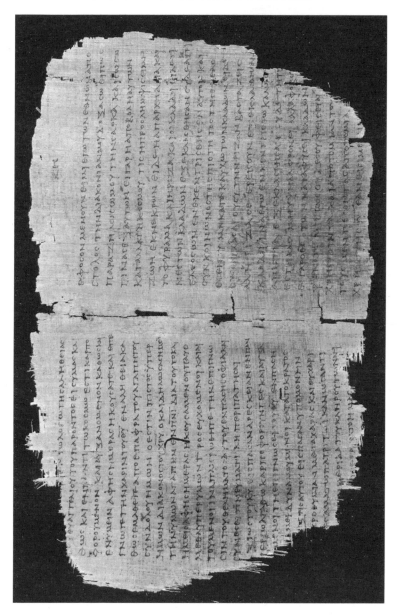

PRIESTHOOD
A life open to Christ
Daniel P. Cronin

The Year of the Priesthood celebrates the life and mission of priests in the Church throughout the world today. Its aim is to highlight the importance of the priestly calling and to support priests, and those in formation, in their daily life and work. St John Vianney is invoked by the Holy Father as patron of this Jubilee Year. The year will serve both to encourage those who are priests today and to communicate the lives of priests who have served God in the past. This book offers insights, for both ordained and lay people, into priestly life and ministry as experienced by 78 priests from around the world – from the Holy Father to one of the newest assistant priests and from the youngest to the oldest.

"I am very pleased to commend this book… its publication is very timely as we seek to respond to the invitation of Pope Benedict XVI to hold a 'Year of the Priesthood'."
Archbishop Vincent Nichols

CANON DANIEL CRONIN is the Parish Priest of Knebworth, Hertfordshire and a former Chancellor of the Archdiocese of Westminster. For some years he was the Director of the Ministry to Priests Programme in the Archdiocese.

ISBN 978-0-85439-762-4   £10.00

ST PAULS Publishing   www.stpaulspublishing.com

IN PRAISE OF PAUL
Edited by Michael A Hayes

This collection of writings on aspects of the life, work and teaching of Paul was originally published as a series of articles during the Year of Paul (June 2008 – June 2009) in *The Pastoral Review*. It is now offered to a wider audience through this publication and may well be of use to individuals and groups in a variety of pastoral settings who wish to reflect on the Pauline Corpus.

Writers include renowned scholars such as:
Brendan Byren SJ
James Dunn
Nicholas King SJ
Jerome Murphy-O'Connor OP
Gerald O'Collins SJ
Bruce Malina
Thomas Stegman SJ
Ronald Witherup SS

MICHAEL A. HAYES is a Vice-Principal at St Mary's University College, Strawberry Hill, London. He is also editor of *The Pastoral Review*.

ISBN 978-0-85439-760-0   £9.50

ST PAULS Publishing   www.stpaulspublishing.com

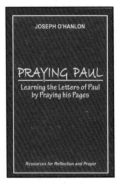

PRAYING PAUL

*Learning the Letters of Paul
by praying his pages*

*Resources for Reflection
and Prayer*

Joseph O'Hanlon

To enter the house of Paul is to enter a house of
prayer. To pray with Paul, indeed, to pray Paul,
to turn his aspirations into our prayers, is to learn
Paul. Every letter of Paul and the letters penned in
the Pauline tradition come to us parcelled in prayer.
They begin, for the most part, with prayer and they
end with prayerful blessings. This little book seeks
to meet Paul where he is best understood and where
his profound thoughts achieve the very clarity of
God. To pray Paul is to learn God.

JOSEPH O'HANLON, a priest of Nottingham diocese,
lectures in biblical studies at Allen Hall Seminary in London.
His books include *The Dance of the Merrymakers*, *Mark My
Words*, *The Jesus Who Was/The Jesus Who Is*, and *Walk One
Hour*. He has wide experience in sharing the Word of God
with adults and passionately believes with St Jerome that to be
ignorant of the Scriptures is to be ignorant of Christ.

ISBN 978-0-85439-756-3   £8.50

ST PAULS Publishing   www.stpaulspublishing.com